Home Fires

Home Fires

A SURVIVOR'S STORY

Shivaun Woolfson

Atlantic Books

LONDON

First published in Great Britain in 2002 by Atlantic Books,
an imprint of Grove Atlantic Ltd

Copyright © Shivaun Woolfson 2002

1 3 5 7 9 8 6 4 2

A CIP catalogue record for this book is available from the British Library.

1 903809 49 5 (hb)
1 843540 82 7 (tpb)

Typeset by Avon DataSet Ltd, Bidford on Avon B50 4JH
Printed in Great Britain by Mackays of Chatham Ltd, Chatham, Kent

Atlantic Books
An imprint of Grove Atlantic Ltd
29 Adam & Eve Mews
London W8 6UG

To Ike Geller, my Pop,
who set me out on the path of truth

To Jesse and Daniel, my sons,
who keep me there

ACKNOWLEDGMENTS

I have thought often about this moment and as I take a long and grateful breath, I say thanks to the following people: Toby Mundy, a tenacious, warm and insightful editor and his staff at Atlantic Books, Alice Hunt and Bonnie Chiang; my agents Shelley Power and Janell Walden Agyman in Europe and America respectively. I am indebted also to the students in my writing classes at Miami Dade and Florida International University and more recently the participants at the Writing the Self courses at Rustique Literary Café all of whom have sustained my efforts and created a home for the work I have chosen. I owe much to my friends in the US who served as readers of this book in its first stages, Debbie Shantzek, Janice DeAngelo, Margaret O'Brien, Josie Phelan, Ruth Rosen, Glenda Jinks, Cathy Burgos and Colin Crossey. I thank also fellow writers Roni Natov, Anne-Marie Hourihane and Stephanie Ellyne for their encouragement. To my brothers, Saul and David Woolfson, my sister Rachel Woolfson and their families, thanks for infinite telephone time, humour, warmth and all the best of what families are made of, and to my sister, a special thanks for helping me find my way into London, my third city. To my mother Jacqueline Geller, I offer thanks for her laughter which has never waned and for showing me that you can step away from the life you were born to. To my father, Solomon Woolfson, I am indebted always for his steadfast support through many difficult years. To Pop, my guardian angel, thank you for being there then; I know you are with me still. To Cece, I loved you then; I will love you always. And finally, to my sons, Jesse and Daniel Quinones thank you for helping me welcome the dawn of each day.

PROLOGUE

⁓

She is three years old and sleeps in a conservatory beside her sister Roberta, an angelic, autistic child with loose brown curls that frame sad eyes. The mother is young and speaks like a grand duchess. She likes to dance, to ride horses, to paint. She has a deep guttural laugh that surprises with its vulgarity. She has chopping, reckless eyes. She loves clothes. She is elegant and flirtatious. She is going insane.

The father is hard-working and studious. He speaks fluent Gaelic and is the first in his family to graduate from university. He is a brilliant young barrister with a prosperous future, but opts instead to work for his father in a flock factory down by the docks. He wears the same suit every day. He travels by train through the night, to save money on the B&Bs, to Germany, to Spain, to Italy, in search of new business. He is determined to create a fairy tale, to turn that factory into gold.

The young wife can't cope with her autistic child. Nana, her own mother, arrives each morning to help her bathe and dress and feed her daughter. Roberta dies before her fourth birthday. Five days later, Nana passes away. The young mother is never the same.

She is told that her sister died during an operation to straighten her legs. Thereafter, Roberta's room remains intact, her clothes and playthings untouched. It is a forbidden space. Even as a child, she knows that she lives in a house haunted by loss.

ONE

—◂—

I'm seven years old.

Standing by a window on a leafy Dublin street. The rain eases from the sky, making curious dripping patterns on the glass. She's gone. Off into the sodden night, down a desolate road, her slight, striding frame eaten up by shadows, carrying the silver candlesticks Nana bequeathed in one hand and an old God-forsaken relic of a vacuum cleaner in the other. Gone.

An hour earlier we were at the large oval table in the lounge that we use for special occasions. And tonight is special: Friday night with its Sabbath candles, sweet wine, roasted chicken and matzo balls, all of which my mother procured shortly before dinner, sneaking in the back door of the Jewish deli in her distinctive dark glasses, with her patterned silk scarf flung casually around her neck. Only I know this. My father assumes she's actually cooked the meal. The truth is, she couldn't prepare a kosher dinner if her life depended on it. I and my younger brother Saul are stationed on one side, my mother and my little sister Rachel are on the other. My father's at the head, rumbling his way through the Shabbos blessing for wine: '*Vayhi erev, Vayhi voker . . .*' My mother, elegant, broken with a ragged beauty, stands like a rod's been shot up her back. Suddenly her eyes catch fire. I concentrate on my father and the words tumbling from his mouth. If I focus hard, the moment will pass. Saul is quiet, stuffed into his chair, his oversized *yalmulke* lopsided on his head, his small neck squeezed against the knot of the speckled dicky bow she insists on even at home. I'm in one of those expensive dresses she gets from Newells, with the lace and fluff that scratch my skin. I look over at Saul. There's fear in his eyes.

I glance around the room. Black leather sofas, heavy brocade curtains, silver wares on a mahogany dresser. But there's dirt too, behind, under, in between. I've seen it. Mangled filth accumulated over time, like the woodworm that eats away at our prized mahogany cabinet leaving a thousand pinholes as it travels, the used sanitary napkins I found when rummaging through my mother's drawers, or the books in my father's private closet with the pictures of naked slaves on the cover and the obscene words between the pages. Our home, beautiful and all as it is, on a tree-lined street in a fashionable Dublin suburb, is rife with disease, a brooding, rotting presence that's never scrubbed out, never found. I'm sensing this as my mother moves away from the table and retrieves her packet of Rothmans from the dresser. She lights one and inhales gloriously.

'Bloody hell, Jackie,' my father says, 'you can't smoke at the Shabbos table. It's just not right. And where were you when I got in anyway? You know it's important to me to observe the Sabbath. If it wasn't for Teresa in there, there'd be no religion in this house. And she's the hired help.'

My mother spits back:

'Religion, you've got enough of that on your side of the family for both of us. Do you know that your mother and your darling sister came over yesterday to inspect the kitchen cabinets? The ruddy kosher patrol, sniffing like dogs they were. As if I was a suspect in my own home.'

'Well, would you blame them? Only a month ago, they found a slab of meat on a *milchik* plate, and what about those sausages you served for breakfast the other day? I could have sworn they weren't kosher. I just don't know what gets into you.'

Her eyes contract, tapering to a point. There's an anxious mania to them like she's landed in a sea of ghosts. They dart around the room, exploding, until they land on his. He halts his garbled prayer mid-sentence.

'For God's sake, Jackie. Not now, not in the middle of dinner, this is ridiculous. Stop, do you hear me? Stop.'

She throws her lace napkin over her plate and pushes her chair back. For a moment she is utterly still, as if the slightest movement will break her. Her body lurches forward. She strides through the door, up the stairs, and into the bedroom. He follows. They argue. We hear muffled sounds, then sharp, vicious thuds. The front door slams. She is gone. My father returns to the table. We eat in numbed silence.

I go to the window and wait.

I don't think my mother comes back that night, or the day after. The next clear memory I have is of her twisting in incongruous motion across the kitchen floor, her squirming slender frame stretched from the Aga stove to the door. Teresa can't stop her, even though she pads her face with a wet cloth, strokes her sweat-drenched forehead and speaks softly: 'C'mon now, missus, the children will get an awful fright if they see you like this, c'mon now, missus.' Mummy keeps on writhing, trying to break out of her skin.

A week later my father asks me to join him for a drive. Just the two of us. Slowly he steers his mint-green Mercedes away from our neighbourhood towards streets I don't know. He's an overly cautious navigator and more than once a passing vehicle honks furiously in our direction. Eventually the car eases through the wrought-iron gates of an impressive estate. We alight in a courtyard surrounded by meticulously manicured flower-beds, then make our way through hallways that smell of old meat, dirty socks and sickness, until we spot her, alone in a corner. When we approach, she offers a feeble smile that makes her lips tremble at the edges. Timidly, she proffers a present in my direction, a small, hand-crafted stool. Burgundy. I hold it gingerly in my arms. Briefly her eyes come to light, back into focus. Then, they go dead.

My mother returns from the lunatic asylum a few days later. Once home she's quieter than usual. She walks from room to room, taking hold of objects – silver salt shaker, porcelain napkin ring, gold-plated knife, glass goblet – the trappings of her life, in her hands, running her fingers along them and letting them go. She seems to be looking for something, but can't remember what exactly it is that she has lost. She moves shapelessly, like a blur at the periphery of our world. She doesn't hit me in those weeks. Doesn't shout. Doesn't leave. Doesn't do much of anything. She just sits by the breakfast table, smoking cigarette after cigarette, drinking one cup of black coffee after another. I want her to wake up, to come back. To thrust her fist in my face, hard. She barely moves. Two weeks into this listless pattern, I refuse to go to school. I wedge myself into the corner of the top bunk in the back room. Resolute as a corpse. My father appears in the doorway.

'Get up, pet, you'll be late for school.'

I'm not sick. I just don't want to go. I know he doesn't have the power to make me. Only she does, and she is sequestered away in her room, with the shades down, as she has been every morning since her return. I have to draw her out. Eventually she comes plunging down the hallway, knocking stools and clothes and lamps to the floor. When she reaches my room, a tall, imposing figure that towers over my father, she yanks the covers from the bed, grabs me by the arm, slaps my face and pulls me head first to the floor. What I remember is not the terror, but a secret gloating that spreads over me as I hit the carpet. I have her back.

TWO

There's fear in our house.

A flat-out dread that clogs the air, clings to the carpets, the drapes, the doors, to every visible inch of living space. It rises up in the mornings. Inside my mother. Travels down the stairs with her. Floats with her towards the breakfast table. Settles into her as she folds into her seat. I wait, coiled in my chair between her and the wall. Saul and Rachel are on the opposite side. My father is getting ready for work. Breakfast is served. We eat in silence. Afraid. She glares. We look away. She breaks slices of unbuttered toast into little pieces and places them abstractedly in her mouth. If Saul or Rachel speak out of turn, or speak at all, she glowers, then flicks a piece of burnt toast towards them. They flinch. I stare at my food. Slowly, I pick up my cup. A spoon drops. She is motionless for an instant. Then she turns abruptly to face me. I see in her eyes everything that is about to happen. My body freezes. Those beautiful long delicate fingers find my head, my shoulders, my back.

I cry.

The hands don't stop.

'I'll give you something to cry about.'

The hands don't stop.

This is how my mornings start. Life itself, its natural sounds and movements, the slurping of a drink, the twitching of an arm, the clanging of cutlery, the mumbling of a word, are all equally treacherous. After breakfast, I am pushed off into the cold with little Saul following behind me. We wait at the bus stop for the 47A to stagger round the bend. There is deliverance in that journey. Once inside the grubby halls of Stratford College I am safe.

Stratford College, one of only two Jewish schools in the city, is a building of hidden burrowed spaces. My classroom is in the basement across from the staff room, where the teachers, Mrs Fricker (Irish), Mrs O'Brien (Maths), Mr Rifkin (Hebrew), Madame Ryan (French, of course) and the headmaster, Mr Walsh, sit at lunch with their homemade sandwiches and cups of tea, their cigarettes, and stacks of books and papers. They are kind to me, these teachers, and approach me with a limber tenderness. They think I am a smart child, and tell me so. They call on me to befriend the strays, like Marjorie, whose mother died, because I am gentle, a good girl, they say. I don't notice that the radiators fail to heat the cold, grimy lavatories. I don't care about the rickety staircases or that the building is decrepit and the grounds unruly. What matters to me is that I am known. I am seen.

In the late afternoon, when classes cease and the sun begins to slip behind the trees, long after Saul has been collected by the household help, Mr Walsh emerges from the building, head bowed. He motions to me and I follow him to his car. Stratford is a mile from my house, up a steep hill, and I welcome the opportunity to be transported in comfort, but even more the chance to sit outside the gates of Tree Tops, where he pulls in, always in the exact same spot, turns off the engine, eases back into his seat and talks to me. What on earth do we talk about, Teresa demands. Her prying eyes shift back and forth behind the curtains. The neighbourhood kids scamper round the vehicle, anxious for me to get out. But I stay as long as he lets me. We talk about families, about books, about school. About home.

I never know which version of my mother will be there to greet me. Sometimes I find her and Teresa jiving across the sitting-room floor, the rock'n'roll blasting from the record player, their skirts high up on their legs, their faces wild. Other times they're in the kitchen sorting through laundry.

'One shit, two shits, three shits,' my mother counts, flinging soiled linen into piles.

'Mummy,' I say, astonished, 'that's not how you say it.'

'Well, it's how my mother said it. After all her years in this country, she still never learned how to speak proper English.'

'Go on now, missus,' Teresa mumbles, 'you're setting an awful example for those children of yours.'

My mother gives a deep throaty laugh.

'If that's the worst they learn from me they're doing well.'

Sometimes when she sees me, she pulls me close and puts her arm around me. Then she laughs chaotically and starts to tickle me, lightly at first. But before long, she has me stretched across the kitchen floor, her hands darting across my body, digging under my neck, under my arms, into my stomach.

I scream.

'I'm going to wet my knickers. Stop, Mummy, stop.'

She keeps going. Teresa laughs. My mother's mouth opens wide as a crater. Her eyes close. I cry so hard that I can't speak, can't beg her to stop. A wet puddle leaks across the floor beneath me. She shouts and sends me to my room. Sometimes she hits me first.

There are other days when she barely gives us a chance to step out of our school clothes and she's packing Saul, Rachel and me into the car with Goldie, the cocker spaniel, squashed between us in the back. We drive out to Dun Laoghaire pier and follow her along the strand. The routine is always the same: we collect five broken branches apiece. Then we stand by the water's edge and watch as she hurls them one by one out to sea.

'Fetch, girl, go fetch,' she shouts to Goldie who dashes across the sand into the icy waters. Moments later she deposits a wet piece of wood at my mother's feet. Other days we collect stones (only the smoothest and the flattest) which my mother sends skimming across the water, shouting with joy as they jump through the air. Her strength is staggering. When dusk falls around us, we make our way back to the car, stopping for a whipped ice-cream from the corner shop. We can never find Goldie when it's time to leave. We march up and down the strand, calling her name over and over, until it's too dark to see. Sometimes she comes trotting back. Mostly we have to go home without her. I fret every inch of that four-mile drive, convinced that she's drowned or lost and that we'll never see her again.

'Don't worry, darling,' my mother says, 'that dog is a bloody genius. She'll be back. Mark my words.' And sure enough, as soon as we round the bend into Tree Tops we spot her, sitting on the front porch, imperious as the Queen herself, with a look that proclaims she doesn't like to be kept waiting. When Goldie dies of a tumour, my mother crumples. My father buys her another cocker spaniel. But the only thing she knows how to chase is her own tail. The trips to the pier stop.

Other days we arrive home to a dark, quiet house. We slink through the downstairs hallways, fearful. Of noise, of movement, of inadvertently doing something that will pull her out of her bedroom, down the stairs. We know if we do, she'll come hurtling towards us, her arms waving through the air like daggers and grab us, by the neck, the collar, the hair, whatever she can get her hands on and beat us. On those afternoons, we play at the end of the garden until after dark. Away from the house. Away from the terror. On those afternoons, I wait for the other woman to come back, the one who laughs and tells jokes, who dances and swerves, who ruffles my hair fondly. I wait for the light to filter back into that dark damaged body, for her eyes to turn soft again.

THREE

Two things make a difference in our house.

Pop and Mr Ed. The pony comes first. Mummy leaves one spring morning, decked out in her riding gear, hard hat, crop and stylish breeches. I wait at the window. I am always waiting at windows. Finally, I spot her across the road, seated atop a large piebald, head held high, eyes unmoving.

'This is your very own pony,' she says proudly, after the animal trots across our quiet, residential street, sails over the front gate and lands mere inches from the glass door. Later, two burly stable-hands arrive in a big red truck with bales of hay.

'Where's the stables Mrs Woolfson?' they inquire.

'Oh,' she laughs, 'the pony will be sleeping in the garage for now; this way, gentlemen.' Moments after his rather impressive arrival, my mother leads Mr Ed (I've named him after my favourite television character) to the edge of the garden, where she's spent the entire week constructing a tremendously intricate jump out of twigs and branches. She stands aside a moment, admires her handi-work, mounts the horse then veers him forward, a look of rare determination on her face. Mr Ed glides over, his hoofs kicking through the air. When they reach the other side, she turns round and sees that the whole thing has come tumbling down. She looks so sad then, I want to put my arms around her. I start rebuilding the jump, picking up branches and twigs, but she has already walked away, leading the huge animal back to his unconventional bedroom. There are nights when Mr Ed neighs so loudly that my mother wades through crates, boxes and buckets in the dark to comfort him. Sometimes she falls asleep tucked in beside his huge brown and black body, and we find her in the mornings with a dreamy, little-girl smile stretched across her face.

My father hates the horse, but not quite as savagely as does Mr Kenny, our gardener. We always think of him as a weathered count, some remnant of Irish nobility, at least that's what he claims. My father tends to believe him, as he himself vacillates between two serge suits year-round while Mr Kenny is always decked out in a top hat, the best of cloth, and a neat waistcoat from which a gold watch and chain dangle. He gardens in those clothes, yet never seems to pick up an ounce of dirt. My father claims that Mr Kenny is the costliest employee in the city because Teresa always has to save the best cut of the roast for him on Saturdays (although he mentions more than once that he isn't that fond of kosher food). He never consumes less than three Rémy Martins with lunch, and usually a glass or two of port afterwards. He spent the summer, prior to Mr Ed's arrival, planting an exotic rose garden and even constructed a wooden trellis to showcase his exquisite display. That year, the strawberries grew wild; the potatoes, carrots, sweet peas and mint yielded their best crops ever, and the stump of every single chestnut tree in the half acre of land we owned was bordered by daffodils and tulips. Mr Ed, it seems, took quite a fancy to Mr Kenny's lush vegetation, and before a month was out, the garden was barren.

A few weeks later, the stable people return to check on Mr Ed and are astounded to find him still residing in the garage. It isn't right, they explain, for a horse to live indoors, with no place to roam; they have no choice but to take him away, which they do, that very day. I'm not sure how my mother explains this to me; I don't remember that she does. One day, Mr Ed is there, tucking into Mr Kenny's prize roses with a vengeance; the next day he's gone. And my mother is off on her next adventure – a multi-coloured racing Mini.

Out of the blue, she arrives at the gates of Stratford College decked out in hipster pants, leather jacket and dark glasses with her hair piled high up in a bizarre sixties do, to rescue me in her devilish automobile dotted with numbers and neon.

'Who is that woman?' the other kids ask. I run quickly to the car, ashamed and, at once, exhilarated by her eccentricity. We drive off leaving a whirlwind of dust in our wake.

FOUR

— ◆ —

She's always been different.

She says so herself. It's not just that she's English, and a snob. It goes deeper, down beneath the bones somehow. She laughs loud and hard like a man. She mimics my father's family, especially his mother, with frightening precision. She couldn't care less about Jewish rituals but speaks fluent Yiddish. She loves clothes, dresses like a model. People compare her to Audrey Hepburn. To me she is dazzling. Especially on Saturday nights when she puts on a red strapless dress that hugs her waist and high-heeled shoes that click against the kitchen floor. She takes my father by the hand, off to one of those fancy supper clubs where they tango, foxtrot and cha-cha-cha, until after midnight. If it's a wedding, bar mitzvah or family event, I go too. I notice that when my mother dances, the world watches. Everything stops. Sometimes on Sunday mornings, I slip into their bed and lie between them, feeling their soft, easy breaths. Sometimes home is a happy place.

Outside Tree Tops my mother's eccentricities are most apparent, especially when contrasted with my father's family – good Jewish stock from Lithuania, as we've all been informed. Grandpa Willie arrived in Ireland at the turn of the century and immediately purchased a horse and cart complete with scrapyard for a mere thirty bob. From that day onward he paved his way upwards with S and S, good old sweat and sacrifice (I always imagined this had something to do with the naming of his favourite son, my father, Solomon Sefton). Old Willie smells of rust, rags and steel and wears horn-rimmed spectacles that shroud cautious eyes that give away nothing. He's a tough one, Willie. Grandma Sarah, on the other hand, is a large, floating entity with soft pale features. I am her *mammela*, her *tattela*, her *bubbelah*, her *Shivonkeleh*, all of the above. Although I never actually decipher what the names mean, they are issued with affection.

Saturday afternoon lunch at Da and Ma's is a mundane ritual. The food is wholesome, dished out on plain crockery. The talk ranges from the price of a bale of rags and the prospect of building a new factory to the *shul* secretary and his impending and rather scandalous divorce. After lunch, Mad Merca, their version of Teresa, flies into the room, stray wisps of mousy hair floating across a bland face, her old tartan skirt hunched up around her midriff. She collects the used paper napkins, at which point Grandma Sarah growls, 'Waste not, want not.' On command, Merca carefully folds the shredded pieces of tissue paper and places them in a drawer for next week, and the one after that. The butter wrappers are scraped through the paper. The juice glasses have the remaining dregs emptied into a big bottle. 'These are good lessons for a young girl to learn,' Grandma barks. 'I know,' I echo, ' "Waste not, want not." '

My mother sits through these weekly escapades with a set smile on her face, a sinister grimace lurking close behind it. Later, when the party shifts three steps over to the couch by the fireplace, my father and his brother Louis migrate up and down in opposite directions in front of the TV set. Louis wheezes as if every breath is his last. His boomerang legs point inward. His thick round shoes almost touch as he walks. My father approaches from the other end of the room. His shoes point inward also, though less so. At the point of intersection they mutter a few words to each other then continue with their pacing. Da Willie sits watching, his hearing aid that whistles and whines like a frantic siren stuffed into his ear. Every time a question is launched in his direction he has to turn the damn thing off, take it out and shout, 'What's that you were saying?' to which my father invariably responds, 'I said why don't you buy yourself a new hearing aid.' 'Buy one?' Willie snorts in disgust, his beaked nose squished up into his eyes. 'Nah, this one's good enough.' With that he replaces it, and the whining continues. Again the conversation drifts – the price of rags, the problem of getting goods through to Belfast, and us kids, racked like slabs of meat on the worn sofa with our eyes eagerly shifting focus, desperate to catch a glimpse of the television set through all those heavy limbs clothed in stiff serge.

On the way home it is always the same. Two minutes out on to the street it starts:

'Solly, your family is simply uncouth, ignorant and rude. That's the last time I'm ever going for lunch.'

'Oh Jackie, that's just their way. You know they are very fond of you.'

'I hate the way your father slurps his soup with that big ugly nose of his right down in the bowl. And the way he takes his false teeth out and leaves them on the side of the dish for all the world to see. And why does he have to drink tea from his saucer? What's wrong with the cup? Can't he act like a normal human being? No, your family has to be different. He's worse than an animal.'

'Well he hasn't done too badly for himself then, hmm, for a savage. I think he's done very well. What about your family? They're above reproach, I suppose.'

'Pop is the epitome of a gentleman,' my mother responds proudly, 'and you know it, and furthermore I don't know why your mother insists on being called "Ma".'

'Because she's always been Ma.'

'Not to me.'

She fumbles through her bag searching for the Rothmans, pulls one out, places it in the gold cigarette holder, lights it and fumes (literally).

'With this bloody Sabbath business, I'm not even allowed to smoke after my meal, if I could just get through the slop they feed me' (under her breath).

'It's a matter of respect, Jackie, simple respect, that's all. Fine example you're setting for your children. Mark my words, they'll grow up with no integrity. Nothing worse than a person without integrity.'

'Oh, I can't smoke a cigarette because it's Shabbos, but you can drive to the office and work on figures and pace up and down with that Dictaphone in your hand while we all sit freezing to death outside. I see making money is fine, but smoking is a sin. And your father with that ridiculous device in his ear, no wonder he can't hear a word. But he manages to pick up the first mention of cash all right. And why does he have to treat us to a view of his scabby legs, week in, week out? Those sores are enough to put a dog off his dinner. Really I don't know how I ever married into such a low-class brood. My mother is probably rolling over in her grave at the very thought of it.'

'She didn't seem to mind when Da and Ma forked out the money for the wedding. Now, did she? She wasn't so grand that she could afford her own daughter's wedding, now was she?'

The differences are out. Mummy holds her bone-white fingers up to her carefully pinned hair. She straightens a button on her chiffon dress. The intense, reckless eyes dart back towards us kids momentarily and then around again, desperate for a way out. I sit glutted by the tasteless meal, the dull talk, and the conflict: their way against hers. All of it leaves my heart chilled. I put my head to the crack above the window to catch some air because although it is cold, the staleness inside the car chokes me. I close my eyes tight and feel the breeze ruffle my hair and blow across my face. Everything else blurs and disappears.

FIVE

—◆—

Pop brings my world into focus.

He enters our home just before my eighth birthday, brightening an otherwise dark, gloomy day at summer's end, surrounded by his wares – boxes of gold candelabras, porcelain plates, gold-rimmed brandy snifters, his onyx and jade cufflinks, pressed gabardine suits, polished shoes, and silk handkerchiefs.

'Shivaun darling,' Mummy says, 'do you mind sharing your bedroom with Pop for a while? He hasn't been feeling too well lately.'

I retire the dolls and toys. I'd never played with them anyway, except for the beautiful black baby doll I got for Christmas (my mother had to pretend it was for Chanukkah). I abandon rough-and-tumble tomboy exploits, like tree climbing, for more domestic pursuits: I help Pop organise his attire in the morning, perfectly matched and colour coordinated, lay out his towels, run his bath-water. At night, our ritual calls for a glass of hot milk laced with a tinge of brandy out of those elegant snifters, after which I listen to his stories. He has so many: the matchbox radio he invented during the war, the fortunes he won and gambled away, how he lost his sight in service and had to work the drills by rote so his officers wouldn't guess he was blind.

He takes great pleasure in lighting his own cigarettes by placing the matchbox at the tip, feeling with his hand for the sulphur, striking along it and allowing the flame to find the cigarette of its own accord. He displays his art collection, identifying each painting by touch, just as he identifies the suit, the shirt, the tie, the cufflinks, the tie-pin for each day, all by feel. He talks about the book he's written which lies in a pile at the bottom of my mother's wardrobe, and explains that he'll have a naked woman, a pack of cards and a wad of money on the cover. And that I can read it when I'm grown up. He advises me about marriage too, says that it's give and take: he gave, Nana took.

My father warns me that half Pop's stories are invented, but that never stops me from listening. Too often his words are interrupted by vengeful coughing attacks, and I lie, scared and still, until the curse has passed and he breathes easy again. A quiet stillness, an ever so fragile clutch on life, fills the air in between those attacks. There's a desperation too that I experience years later watching a friend on a life-support machine – the in, out, in, out, and the interminable dearth of breath in between, a long, splintered pause that can't find its way back to natural rhythm.

Every Saturday, at nine o'clock sharp, Henry the chauffeur squires us away to Adelaide Road synagogue, where he parks Pop's silver Rolls-Royce at the corner, so we can walk into the hushed silence of the place like observant Jews who don't drive on the Sabbath. I hold tight to Pop's arm as he strolls down the aisle issuing salutations with uncanny accuracy. I am special: one of the only little girls amongst a horde of bowed men covered in white silk. I'm too young to sit upstairs by myself, Pop says. And besides, who would help him find his place in the prayer book if I wasn't there? I smile when he says this because he knows all the prayers by heart anyway. Upstairs feels so remote, so cold. Downstairs is warm. When we arrive at our destination, the row of seats right behind the *bima*, Pop removes his cashmere overcoat, his Paisley scarf, his kid gloves, lays them to his side and proceeds to don his prayer shawl. He looks so regal beside me, so linked to his space, and when the cantor begins to sing, Pop's voice joins him. Those mornings in *shul* are the safest I have ever known.

After *shul* Henry deposits us at the barber's in Johnston's Court. I sit propped on a small stool as old men in starched white coats shave traces of stubble from Pop's face. They snip his hair with steel scissors, then apply hot towels to his smooth skin, followed by a dash of aftershave. I love the smell. The way the old men move, with such care, such precision, and such speed. Most of all, I love how they address Pop, as if he is king, his own brand of royalty. When they're done, I lead him to the gourmet deli next door where the owner shoves a giant gherkin into my hand.

'Remember, Shivaun,' Pop says, 'you must develop a taste for the finer things in life.' The men cut slices of smelly cheese and place them in white wax paper. They select olives from porcelain bowls and drop them into round containers. It is my job to carry our purchases to the car. Back at home, Teresa unwraps the packages and prepares lunch.

Many years later, I receive a copy of a worn video, entitled 'Woolfson Home Movies', filmed on Uncle Louis's antiquated reel-to-reel contraption that he carried with him to every family event. In it, I see us as children, dashing back and forth with our cousins, on beaches, running races, at Da and Ma's for those Saturday afternoon lunches. At the very end, there's a shot of the garden at Tree Tops. It's my seventh birthday party with a Punch and Judy show, a massive marquee and Mr Ed being led by a young man, ferrying children around the grounds. Suddenly the camera shifts to the house, and it catches my mother and Pop walking towards us. Pop looks around, trying to get his bearings, then places his arm through his daughter's before moving forwards. Even in the video I see that it is her father who ties her to the ground, that without him, she will lose her place.

SIX

And she does.

No matter how she tries, she'll never be like the other mothers. She purchases brand-new clothes to contribute to the Ladies' Society jumble sale, rather than fumbling through our wardrobes for cast-offs. She invites begging travellers in for tea. She discusses her sex life with Teresa over morning coffee. Her quirks extend, like creeping vines, over her children. Once, for a fancy-dress Purim party, she decides she's sending me as Charlie Chaplin. Even though he's one of my favourites, I want to go as Queen Esther like all the other girls. But she's insistent, has me decked out in one of my father's old suits, Pop's top hat and cane, practising that wobbly walk up and down the hallway for weeks. Paints my face white with the stuff you use for tennis shoes, blackens my moustache with boot polish and drives me down to Stratford. By the time I get there, my face is streaked with tears. I want to be the Queen. Especially when I see all the other girls, with their velvets and lace and mock tiaras. I run back to the car. But she forces me out, sends me up to the auditorium and makes me parade up and down in that agitated walk I've been practising so hard.

I win first prize.

Her tastes always run against the grain. She doesn't listen to jazz or classical music. But she does escort me to see the Beatles when they perform in Dublin. We take our place in the concert hall alongside all the other screaming females. She's got her bell-bottoms on and the hippie scarf, the dark glasses, the suede jacket. Afterwards, we eat fried chicken and chips out of little red baskets in one of those trendy city restaurants. She sits for a while, surveying, then removes her glasses. Her eyes swallow the room.

The waitress deposits a drink in front of her, pointing to its source, a tall, elegantly attired man with silvering hair, who stands alone in the corner. My mother smiles in his direction. 'An actor,' she tells me, 'quite famous. And very good-looking, don't you think?' There are many nights like these in fancy restaurants where she flirts with handsome men who pay for our food: crab and prawns and non-kosher meat, which I'm not supposed to eat. At home, she retreats to the garage where she paints in wild, vibrant colours on canvas. Or she dances in the living room, moving her body in bewitching motion, her head thrown back, her hair wild. She lets go. I watch. My mother is different, very different – exotic, eccentric, unhinged. I know this, as well as I know anything, but I don't know what it will feel like when she's gone.

My father arrives home from work early one night. As usual he's transported the entire factory along with him. He sets himself up in the study, with his bottle of Rémy Martin, the mounds of paperwork, the ever-present Dictaphone, and begins his frantic pacing back and forth, spitting words into the hand-held machine as he marches: *Dear Harry: Reference your correspondence dated 14th of August, we cannot accept the price you quoted for fibre.*

From the doorway my mother launches into quite a performance about having a nice girls' night on the town, just me and her, she says.

We arrive in the lobby of Jury's in Ballsbridge just after dark. A man approaches.

'This is Mr John Marley. Doesn't he look just like Paul Newman?' my mother remarks as he rushes over to her. She lets go of my hand and turns her face towards his. The jolt that passes between them shocks me.

'This is my daughter, Shivaun,' she says.

'Hello,' he answers in a shifty voice. He sounds like he's from the north.

'You're a very pretty girl,' he proclaims once we're seated around a small table in the bar. 'How old are you?'

'Eight.'

'My goodness,' in that same, sharp, nasal tone. 'You're such a nice size. When my sister was eight, she weighed eight stone. Can you imagine that?'

'That's very big,' I tell him after giving the matter serious consideration. 'How old is she now?'

'Twenty-four.'

'And does she weigh twenty-four stone?' I ask.

'Oh, no,' he replies, chuckling. 'She's slimmed down a bit.' Then to my mother, 'Jackie, dear, you have a charming daughter.'

Charming and all as I am, they walk off down the hall, leaving me in the company of a soft drink and a plate of pastries. I sit for hours thinking about his slicked-back hair and thin lips and imagine what they are doing to my mother.

At home, my father corners me in the kitchen.

'Where the hell were you two until this hour?'

I watch my mother from across the room. She's mouthing words. I strain for them, but I can only make out 'cakes' and 'kosher'.

'Out,' I say, terrified, 'out with Mummy, for dinner, like she said.'

'What did you eat? Where did you go?'

'I ate cakes,' I tell him, 'cakes and fish, only kosher. We didn't do anything wrong.'

My mother stands off to the side, her body still twisting with a crazy fire for the man of the hooked nose and shiny head.

She gives birth to my youngest brother, David, in the summer. I don't remember her having a belly or that I was even excited at the prospect of a new brother or sister. I do remember getting the news. I take Rachel down the garden to pick roses for her. The thorns prick me and I begin to bleed. I carry on, plucking stems from the bushes.

'You're hurt. You're full of blood,' Rachel screams suddenly. 'Let's go back inside.'

'It's nothing,' I say. 'Nothing compared to the pain of giving birth.'

That afternoon we visit my mother in hospital and I lay the roses on the starched white sheets of her bed. In the corner in a bassinet lies David, his long, thin body wrapped in blankets. I ask if I can hold him.

'Go ahead,' she says, 'you're a big girl now.'

I take him in my arms and pull him gently to my chest. His soft baby breath touches my face. In that moment, I know what it feels like to be a mother. There are many nights in those first months of David's life, when Teresa's gone for the day and my mother is out, that my father watches nervously as I rest my brother on their large double bed and struggle with the huge nappy pins. Neither of us is much good at changing diapers. Soon enough, he hires an au pair from Spain who steps gracefully into the role.

As summer progresses I become my mother's accomplice. It's not an easy job. Everywhere she ventures, I go right along with her. My father's cross-examinations intensify. He's getting desperate. I never give her up, not once, but I begin to avoid contact with him altogether.

In August we visit the horse show as Marley's guests, with special passes to all the events and the best seats for the competitions. He leads us into the stables and introduces me to his prize horse. I feed him oats and stroke his mane and feel so important in there with all the trainers and champion breeders.

We set off in the rain under a huge umbrella towards the winner's lounge, where he's arranged a luncheon in our honour. We pass a rusty blue car stationed off to the side. I notice three little faces peering out. Two boys and a girl bang on the wet windows. I see their mouths stretch open, moving, but I can't hear them. Marley glances in their direction and, without changing expression, charges forward.

'C'mon, now, or we'll be late for that wee luncheon of ours.'

I stand there transfixed by the image of those forlorn children. My mother pulls me along behind her.

'They're his children,' she says.

'But when are they going to eat?' I ask.

'Oh, we'll bring them back some sandwiches later.'

All through the wee luncheon I think of them suffocating in that damp air, cold and shivering with their scruffy coats pulled up around their necks and their tiny fingers drumming up and down on the wet window-panes.

It is during this time that I find a newspaper clipping tucked away in a drawer under a piece of lace and a few mothballs, which displays Marley and my mother standing proudly together in the winner's circle at the Royal Dublin Show. Attached to it is a report from a private detective which cites Marley as 'irresistible to women'. Next day in school I ask my teacher what irresistible means. And that night as I stand in the doorway to my parents' room I find my father hunched over his bed with the clipping in his hands. His head is down, and he's crying like a baby.

SEVEN

—◆—

She walks off.

Straight into Marley's arms. At least that's what I suspect. What we're told is that she's taking a break and has moved herself into a lovely flat at the bottom of Orwell Road, where we can visit her on the way home from school. A 'separation' is what my parents call it. What they don't mention is that Marley has taken the flat beneath her. Maybe my father doesn't know this, but on the day that I choose to pop in unannounced I can't locate her. Finally I ring the bell of the flat below. When she opens the door, she is surprised, but invites me into a room littered with boxes and crates filled with men's clothes.

'Don't say anything to your father,' she says as she picks up a pair of slacks and hangs them in the wardrobe. 'He doesn't need to know everything, right?'

I nod.

The next time I visit, I find her impounded in the toilet of her own flat, unable to move. In her hand is a piece of tissue paper covered in thick bloody clumps.

'I'm bleeding,' she says. 'What should we do?'

She's shaking. I'm afraid for her. I want to cradle her and neatly wipe the blood away. I want to carry her home.

I will be sensible. I will fix it. I will fix my mother.

'Maybe we can ring Dr Robinson,' I say, thinking of the kind old man who visits me when I have a temperature and always gives me a shilling.

'No,' she almost shouts. 'We can't ring him. He'll tell your father.'

She fills another tissue with even chunkier clumps of blood.

'Maybe it's a very bad period,' I say. The authority in my voice surprises me. In the end, the blood stops. Whatever's come out of her is flushed down the toilet. It's grown dark outside, and home is a mile away. I leave her stretched on her bed, under the dim light of the lamp, with the covers pulled up around her neck, shivering and pale.

'Go on,' she says as I linger in the doorway, 'Go on home now, or your father will have the police out looking for you. That's all I need.'

All night long, I imagine blood oozing from between her legs. I see red, tangled sheets and her beautiful thin face growing whiter than the porcelain toilet bowl upon which she spent the afternoon. All night long, in my mind, she fades until there is nothing left of her.

Through it all, Pop is the anchor that affixes me to the world. As my mother moves away from us, he fills all the fissures where her absence lives. I still sleep on the small fold-out bed beside his. Even though my mother has gone, there's no question of him leaving us. My father never even suggests it. Pop is dying. At night, I lie awake listening to his relentless coughing. I watch him sweat. I hand him his medicines when he calls for them. When it is too much, I knock on my father's door for help. Exhausted, he sits at Pop's bedside. Sometimes he stays all night.

It happens in June. About a year into the trial separation he is taken to the hospital. I am allowed to visit him only once. When I walk into his room, he tries for a smile. He knows I am there even before I speak.

'My beautiful bandit,' he says, 'I hope you are keeping the bed warm for me at home.' I never see him again. My mother shows up for the funeral in a black miniskirt and a wide-brimmed hat, a stranger in her own home.

'He died of a broken heart,' she tells me. 'Because I left him.'

EIGHT

—◆—

The trial separation seems to work out well for my mother.

She never comes back and I become everyone's favourite orphan. I eat cakes at Ruth Cohen's house, while fending off the advances of her brother Harold, a maths whiz who masturbates in the desk behind me at school; go on camping trips down to Brittas Bay with the Krone family, where Renata and I pore over her father's pornographic magazines while listening to his jazz violin solos on the scratchy record player. Hal Krone is from some foreign place and has played with the likes of Yehudi Menuhin, which impresses my father no end, but means very little to me. I'm far more interested in his customised magazine collection. Saul, Rachel, David and I are regularly shipped down to Brittas Bay with our cousins. We hate these trips because Uncle Louis drives so slowly that we all get carsick. We are always desperate to get back home even though the rare moments we do spend there we have to put up with a succession of demented housekeepers to whom our father entrusts our care. We imagine at times that he gets them through a mental home rather than a domestic agency because despite the fact that he places thoughtful ads in the Help section of the *Irish Times*, only the creepiest women respond.

Of these, the most memorable are Mrs Higgenbottom, who

refuses to cook or clean and who wakes us all up at dawn and makes us stand to attention in the corner of her room in the dark as she sleeps; Francis who takes us to the racetrack instead of to the pictures or the zoo or wherever it is she's supposed to take us, and who arrives home after her days off covered in bruises and scratches. There's also the self-titled pixie twins, who claim to be nieces of Edna O'Brien, and the woman who crashes three cars in a row. Other nameless creatures arrive who belt out commands in Russian or French or Spanish, and who lock us in the playroom while they go off about their business. Home is an awfully strange place as we rifle through household help like day-old underwear: Saul develops a fierce temper, Rachel has night terrors, David has no clue who his mother is, and my father works non-stop.

We survive.

We put on acrobatic shows and plays in the living room for the neighbours, ride our bikes down dirt tracks and across dangerous waterfalls in the park after dark. There are no rules. We're the wild kids from the big old house on the corner whose mother has disappeared. At night, we bunch together on the floor of my back room like the strays that we are. There's hope to the time we spend together. We will always have each other.

After they've gone to bed, I lie in the dark and try to imagine what life holds for me. Sometimes I see myself in New York or Paris, sitting at an outdoor café, dressed in chic garb. I always have a cigarette in my hand, a glass of wine in front of me. I am always a writer. Always famous. When morning comes I see that I'm just an eleven-year-old girl, on the stocky side, who doesn't have particularly nice clothes.

NINE

In my early teens, I find that Ireland grounds me.

There's something in the landscape itself and in its heavy incessant rains that drains away sorrow, a lyric, almost mythical quality
that gathers itself about the forlorn. I start catching the bus out to
the coast where I sit by the seawall and watch for hours as the
waves crash against the rocks. I see myself in those hours as an
essential part of my island's topography, cut off from the rest of
civilisation, as lonely and isolated as the ground beneath me. But
though I long to slip into the surroundings, to merge into their
shape and form, to be taken in, held fully by their rhythms, I never
feel like I fit.

Yet, there's something in the Irish way, a quiet defeat that lets life
seep slowly into the abyss of a beer bottle, which comes as second
nature to me. I understand the ebbing away of promise and of
hope. I grasp the essentials of melancholy. What I don't get are the
notions of exclusivity that my fellow Jews seem so comforted by. I
don't want to stay among my own kind. And I don't. I make friends
with Nuala and Dermot, a brother and sister duo from across the
street. We go everywhere together, so when my father asks me to
attend the Zionist National Fund 'Christmas' dance, I invite them
along. Dermot and Nuala, blond, blue-eyed and freckled, contrast

sharply with the sea of olive skin. We're in faded jeans and cheesecloth shirts. They're in spiffy suits and long-sleeved dresses. At the door, Alan Goldberg, junior Jewish National Fund treasurer (he groped me once on a dark staircase) halts us.

'You know better than this, Shivaun,' he says. 'This is a Jewish event.'

I remind him that we are in Ireland, a democracy after all, and that his is the very behaviour Jews themselves are always complaining about.

'This is a Christmas dance, for God's sake, in celebration of Christ himself.'

The very mention of Christ catapults him over the edge. His face goes scarlet and the veins in his neck engorge to bursting point. Quite suddenly his anger is replaced by a sneering grin.

'I wouldn't expect any better from a girl who's raising herself, from the daughter of a tramp,' he mutters. We never even make it through the door.

I give up on the Jewish scene after that and become a regular at O'Donohue's. It's my first real taste of Dublin life: men play the spoons and sing in mournful voices. Women sit huddled together, drinking whiskey and Guinness. At thirteen, I am far too young to be spending my Saturday nights in a pub, but the fact that I have a pair of knockers that rival Mae West's and an attitude to go right along with them, must account for something. The bartenders serve me pint after pint of lukewarm Harp until I puke my guts up. In O'Donohue's on Saturday nights, I reinvent myself as a surefire patriot, drinking with the best of them, singing along with nationalist fervour to the songs that made my country famous: 'Danny Boy', 'Give Ireland Back to the Irish', 'Dirty Olde Town': I know them all. Often I meet bohemian types from France or Holland, who look at me in a confused, probing manner like they half believe I'm old enough to drink, to kiss, to fuck, even though

I'm probably younger than their daughters. I play with the possibilities. I always drink. Sometimes I kiss. I never fuck.

Back at home, I miss my mother. Her wacky, subterranean laugh, the off-colour jokes, the smoky breath, the dancing, all of it. Sometimes I think about the beatings. But what I end up with always is an image of a beautiful young woman turned acid. More than anything I want her back.

I spend much of my time locked in my bedroom, remembering. Gazing out the window, I get lost in the dense mist that steals across the Milltown golf course (they don't accept Jews). I get a perverse pleasure from the fact that half their golf balls end up in our garden anyway, which we, enterprising young Jews that we are, collect and sell back to the golfers at considerable profit. My mother and aunts played golf, and boasted impressive handicaps to boot. They couldn't play there. Instead they played at Edmunstown, the Jewish golf course on the edge of town. My mother wasn't happy at that club.

'I don't think I'm Jewish enough for them,' she'd tell my father, 'and they make fun of my English accent.'

'Don't be so bloody ridiculous,' he'd say, raising his head briefly from a mound of paperwork. 'You're imagining things as usual.'

'What would you know? All you care about is making money, the bloody factory.'

'Well who else is going to cater to your expensive tastes, your nights out? I don't even know where you are half the time.'

There are so many scenes to remember: Marley's car slipping noiselessly up to the front gate, glistening in the moon's light; her slight figure scurrying down the path towards him, the swoosh of the tyres against the wetness of the road. And the next night my father pinning her to the floor in the downstairs hallway, forbidding her to move, while we sat and watched from the stairway. Her arms flailed against him. Her screams pierced through the house. We begged him to stop. Finally, exhausted, he let her go. Then we drove into the city, her and I; he made me go with her. We booked a room at Jury's, ate a lavish meal. She slept. I stayed by the phone all night, rang my father every half-hour to make sure he wasn't too sad. She laughed at me, called me a Daddy's girl.

These are the images that swell in me as I gaze outward.

Eventually I turn away from the window. I lie on the bed and cry myself to a stillness. Sleep never comes easily. She appears at the edge of my dreams with turbulent gestures and mangled speech: a woman always on her way out, never on her way back. In my waking moments I can't accept she's gone for ever, not fully, not until that final dream, after which the pretence dies. In it, she's sitting by my bed, so close that I can smell her perfume and feel her smoky breath. She speaks slowly.

'I'm coming back to stay, darling, because I miss you too much.'

But when I look down, there's no chair beneath her, only air.

I wake myself up screaming. My father hurries into my room. He tries to calm me. I rage against his fragile arms. I swear she's been there. I demand that he bring her back. He makes a series of phone calls. She does appear that night, summoned by a daughter's anguish, and promises me that she'll come back to stay. Next morning I awaken to a heavy truth: she's gone for good.

TEN

My father disintegrates around the holidays.

When his factory is closed, and there's nothing to cling to, no deals to be brokered, he gets this sad, beaten-down look about him as he wanders through the house like he's shaking off phantoms. At odd moments, we find him sitting in corners, asking himself, 'Why me, why did this have to happen to me, why our family?' When he notices us, he jerks his head back into place, and sets about movement: to the desk, the pile of papers, the brandy glass, the fat cigar. None of us have the answers. We trail around the house, avoiding the question, avoiding each other.

A few Christmases after she leaves, he packs us into the new Mercedes and carts us off to some holiday emporium in Kerry with buffet tables, evening sing-songs and masses of kids running back and forth. People are always asking questions. About our mother, and why she hasn't come. They comment on how grown up I am, lifting David up and ferrying him through the corridors, feeding him. 'Only a child herself,' I hear them say. At night, in the hotel lounge, Saul gets up on stage, in his ill-fitting clothes with his hair brushed comically upside his head and begins to sing 'I'm Nobody's Child'. Someone's always moved to tears. Later, I sneak into the bar and sit amongst the countrywomen who drink their whiskeys back to back. The priest orders his double. With a Consulate menthol smoke dangling from my lips, the alcohol-tinged Pussyfoot in my hand, I observe from my corner table. I feel grown up sitting there, with the sounds of forced, drunken laughter, the slapping and reslapping of hands on backs, the tinkle of glasses and the high-pitched, accelerating fiddle. Suddenly I can't breathe. I run out across the grass until I reach the winding country road. In the distance I see a string of city lights blinking. I imagine it is Dublin, beckoning me home.

On one of these winter forays we're sitting at the back of the ballroom staring at the stage. Into the spotlight steps Moira in a white sequinned dress. There's a strength to her. Her movements, her voice, her presence reach all the way to the back and the top of the room. My father sits up, alert, and when the song is over, he claps harder, longer than anyone else. Back at Tree Tops, a week later, I hear the housekeepers laughing as they wade through his dirty laundry.

'Oh be Jaysus,' mutters Nuala (the latest) to Teresa (who's down to two days a week), 'this looks like lipstick stains on his collar. Can't imagine who put them there, get a whiff of this suit. Lady's perfume to be sure.' I hold in my breath from behind the door and wonder, whose lipstick, whose perfume?

A year later, I find out. Another Christmas retreat, this time the Green Isle Hotel on the outskirts of Dublin. We're in bed. The lights are out. My father slips into view. Behind him a woman follows. They tread across the darkness, lay a batch of presents at the foot of our beds, and creep out. Through the shadows I see their hands touch and hear the faintest sounds of laughter. Next day, I question my father.

'Who was that woman in our room last night?'

'What woman are you talking about?'

'The lady who put the presents by our beds.'

'Just a friend, that's all.'

Moira enters our life in the form of hushed phone calls. My father starts going out at night. He wears cologne. He buys himself a new suit. Then there are weekends away. Gradually, Moira cements a place in our world. She purchases our clothes, takes us on holiday, plays with us, sings to us, cooks for us (matzo meal omelettes, the recipe of which she gets on the back of the matzo box).

SSW (as my father prefers to be called) continues his gruelling work schedule, has two open-heart surgeries before his thirty-fifth birthday, almost dies, comes back to open an even bigger factory. And Moira, through it all, is there. Leading him to the bathroom when he can't stand by himself. Bathing his wounds. Yet, at Saul's bar mitzvah, in front of the entire Woolfson clan, she enters through the back door like the hired help, makes her way to the stage, where she delivers a stunning performance of 'Sunrise, Sunset' (my father's favourite) and a host of Jewish numbers she's learned especially for the occasion. She exits just as she's arrived with a weak, knowing nod from my father.

Back at Tree Tops, I hear them argue.

'I feel like an employee, not a girlfriend,' she says.

'Moira, you know my circumstances. I'm a well-respected member of this community. Now how would it look if I were to be openly seen with you? You're asking too much of me. I have my children to think of, an example to set for them, my reputation. It's bad enough Jackie walked out on us. I can't be seen to be involved with a non-Jew.'

And there it is, one of those eternal clashes that set belief against behaviour, word against action. The Jewish man, the respected community member, with the *shiksa* girlfriend. Disgrace, shame, *shonda*. There are a lot of names for men like my father, and I'm not sure how he replays them all in his own head. Whatever he does with them, they metamorphose into a mandate to us: to be more Jewish than Irish, to stay among our own, ward off those on the outside. What he doesn't realise is that we are being formed, day in day out, by the anthems that Moira sings late at night in our Jewish kitchen with its milk and meat plates, its separate sets of dishes for Passover. We are surrounded by Irish women. Because they take care of us, we are drawn close to the cadence of our country. It's an osmotic process, through which, even under my father's watchful eye, we become more Irish than Jewish. Perhaps because he senses this he recoils beneath the shadow of prayer and ritual. He begins to attend synagogue regularly (something he has never done before), clings tighter to the trappings of his faith, and develops an almost obsessive awareness of matters Jewish: the state of Israel and its flimsy borders, the Jewish dances that we should be attending, the community groups to which we just have to belong.

Briefly, in an effort to please him, I become immersed. I refuse to be driven on Shabbos, eat only kosher food, and insist on going to a B'nai Brith summer camp in Bournemouth. But I feel coldly displaced among the teenage boys and girls and the rigid camp counsellors. I know all the Hebrew songs, the prayers, the Friday-night ritual, but I can't find a way in. The boys view me as a misfit, perhaps because I can handle more wine than they can, can kick a football harder, and know more dirty jokes. The girls move away when I approach, lower their voices to a hush, and fail to make space for me at the dinner table. I spend two miserable weeks attempting to feign nationalistic fervour when we sing Zionist songs and, equally, to rein in my horror during racist discussions on how to maintain the Jewish state.

'We've got to stick together, stay among our own. Otherwise what happened with Hitler can happen again,' one of the counsellors comments one evening over dinner.

'I'd disown any child of mine who dated a non-Jew,' says another.

I think of my father and Moira back home. Of the Catholic friends I've made up the street, of Teresa, and of my own mother, off in her new life with Marley.

The counsellors bat words across the table: *shiksa, yoch, goy*.

'What about kike, yid?' I ask. 'What happens when people call us that?'

'That's different. We're the chosen people. God's chosen people. Better than all the others.'

I want to go home.

ELEVEN

Addresses don't make homes.

In the few weeks away, I'd convinced myself I had something to get back to. The truth of it is this: I'm steadily working my way towards womanhood. Have the breasts, the monthly cycle and the attitude to prove it. Not to mention a ghostly resemblance to my mother. I want to be just like her, want to swish and sway and adopt sexy wiles, lower my eyes, flirt. Most of all, I want to move like she does, with a raw abandon that leaves nothing unspoken. But I've witnessed where that leads: to a grown man sitting on a bed, crying uncontrollably, who wanders his own house asking questions to which there are no answers. And to a woman who ends up on a toilet in a dark flat a mile down the road from the home she created, staring at clumps of her own blood. Sex is dangerous. Being a woman is dangerous. So I become a tomboy, shroud my female self in baggy boys' clothes. I adopt a manly swagger, play boy games, climb trees. In the evenings when the housekeepers are busy, I dress up in my father's suits and stand in front of the long mirror in his room. Behind that dark cloth, under the layers, I feel protected from his wrath and hurt. But no matter how I try to conceal my woman self, my father finds it anyway. What he sees in me always is the reflection of the woman who left.

When he stares at me, a doomed look settles in his eyes. There are words to accompany the look: slut, tramp, trollop, traitor, unreliable – just like your mother.

And I become her. I do nothing right. Every time he appears in the doorway of my bedroom, hands thrashing in distress, momentum building in his voice, every time he balks at the lack of order, belittles my choice of career (writing), bemoans my style of dress (or lack thereof), derides my choice of friends (hooligans and misfits), a little piece of me goes missing.

At night, I venture towards the doorway of his study, my notebook tight in my hand. Breaking into the muffled monotone and screeching rewinds of his Dictaphone, I ask, 'Would you like to hear some of my writing? I think it's quite good.'

He responds by delivering a diatribe on corporate enterprise, the benefits of attending a Jewish school, the irrelevance of creative pursuits, and the imminent possibility of my seeing a psychiatrist. I turn away dejected and make my way up to the little back bedroom. Big and all as Tree Tops is with its five bedrooms and maids' quarters, it's still too small for my dreams.

I begin to frequent the nightclubs along O'Connell Street – he calls them firetraps – with their powder rooms jammed with expectant females clamouring for space in front of dusty oblong mirrors. These girls with names like Agnes and Deirdre and Concepta are dolled up to the nines, with heels so sharp they could cut diamonds. Among them, for the first time, I sense that the birth name I'd assumed was exotic, a trifle French, when set against the Sarahs and Rebeccas at school, and the Saul, Rachel and David of my own brothers and sister, is common as muck. Among Jews, I am considered unique, the only one in the community with a Gaelic label. Outside that domain, there's a different world, in which every other girl bears my moniker. From the slums in Ballymun to the tower at Ringsend, 'Siobhan, Siobhan, Shove on your knickers.

Your mammy's coming,' is the anthem. But even in that, there are nuances that thwart incorporation.

'Whyddaya spell your name like dat,' inquires the burly doorman at Sloopy's disco one night when I sign 'Shivaun' in the guest book. 'Are ye a Yank or a Brit?' he asks, at which point the mile-long queue behind me turns to stare. I begin a long-winded explanation of how my mother, an Englishwoman, and my father, one of the first Jewish scholars of Gaelic, arrived at a compromise: the Gaelic name with the phonetic English spelling. Halfway through my discourse, I lose him. That very night a young man with a winning smile and a certain flashy allure approaches me at the bar. We strain to hear each other over the music.

'What are you doing in a place like this?' he asks.

'Same as you, probably,' I say, trying to act all casual.

'Where are you from?' he asks, like he already knows the answer.

'Rathgar, the south side.'

'I knew there was something different about you. You snooty types, with your uppity accents and hippie clothes, think you don't even have to dress up. You come down here gurrier shopping, thinking you have it made in the hay. What makes you think I'd be with the likes of you anyway?'

I want to tell him how ostracised I feel, how diminished by the 'Come as you are' look I've perfected, an outgrowth of my tomboy days that I haven't yet managed to mutate into femininity because I simply don't know how. And I wonder when I will find a place where my accent, or my address, or lack of feminine wiles don't give me away off the bat.

Once or twice on the way home from the club, I let the taxi man feel between my legs and stroke my silky knickers up and down as he drives. My mother did the same thing. My father told me so. The spidery touch of those fingers keeps her alive in me.

Eventually, my sorties to Sloopy's bear their own reward: the night I meet Pat who is titillated rather than offended by my uppity accent, and the fact that I order pints, smoke unfiltered French cigarettes and don't dress up for dates. Architect student, part-time musician, Catholic from Ballyjamesduff. Everything about him draws me in: his dismally old-fashioned plaid jacket, his stammer, his infectious laugh and those bright smiling eyes. My father, needless to say, isn't quite as taken with the notion of Pat as I am. He flat out forbids me to see this new 'boy' (Pat is twenty-two) as he titles him.

We argue.

'How can you tell me not to see him, when you're going out with Moira?' I demand.

'Now that's a different matter entirely,' he says

'Oh so it's do as I say, not as I do. Typical Jewish hypocrisy.'

'You won't be happy till I'm dead in my grave.' His hands flap at his sides. 'You won't stop until I have a bloody heart attack. That's what you want. To kill me off once and for all.'

And on it goes. For her part, Moira tries to intervene.

'Ah now, Solomon,' she says (adopting the mothering tone she uses when he's acting even more unreasonably than usual), 'you can't very well have a relationship with me and prohibit your daughter from seeing this fellow. Why don't you meet him? Have a drink with him. See for yourself. Shivaun has good judgement. Isn't that the way you raised her?'

'I will not, under any circumstances, under no account, go out with Shivaun and this "fellow" as you call him. She knows how I feel. She knows what's right, and that's all there is to it. As for raising her, I wasn't the only one involved, and you know what her mother's like. God knows how she'll end up if she follows her example.'

What about his example? Maybe he starts wondering himself because we see less and less of Moira. Her drinking twists to new heights. We hear about a roadside skirmish in which her car smacks into a wall. And an awkward spill into a pool after a performance in some country hotel, as a result of which her vocal cords, not to mention her confidence, take a beating. We hear too about trips to doctors for an obscure ailment she titles the 'complaint', some woman's malady they never pinpoint. When we do see her, she's in a drunken state on her way back from a show at the Gaiety or the Olympia. The kind my father conveyed us to with such enormous pride only a year or so previously, where he'd clap gleefully the moment she stepped under the white stage light, and continue doing so long after everyone else had stopped. Their disengagement process is gradual, ruthless almost and, if the truth be told, prone to reversal. After close to a decade together, SSW coldly and systematically sets his sights on what he's probably always hankered after: a bona fide Jewess, to replace the one he lost. Some weeks he seems to have moved on from Moira, others he's back, getting that exposed look on his face on the phone, which signals that it's no business associate on the other end.

None of this helps with the Pat scenario. In fact, it makes it worse. Now that he's given up on Moira, my father is even more adamant. In response, I become adept at a level of subterfuge that could topple governments, lying about my whereabouts, fabricating events which I just have to attend for this youth group, for that school organisation. The only truth to my life is the time I spend curled up next to Pat in his single bed on the top floor of the flat in Churchtown. Without realising it, I have become my mother: a double-dealing female bent on deception. God knows, I've certainly had the training for it. I think to myself that these are the compromises you have to make in order to find and keep love. They are the minutest concessions to honesty that demand that I stare my father straight in the eyes while telling him a barefaced lie, that I lie to myself so often that eventually I no longer remember what truth is. I suffocate under the false notion that Pat loves me completely, that he will ask me to marry him, that I will leave my father's house and walk out on my own, just as my mother did.

It doesn't work out like that: one spring afternoon Pat asks me to meet him in Kehoe's in town. I don't like off-the-cuff meetings, curves in the road that I'm not prepared to navigate. This one is no different. I've never told Pat that I'm still a schoolgirl, have pretended since that first night in Sloopy's that I'm in Trinity. Normally, to meet him, I have to cut classes and leave Stratford mid-afternoon, get on a bus and travel into town. I've done this plenty of times before, even once after a particularly rowdy bout of hockey, when I had to change out of my sports uniform into a pair of clean pressed trousers in the toilet, with no time to remove the muck and grime of the hockey field from my thighs. Usually, I get off at the back of Trinity and walk my way to the front gate to meet him as if I've just emerged from an enlightening lecture on seventeenth-century literature. On this day though, sitting on the upper deck of the 15A on the way in, I'm nervous. I didn't like the sound of his voice on the phone, and he's been acting weird lately, distant. I arrive early and order a pint of Harp. He walks in a while later, worn down, battered looking. He's anxious, I can tell, because he's stammering more than usual, talking about his job at the architect's office, the band rehearsals he's scheduled with some new fellas: anything but the matter at hand. Finally he musters the courage.

'I don't th-th-think we can ssssee each other any more,' he says.

I've been dreading these words since the moment I met him. I lean forward, close enough to kiss him, to smother whatever he's about to say next.

An inevitability hangs between us that means I have as much chance of changing this as I have of fixing his stammer.

'I can't take on this whole ffffamily saga of yours, with your

ffffather being ssssso against us. It's too much responsibility for
me.'

'You don't have to feel responsible,' I say.

'Listen,' he blurts out. 'I don't know wwwwhere I'll be in six
months.'

'Where would you be?' I ask. 'I thought you wanted to live with
me.'

'I don't, Shivaun. Not now.'

'Please don't do this,' I say. 'Don't leave me.'

'You don't have to beg for love. I'm very fffond of you. I even
think I love you sometimes, but I'm not ready for that. I think I'd
like to date other people.'

'Other people?' I ask. 'Like who?' Then desperately, before he has
a chance to answer, 'You could date me too. It doesn't mean we
could never see each other.'

I'll share him, I think to myself, just so long as I don't lose him.

The bar is smoky now and noisy. I've had three pints in about as
many minutes and my head has started to throb. I don't know
where to put what I feel. Suddenly I realise I'm late for a meeting
with my father over at the Unicorn restaurant. I leave Pat sitting in
the snug, sipping his Bass. Once out on the street, I'm blind. Even
though the Unicorn is five minutes away, I get lost and almost
knocked down by an oncoming lorry. I stop four times to cry. By
the time I get there, my eyes are raging red. Saul is standing outside
against the wall.

'What's the matter, Shiv?' he asks as soon as he sees me. I can
never hide things from him.

'Pat,' I say. 'He broke up with me.' Saul puts his arm around me.
There's safety next to him. He's fifteen, with long tangled hair and
big brown eyes just like my mother's.

'Don't worry, Shiv. Let's get dinner and see what Daddy wants.
Do you know why he asked to meet us?'

'I've no idea. But it must be important because he sent Rachel and David to be minded. Said it was a grown-up matter, just for me and you.'

There's awful chaos inside – something about over-booking – and it takes an hour to get seated. The waiter hovers nervously over the table. 'Yes, Mr Woolfson. Of course, no meat stock. Which wine is that again?' There's tension as soon as we sit down. My father picks nervously at his food. Finally, he embarks on his little speech.

'Eh . . . eh . . . I invited you out tonight because I wanted to tell you that I'm getting married.'

'Married? To Moira?' I ask.

'No, not Moira, Adele, the woman I met through your Auntie Jill, from Leeds. A very nice widow, with one daughter.'

'Does Moira know?' I ask.

'Well, not yet, not exactly no. I thought I'd tell you two first. I want to make sure you approve.'

Approve? Right now, I don't know if I can live another five minutes. It's taking all my resources not to cry into the bowl of green pea soup set in front of me. Had he proposed this on a night when I still believed in love, in possibility, I might have conjured a more informed response, but on this occasion, I offer only silence, which I've no doubt he interprets as acquiescence. I'm stunned. I know absolutely fuck all about this woman with the one daughter from Leeds.

'Well, who is this Adele anyway?' I inquire.

'You remember the lady I escorted to the New Year's Eve dance this year?' I remembered all right; she'd materialised out of some extremely thin Jewish air, the cousin of a friend of a friend of my aunt's they'd fixed him up with for the night. His family were all at it in those days, setting him up on dates with Jewish women. They were that desperate to rid him of Moira. At the time I hadn't paid her much mind. She'd spent all of ten minutes in our house, ushered in and out, leaving the whiff of extremely strong perfume behind her. She was tall, thin, very English, a little uptight, with heavily lacquered hair pulled up in a tight bun. Well, the plan, it seems, had worked and here we were speechless in a crowded restaurant.

Across the room, at that moment, we hear a familiar voice. Staggered, we watch Moira enter with her brother and sister-in-law. My father takes two rapid swallows from his wineglass. As far as we know he hasn't seen Moira for months. Certainly she hasn't been at the house.

'I didn't know they'd be here. I wonder what the occasion is,' he says.

'Probably her birthday,' I tell him. 'It's June the sixteenth today.'

'Of course,' my father says. 'I got her a lovely gift. I didn't forget, but what a coincidence.'

What ensues is a highly complex version of musical chairs, with Moira approaching our table, us leaving to sit at hers, the waiters becoming even more confused in the process, delivering the braised lamb to my father, who almost faints at the very sight of the non-kosher meat, the poached salmon to Tony, Moira's brother. The red wine goes where the white should be. Overall it's a disaster. By the end of it, I'm sitting in front of Tony, and the tears that I've been holding so bravely roll down my face.

'Is it about your father?' he says, having just been informed as to the reason for our presence in the damn restaurant in the first place.

'That,' I say, 'but it's Pat, too. He broke up with me today. Just before I got here.'

'Aww, pet, little Woolfcub,' he says (that's what he always calls me). 'Don't worry, it'll turn out right.'

'Right,' I say, and as if in confirmation of the absurdity of the notion that anything could ever possibly turn out even halfway right, at that very moment I look across to my father's table. From the body language and the facial gestures I see that he has just imparted the dramatic news. Moira sinks back in her seat. Her face turns white, almost translucent. She grabs the wineglass, guzzles recklessly until it's drained, at which point she pours herself another.

Dinner dispensed with, we make our exit. My father invites Moira back to our house for a drink. To talk, to explain, to say goodbye? Whatever the reason, she accepts. En route he produces the present: a gold watch.

'It's very expensive,' he says as he hands it to her. 'Cost over a hundred pounds.'

'Oh, it's beautiful,' she answers, 'but Solly, you left the price tag on, and it says forty-five pounds.'

At this we laugh, us Woolfcubs in the back. It's so like him, to give her a watch, boast about its price and forget to remove the tag. Back at home, I retire immediately to my room. I lie on the bed in the dark. I want to screen myself against what I know or, at the very least, to engage in some manner of psychic wizardry that can transform the story into a better one that doesn't hurt. But, no magician, I just lie there waiting for the facts to wash over me and travel on elsewhere.

'I'll get through this,' I say, out loud, 'just like I get through everything else.'

The taut, hard line that holds my centre together with the grip of steel, that instinct for survival, born, I think, during those awful summer afternoons before my mother left, when she beat me stupid and I'd slink away like a wounded puppy, head down, feet dragging, to find myself alone on the top bunk-bed, crying until my breath stalled, time disappeared and I entered a safe, white place, a space from which no one or nothing could move me. I enter that place now.

There's a knock on the door.

'Come in,' I say.

Moira sits on the edge of the bed and, in the darkness, takes hold of my hand.

'Tony told me what happened with Pat,' she says. 'I just wanted to make sure you were all right.' I cry then, deep, harrowing sobs. She turns on the light. Her piercing blue eyes are bright and wet.

'He'll phone you, Shivers,' she says, 'he'll come to his senses. He'd be crazy to let you go. He's scared is all. Men, they get scared. They make rash decisions. They look back and if they have any sense whatsoever, they make it right.'

'Will Daddy make it right?' I ask.

'I don't think so.'

Moira is correct on both counts. Pat rings two days later, probably a whole five minutes after he receives the gut-wrenching missive I've launched in his direction.

'I miss you,' he says simply. 'Maybe we can work it out. I'm not so happy on my own.' In an instant, my entire world shifts to smoothness, like I've been driving, got the clutch stuck in one of those horrible, throttled moments, and finally managed to get back into gear.

We amble along dubiously for another six months until Pat and a group of friends form a band, a Doobie Brothers, Eagles knock-off deal that's bland as all hell. They play in corners at all-night parties and do a whole lot of talking about giving up their day jobs. I'm not convinced they have much of a future, until the afternoon Pat tells me to meet him at a flat in Ballsbridge.

'Whose is it?' I ask.

'Some guy named Geldof, I don't know him that well.'

When I arrive, a tall, thin girl with long black hair and an exotic face opens the door.

'They're down there,' she says, pointing to the garage at the edge of the garden, like she is used to these intrusions.

Then I hear the music, a fast-paced cover version of Bob Marley's 'Trenchtown Rock'. I open the garage door. I'm shocked. This Geldof guy is tall with mad skinny legs, dressed in a tailored dinner jacket, moves just like Mick Jagger, and is singing his guts out, even though there's no one watching him but me and the band. This isn't mild Doobie Brothers shit. This is good. Afterwards, I tell Pat:

'You guys are going to be famous. You'll be giving up the architecture after all.'

'You really think so?' he asks.

'Hell yeah!'

It isn't long at all before the Boomtown Rats are being hailed as Ireland's musical ingénus. I manage to follow them pretty much everywhere they go, up and down the countryside to bars and clubs, student halls and university auditoriums, becoming increasingly disenchanted by the hordes of screaming girls who continually trail them wherever they go, and whose attentions Pat is enjoying a little too much. Once or twice, in some remote country town, the guys in the band point out a dark-clothed man in a corner who looks suspiciously like an undercover agent and whose gaze seems to follow my every step. I remember the printed report from a detective agency I'd spied in my father's drawer detailing my mother's activities with Marley. There's something wonderfully debauched in that parallel.

Eventually, Pat and his Rats depart for London to hit the big time. On a dark day in January, I follow him out to the boat, the mighty winds flapping at my coat. Suddenly we're on the plank, the piece of wood which for me represents the bridge to nowhere, the transit with the luminous power to disconnect me from myself. He turns to me briefly. Then he is gone. I tramp back across the docks, barely conscious of the rains that drench me. Hours later I sit in the Bernie Inn alone, senses blurred by too many pints of

Harp, and wonder how I am ever going to deliver myself from the pit of gloom I've landed in.

We write back and forth, long emotive missives from me which prompt clipped responses from him. We talk on the phone, late at night, after my father has retired to bed. Often when I ring, he's 'busy', one of the lads informs me, or out. I refuse to give up. When summer arrives, I lie to my father, telling him I'm off to London to make some money with a college friend.

I arrive at Paddington Station just in time for rush hour. I'm dwarfed by the throng of people, the mass of movement and the noise. I look around, unsure, then wade through the crowds towards the kiosk. Pat is standing to the side, just as he said he would be. A wave of relief washes over me. He smiles, hugs me, takes my bag and leads me to a taxi. Hours later I'm sitting in a big old house in Chessington, on loan from the record company, with Pat, Fingers, Geldof and the gang.

It's a crazy life, populated by reporters, record company people, groupies and roadies. In Dublin I'd got on well with Geldof. He was funny and bright and seemed to enjoy my company. Often I'd sit watching him as he worked through his songs on the guitar in his tiny kitchen in Blackrock. But here he's all business, on the phones, in the rehearsal room, lining up gigs, giving interviews, even cutting the band members' hair (and mine once or twice). I feel unwelcome. In the way. The band spend much of their time on the road and the resident girlfriends and I travel the length and breadth of England to tiny hovels with stages five foot wide to watch them play to audiences of twenty or so. It's 1977, the year that my tennis hero, Virginia Wade, wins Wimbledon, but my joy at being away from home, close to Pat, a big girl all grown up, in a big town, is marred by a nagging sense that it's all about to unravel.

One afternoon Pat and I are stomping around Piccadilly Circus. Liberated momentarily from the jaded, cynical gaze of the

Chessington crew, we laugh and hug, silly as two kids on an outing. It all seems so unreal right then, the money piling up in the bank, the screaming adulation of total strangers. I spot the magazine on the news-stand. It shows The Rats in full colour on the front cover. Excited, I grab a copy and start to read. At one point, the interviewer asks Geldof how he deals with all the female fans, to which he responds, 'Oh, I don't have to worry about that. It's Pat who gets all the women.' The joy of the day trickles away from me. I walk off blindly and find myself, moments later, cowering in the back of a dark clothing store. All around me, beautiful, trendy girls are fussing over their make-up, fretting with their outfits. I look at myself in the mirror. The reflection that stares at me has nothing to offer. Back at the house, I try to slip in unnoticed, past the unknown couple sprawled on the couch, the record execs in mid-conversation at the table and the band members laughing hysterically in the corner. Halfway up the winding staircase, the dreaded words hit. 'Don't take it so seriously, Shivaun. He hasn't had that many. It's just good PR, that's all.'

Are they lying?

Am I crazy?

I'm trapped in the noose of conjecture.

As it turns out, the evidence is right there in the diary, the beautiful leather-bound journal I'd given him as a going-away present, the gold lock of which I burst open one gloomy night when he's off playing one of those tiny northern English hovels. I have to know. And I find what I'm looking for. Thereafter, every painted face, every glint of the eye, every breathless approach is a truth that mocks my ignorance. When summer ends, so do we. I leave for the airport alone and arrive back at Tree Tops a whole lot sadder than when I left.

TWELVE

Nothing for it but to trek off in search of a dress for my father's wedding.

I have the hardest time finding the right outfit. Can't seem to look ladylike in anything with my bundles of flesh sticking out in all the wrong places. Finally, I settle on a midnight-blue velvet number that's pseudo-sleek at the right angle. But no matter what angle I resort to I can't escape the sadness. It's settled in me like a bad cold. To top that, the wedding is in Leeds. The hotel is chilly, just like the city. What's more, us Woolfsons feel like orphans, probably look like them too, following SSW from room to room, listening, watching, waiting to see where we fit.

The night before the ceremony, there's a dinner in honour of the happy couple. My brothers, sister and I are to one side of the table. Adele's parents, her daughter, Elissa, and a bunch of people we've never met before face us. The strangers toast the bride and groom, drink to their happiness, and suddenly I'm standing myself, a glass of champagne in my hand.

'On behalf of my brothers and sister,' I say, all grown up, though I feel about five, 'I'd like to make a toast to my father and his new bride. We will do our best to make this marriage work.' I think, as I stand there, of my own mother, on the other side of the sea, with her five new children by Marley and her little life out by Glasnevin Cemetery. I think of Moira and her lovely voice, her laughter and where that landed in our decaying world. I remember too the last time I'd seen her, on the doorstep of Tree Tops, drunk, dislodged. I look around at Saul, Rachel and David. Their earnest faces proclaim, 'We trust you, Shiv. We'll try too.'

While the happy couple jet off on the honeymoon we stay in a fussily adorned terraced house with the parents and the daughter. It's an absurd circumstance, this forced coming together of families, which we navigate with no small measure of disdain for a week until we're packed off back to where we came from: Tree Tops.

Her second day there, Adele is parcelling up little bundles packed with delicacies in the fridge that bear small plastic name-tags with the words: *For your father only*. She places other treats in a freezer in a locked garage and proceeds to feed us canned tuna fish sandwiches every day for lunch. Then there's the issue of the thirteen-year-old daughter who's moved in along with her and who's revered like a prize possession, driven to and fro by my father, while we, his own children, walk in the rain. Even though she's the same age as Rachel, she's treated like one of the adults. She eats salmon and steaks and sits right up beside my father and Smelly (as we've named Adele in reference to her unusual love of cleaning solutions), at the top of the dinner table, while we, relegated to the fringes, are doled out scraps of stringy meat, stewed beyond edibility, that require a pair of Mr Kenny's gardening shears in order to be hacked apart. Sometimes, over dinner, I glance at our new step-sister and see that she is as uncomfortable as I am.

For visitors, lavish meals are prepared and everyone marvels at the new bride's culinary prowess and her benevolence. They would never guess that we resort to some serious espionage tactics, that we've found a way to pick the lock of the door to the garage containing the forbidden freezer which we steal from religiously, or that we hijack the delivery vans for bread, meat and vegetables a block from our house and purchase our own food (on my father's account, of course), which we prepare in haste whenever Smelly ventures off to the hairdresser.

Somehow we never manage to convince extended family members that us Woolfcubs spend most of our time corralled in the playroom, which has been transformed into the domain of Princess, the step-cat: we know this because her name has been tacked to the door, her feeding bowls, playpens, kitty cot and stinking litter-boxes spread out across the room. Even the television, hitherto a fairly even source of entertainment, has suffered a hostile take-over. Once, while we were watching a particularly close Wimbledon match, Princess ventured up on the shelf behind the set, sprang forward, as only cats can, perched herself between the antennae and proceeded to urinate into the television, which was never quite the same again. This charming act became a standard aspect of evening viewing, to the point that we've stopped watching TV altogether. Saul is terrified of cats, and spends most nights diving from the sofa to the seat in the corner and back on to the armchair in his efforts to escape her, all of which has become a source of tremendous amusement to neighbourhood friends whose visits are inevitably punctuated by the high-pitched sounds of Smelly running around the garden clapping and shouting, 'Princess, Princess darling, come on in,' with my father, steadily behind her, snapping his fingers and becoming only mildly agitated, calling 'Princess, now that's enough, pet.'

We marvel at this because he never liked animals and fought viciously with my mother over every creature she dragged into our house. And here he is, night after night, prowling through his own garden, tracking a spoilt bitch of a feline, who's displaced his own kids from the one room in the entire house they actually feel they belong in. Even there our tenure is short-lived because Smelly decides that the cupboards and desks built precisely for our use, years earlier, are just right for stocking her unparalleled array of canned goods. On any given night, as Saul, Rachel, David and I sit with the neighbourhood gang, listening to The Doors, Joe Cocker, Fleetwood Mac, and sometimes, when we're in a melancholy mood, The Carpenters or Minnie Ripperton, Smelly lunges through the playroom door shouting, 'Just move, just move, just move.' We all topple out of the way and sit in silence until she's rifled through the cabinets, found what she's looking for and departed, without a word. We spend many nights like that, precariously situated in our own home. It's hard to fathom that though we have lived there all our lives, we have no sovereign space and no one to protect us.

Where is my father while all this is going on? Doesn't he hear her scuttling through the hallways at midnight, slamming doors behind her with kinetic aggression, or shouting, 'Their mother is a whore, a slut,' in a dirge that renders sleep all but impossible? Doesn't he see her standing naked at the top of the stairs, backlit by the moon, howling, 'They're evil, evil, evil'? Doesn't he know that she has wedged a piece of tinfoil into the garage-door keyhole so that we can no longer pick our way through it to the food-filled freezer, or that before they leave on their two-week-long trips to Israel at Christmas she turns the central heating down and bolts the boiler-room door with a padlock? Doesn't he know that while he lounges on a beach in the sunshine, staring lazily out over the Red Sea, his children sit huddled round the kitchen table in jumpers and woollen socks to ward off Dublin's winter? Does he realise that David sleeps with a kitchen knife tucked under his pillow because he's afraid she will kill him? The fact is, there's no talking to him. He doesn't want to know. Doesn't want to hear, and there's no one else to tell. The relatives are overjoyed about his new marriage: Moira is gone and Smelly's made mighty quick work of all the remaining housekeepers, whom she's replaced with Edie, a little old woman who comes twice a week to push the Hoover distractedly from room to room.

I attempt a series of coups, raiding the forbidden cupboards when she's out, squirrelling away food to give to Saul, Rachel and David when they arrive home from school exhausted, cold and hungry after the long walk. But it's when Passover comes that the shit, as they say, hits the fan. The boxes from Baila Earlich's deli arrive in advance, as always, filled with matzo crackers, cake mix and coconut macaroons, tins of gefilte fish, jars of matzo ball soup. It's legendary in our house, this Pesach business, a time for unchecked food consumption. Only this year, Smelly hoards it all away, and by the eighth day, the cupboards are still full. She's upstairs. I hear the swishing of water. Saul, Rachel and David are in the kitchen, making little matzo sandwiches out of whatever food they can find, and it's a dismally slight offering. I spy the cake-mix boxes on the top shelf. I take them down, start mixing the batter, turn the oven on. I'm determined to get these cakes made. Suddenly she's there, swinging in through the kitchen door like a bat, pulling the bowl out of my hands, pushing me away from the oven. I'm not about to be moved. The front door opens and my father's standing before me. He rushes forward, takes a swipe at my head, makes contact with my ears, which start to ring loudly. He pulls me away from the stove, out of the kitchen. Saul forces his way between us. He's taller than my father now and threatens him with a clenched fist.

'Don't hit her,' he shouts. 'Don't you dare hit her. She was only trying to help, to make sure we ate, for God's sake.'

My father shoves past him, back in front of me.

'Why?' I shout. 'Why can't I make the cakes? It's the last day. What is she saving them for? For you, for her daughter, for herself? What about us?'

'That's enough,' he says. 'You're impudent, and rude. Adele is my wife and you'll do as she says, or you'll leave.'

The cake mix, a golden brown soggy liquid mass covers the floor, the oven, the counter tops. So much for Passover.

I walk away from the house in the knowledge that my father has replaced one disturbed spouse with another; only this one doesn't seem to have a sense of humour. But I have nowhere else to go. So, after hours of walking through the city, I catch the last bus home.

THIRTEEN

◂━▸

Adele, I discover, has her merits.

She distracts my father. Diverts his focus. In her presence, the memory of my mother is neutralised, as a result of which he no longer locates the woman who left him in my every movement. He stops cornering me in the doorway of my bedroom the way he used to when Pat was a feature, with that sickly beleaguered look on his face, stops the whore and slut references. Calms down. He doesn't seem to care so much where I go, what I do, when I return. That suits me fine. But we fight about my choice of career. He wants me to study law.

'You'd be a great prosecutor, you're always asking questions, digging, never give up, always have to have the last word, impertinent, tenacious.'

I want to take English.

We settle on history and political science. But I don't make it to the first lecture. I'm lying in bed, covers draped around my neck, shades drawn, daylight tucked behind the windows. I don't want a future. Suddenly I hear Auntie Lily's high-pitched voice rising up the staircase.

'Is she not up yet? Isn't this her first day at college? She has more brains than sense, that girl, with all the honours she got. Her father will be so disappointed, and the fees he's paying. Getting into Trinity is a privilege. Let me at her.'

The voice travels closer.

'I don't know what she's doing,' Adele says, 'she comes and goes of her own accord.'

Hours later, I scuttle across the cobblestones on my way to class. I feel invisible and just as much of a fraud as I ever did as I sit in the cavernous auditorium which is lifeless, save for the odd cough or shuffle of papers. I am, by my own standards, an obtuse, dim-witted intruder who's conned the system. By mid-afternoon I've managed to befriend a beautiful student whose father is head of pathology or something. She's tall, slim, elegant and erudite. Beside her I look like a blundering oaf.

With every passing day there I feel more like an interloper on a weekend pass who can't quite get her bearings. And I can't forget Pat. Instead of studying I hang around the likes of Brown Thomas's on Grafton Street where I spend hours picking out flowing gowns. For the wedding, I tell myself. Then I saunter over to the men's section, find a suit, stand in front of it, and will Pat towards me. I dwell almost exclusively within the confines of my own head, and nothing, neither reason nor sheer fact, can dislodge me from illusion. Desperate, I walk back and forth over the Liffey bridge, trying to lose myself, as I've always done, in the mists that rise off the grey waters but feel stifled by the thick, acrid air. I trudge through the streets, frantic for a glimpse of a face I know, a partial smile even, and find none. I keep thinking I see Pat, keep imagining I hear his voice, his laugh. I venture into bars and sit alone, hide in corners, or laugh too loud, and most nights I end up on the floor of a bedsit on the north side of Dublin, lying next to a tall, bony man who repeats my name over and over. I drink too much, too often, listen to music that's too loud, and I'm so hung over in the mornings that I can't even make the two o'clock class.

On June the 3rd, the night of my nineteenth birthday, I sit alone in a corner of the Bernie Inn and size up the scene. I've neglected to take two of my exams and have failed one entirely. I haven't spoken to my father in weeks. It occurs to me then that if my life does not change for the better, and quickly, I can simply cancel it. There is power in that thought.

The next morning, walking across those gruelling Trinity cobblestones, I happen upon Jerry O'Connor, a dwarf-like creature with a tuft of red hair, scraggly beard, infectious smile and a visibly long penis that slopes down one side of his jeans. Why do I notice this?

'Show us your knockers,' he mutters, as he slides past me on his way through the gates. 'You've got a vicious pair on you. Show us.'

He's fucking crazy, I think.

'C'mon,' he says, 'don't be so bleeding shy. Bet you're dynamite when you're worked up.' Truth be told, I feel like a sack of potatoes, as I do most days.

'Tell you what, I'm opening a nightclub down the road, McGonagle's. Come over tonight and I'll give you a job. How's that?'

Within hours, I've taken up residence as the door-girl slash manager. Meet rock star wannabes like U2, who are just starting out, DJs, journalists, and a cast of groupies of the male and female variety. I also encounter, my second night there, a bedraggled, hippiefied ensemble who claim they are followers of Guru Maharaji, and who possess, en masse, a curious calm. Jerry's a *premie* (devotee) as it turns out, and so are the chef, the waitresses, the security guards, the girls who take coats and tickets, in fact everyone else in the whole damn place but me. In a matter of days, I move into a big old ashram on the edge of town. I'm attending *'satsang'* (devotional meetings) nightly and instantly forgo my drinking, drugging, fornicating ways. Maharaji seems to offer not a way out, but rather a way in, through the 'knowledge' he grants, a point of connection to the self, where mine has been harshly severed.

Through Maharaji I begin to believe in the possibility of grace and divine presence, in a Creator who won't cut me loose. I see for the first time that reality, which I have always identified with pain and misery, can equally be comprised of happiness and joy. It's as if I have finally found a suit to fit, but as I travel closer to my own core, I distance myself even further from the mainstream, viewing others as unevolved, mercenary and materialistic. The mundane details: getting a job, cleaning the house (which I'd never been adept at to begin with) take second billing to the far more momentous tasks of staying in the moment, living in the flow, recognising the bliss in every instant. And as life itself becomes a consuming, breath-by-breath experience, I, along with a million others, identify Maharaji as the integral connector, without whom our very lifeline will expire. My world becomes translatable only through a series of Indian words: *satsang, darshan, ashram, jat sat chitanand*, all of which speak to me with the promise of redemption, even as they disengage me from my past.

On the day I finally receive the 'knowledge', after months of diligent attendance at 'aspirant' meetings, I am escorted to a beautiful house on the edge of town. There, amid a kind of luxuriant hush, made all the more conspicuous by the floating scents of flowers and incense, a Michael Caine lookalike, the initiator at the event, and a group of dreamy disciples, far more devout than Jerry and his crew at McGonagle's, I, and seven other inductees, await 'transformation'. The windows are sealed shut with black tape, the curtains drawn, the doors locked. Several hours later, we emerge, floating, 'knowledge' installed. As I am led from the dwelling to the van that waits to escort us to the city, my father's silver Mercedes screeches to a halt on the front lawn. He bails out from one side,

Uncle Louis from the other, wheezing, and together they lunge towards me, grabbing frantically at the unlikely flowery dress I've borrowed for the occasion, which, in the scuffle, rips right along the breast-line exposing my skin. With my body wedged halfway into the back seat of their car, my feet scrabbling for contact with the grass outside, I pull back, free myself and make a rush for the waiting van. What ensues is a high-speed chase through Dublin's rain-drenched streets that raises more than a few eyebrows. In the end, my father simply gives up.

I know that home is no longer a place for me, but I've been sleeping for months on borrowed beds, dressing myself in loaned out clothes, and I suddenly need my own things around me. So, a few nights after the 'knowledge' session and subsequent car chase, I slip into my old bedroom after dark and set about organising my belongings: clothes, books, records, birthday cards, the markers of my life. I feel safe in the quiet of this room with the stencil of Charlie Chaplin, the photos of Judy Garland and Edith Piaf and the Ugly Ducking poster tacked to the wall. In this very space, with its olive-green walls, lopsided bed, and crammed bookshelves, I have travelled away from childhood.

Exhausted, I lie down, wrap myself in that familiar-smelling bedcover, sink deep into the dip on the left side that my own body has pressed out over time. I fall asleep. With sunlight come the usual household noises: the vacuum cleaner, my stepmother's abrasive voice barking orders at Edie, the sloshing of water and the rhythmic motion of her state-of-the-art washing machine. I feel oddly like a prowler and yet, at the same time, so comfortable. Placing a sheet over my head, I begin the ritual meditation that I learned just days before, becoming so engrossed in my breathing that I don't hear Adele enter the room, not until she begins to shriek.

'Get out of my house, you heathen,' she yells, breaking into my private world. 'Stop this witchcraft under my roof.' She runs to the phone and within seconds it seems, my father, Uncle Louis, her cousin Kitty (a woman I've met only twice in my life) and Adele herself are standing in the doorway. All I know in that moment is that I have to get the hell out of there.

'You have no family now,' my father screams. 'That Guru is your father now, and you'll go to pot like all the other poor fools who sit under blankets all day long and starve. How could you do this to me? I always said you wanted me dead.'

Suddenly his face is dangerously close to mine. I draw back as he clouts my head hard. It hits the wall with a loud thump. I bounce back into place only to find his fist ready to strike me again. They are screaming: my uncle and Kitty and Smelly, their voices merging into a fuming mass. My head is pounding and my cheeks and eyes begin to ache. Throughout, I hold tight to the breath rising and falling inside of me, and I remember how I managed, as a small girl, to journey from one side of my mother's beatings to the other: by telling myself over and over that it would end soon and that I would emerge, still living. Suddenly, I hear Nuala, my friend, blasting the horn of her moped outside. Grabbing a few possessions, I stare resolutely at the group planted like trees in the doorway.

'I'm walking out of here.'

Like the Red Sea they part. I don't look back. Outside, Nuala sits with her legs slung casually over the bike and a grin on her face.

'Need a ride?' she asks. 'What the hell happened to you? You're full of bruises. Look at your arms, and there's some on your neck too.'

I look down at the purple blotches. I am shocked. I'd been beaten worse and come through without a mark.

Not knowing what else to do, Nuala heads straight to Bugs' and Sinead's sprawling Georgian mansion/ashram on Harcourt Street.

With its wobbly staircase and subdivided flats which house an eclectic group including Harry the dope-dealer, Alfred the old English carpenter, Sinead, Bugs and the kids, who run the vegetarian restaurant on the second floor, number 424 has become my second home. Once we are inside, Sinead, always the mother hen, offers us a cup of tea. Someone picks up a guitar and begins to strum; someone else lights a joint. I'm in the process of describing where I acquired my bunch of shiners when two Starsky and Hutch types, too cool for their own good, tumble up the stairs. 'Drug raid,' they announce.

Next thing you know, I'm being carted off to the police station, and placed in a courtroom in front of a wiry-haired judge. I spot Uncle Louis hunched under a thick raincoat in the corner. He nods to me. His eyes say that I have disgraced the family. Again. I can't imagine how he knew, or why he's there instead of my father.

'It wasn't mine,' I tell the judge, 'that stuff wasn't mine. I don't even live there.' He lets me off with a warning. The press, desperate to catch something newsworthy, hang around the courthouse as I emerge.

'Name, address.'

'Go away,' I tell them.

But the report appears on the front page of the morning newspaper anyway, under the headline, 'Daughter of Jewish businessman arrested for cannabis possession'.

FOURTEEN

Something fundamental dies in me that day.

Looking around, I find myself stranded at the centre of the only world I've ever known. I can't go home again, and the places that I've conjured as stand-ins – borrowed couches in college dorms, floor space in grimy bedsits, and Harcourt Street itself – are equally hazardous and just as lonely. So I opt for exile, a passing fancy masquerading as escape, as simple as several items of frayed clothing flung into a discarded case of cracked leather, a few quid, a ticket, and a vague destination – in this case Miami, courtesy of the fact that Maharaji has scheduled a birthday programme there and half the Harcourt Street ashram are heading off. In truth it's the kind of exile you never return from. But by the time you realise it, you are no longer the person who left.

It's November 1979. I'm twenty-one years old, with exactly a month to find the money for the trip. I gather all the books, records and every last piece of clothing I don't wear on a regular basis, and open up a stall in the Stephen's Green flea market. I can't believe that people want my cast-offs, but they do: shirts and shoes and dresses. The books and records are the hardest to part with, but I get used to it. The last thing I sell is my *A Tonic for the Troops* album by the Boomtown Rats. I get £20 for that because it's inscribed with the words, 'You Are Somebody, love Pat'. I had to fight for those three words when I'd met him months before in the Bailey. He was only in town for a few days and I was nervous about seeing him. As soon as I sat down, he handed me the album.

'Write something on it,' I said.

'What?'

'I don't know, something that lets me know I am somebody to you, that I meant something.'

You are somebody.

I wrap it in a brown paper bag. There's nothing left of us now, I think as I pass it over. Not even words.

The fact is I've run out of things to sell, and I'm still short. To raise the final funds for the ticket, I and Trisha, a wacky Dublin girl who's taken to stopping by the stall of a Sunday, and with whom I feel an unusual kinship, sign up for a rather unique job: selling periscopes for the Pope's Irish tour. For ten days, we travel from Dublin to Kerry in the back of a loaded van belonging to Deirdre, the first lesbian I've ever met. Crushed beneath box-loads of cardboard, we cross the country in the dark, down long, winding roads, through cramped villages. Sometimes we stop at a local bar for a few drinks, at which point Deirdre gets loud and frisky and makes suggestive comments, which Trisha and I nervously ignore. Eventually we arrive in Knock, the sacred site where the Virgin Mary once appeared, and sell our hand-crafted periscopes to the travellers and gypsies who arrive in droves, dressed in their best, with their coloured shawls and beads, their long hair, rugged features and harsh voices. They stand aside with solemn humility, these men and women, and their children who are used to begging and brawling as Pope John Paul II is driven through the valley in a makeshift motorcade. All around him there's a palpable silence, so gentle it ripples through the air. The travellers are touched by his presence, visibly so, as their faces become soft and warm, reflecting a supple and beautiful light. I say a silent prayer as I watch them, to Maharaji, and to the God I summoned as a little girl back in Adelaide Road synagogue. I ask them to take care of me, to watch for me in the years ahead, because I know that I will never again be the person I am on this day. I know, too, that I am leaving behind a place, a setting, however garbled, however hurtful, that is the only place I will ever call home.

FIFTEEN

The last time I see my father in Ireland is the day of my brother David's bar mitzvah.

He warns me on the telephone not to set foot in the synagogue. Not while I'm still involved with that cult, and definitely not when I'm planning to leave for America in a few days' time. He won't hear of it. I'm making the biggest mistake of my life. The night before I take David and his friends to see *The Champ*, a sad movie with Jon Voight about a boxer who dies. Outside Tree Tops, I hand him the skateboard I've saved up for weeks to buy. A gracious smile crosses his face.

'I don't care what Daddy says,' he tells me, 'I want you at my bar mitzvah . . .'

The next morning I catch the bus out to my Aunt Jill's (Uncle Louis's wife). When I arrive she points out that I have a grey line of dirt around my neck and that I need a bath, bad. I'm ashamed to tell her that we don't have running water at Harcourt Street and that I bathe periodically (every other week at best) in the homes of friends. After I've showered, she pulls a stylish blue gown from the wardrobe and orders me to try it on. I can't believe what I see in the mirror. I look normal, like an elegant Jewish woman en route to her brother's bar mitzvah. Nikki, my cousin, applies the make-up,

Andrea, the perfume, and I'm set. Walking into Adelaide Road synagogue is hard. The formality of the place has always silenced me but, as a little girl, I had my Pop to cling on to, his hand to press in mine. Now I am greeted by the self-righteous, indignant stares of men and women who have probably read the newspaper article and pegged me for a loser. I forge my way to my seat upstairs, right in the front row, that my father has continued to pay for, even though I haven't set foot in the place in years.

'Thank God you've returned at last,' says Mrs Felshen, an elderly dame covered in freckles. 'There's nothing to block the draught when you're not here. I asked your father if you were coming, just this morning.'

I try for a smile. Then I sit and listen as my brother, with his soaring voice, recites his *Haftarah*. I see my father, my uncle, my brother, Saul, up in the front by the Ark, where they always sit, and in his top hat and tails, Mr Kenny, whom I'm sure people mistake for some important dignitary. I see all the people who have populated my life from the day I was born, except my mother. She wasn't invited.

Later, at the reception, my father approaches me.

'You look nice,' he says. 'Better than expected.'

'Did you think I'd arrive here like some drug-addicted flake and let you all down?'

'I never know what to expect from you. I didn't think you'd come at all,' he says. I notice as he speaks that a place has been set for me at the head table. We stand together in the centre of the room encircled by prattling relatives: the hair-dos, the styles, the business ventures, the Jewish school, the holidays, the washing machines, the divorces and, even, 'Doesn't Shivaun look good? I'd heard she'd gone off and joined some cult.'

It's all talk.

My father is standing a breath away. He leans towards me; his hand reaches across my back, stays there, and then he gets that forlorn, liquid look in his eyes that I've come to identify with too many brandies. It tells me that he wants to love me but doesn't know how. It says I am still too much like my mother. I walk away that night, not knowing whether I will ever see my father again.

SIXTEEN

'Thanks be to fuckin' Jaysus, we're out of that hellhole at last,' Trisha announces a few days later, as we settle into our seats on the Boeing 747. 'The fuckin' cold, shrinking me bones it was, had arthritis in the kneecaps, the fingers too. No wonder I couldn't find a daycent job, any job for that matter. Off to Florida: sun and palm tress and a few suntanned hunks into the bargain. I'll drink to that,' she says, knocking back a double Paddy's. I look over at Trisha's twisted fingers and shrinking bones, her befuddled, hypochondriac kneecaps. It's just like her to leave it all behind, then justify a lifetime of missed chances with a few whiskeys.

'I'll miss Dublin,' I tell her, 'the bleakness, the rains, the dreary streets, they're all I've ever known. I'm not so sure I'm up for all that sunshine. You know, I'm not one for the heat.'

In response, Trisha inhales her fourth shot of whiskey, getting lost in her own thoughts.

We disembark from the Aer Lingus jet around noon, and instantly reel from the rush of Miami heat that sweeps over us; it's a sluggish, vapid film that clings to the lungs, stalls the breath, bounces brilliantly off buildings and cars, everything visible, slowing the world to a standstill. Walking down the steps in search of land, I find myself jammed into an unknown border space, a detached, marginal landscape, which, in the instant, fails to reveal a point of entry. I am stuck, someplace between the new and the old. It's hard to push myself forward. I feel encumbered, slow. My clothes stick to my skin, sweat drips down my face and into my eyes.

I am afraid.

My newness, the novelty and rawness I feel is reflected everywhere: in the faces of the stiff airport officials who question my motives for entering the US (loss, disintegration, desperation, hopelessness, where should I begin?), in the dangerous, sensual stares of dark-skinned men lined against the airport walls. Their tall, languid bodies beckon as their eyes blister through my whiteness. Casually they finger their scrotums. Their senses sharpen around me.

Emerging from the airport intact is a feat in itself. Once outside, in what passes for air, though it certainly does little to enhance breathing, I am intrigued by such oddities as the sound of crickets chirping, the particular timbre of American ambulance horns, police sirens and ringing telephones. Here I am breathing in, physically inhabiting, a world I have only ever known from Marcus Welby reruns in the playroom back in Dublin.

That night, I and the rest of the Maharaji followers are transported to the beach on a Greyhound bus. In those first few hours America, to me, is the cashiers at the all night Seven Elevens who really do say 'Have a nice day' to every single customer, usually in a growl, no matter what time of day or night it is. It is the old black men who stand outside those shops, sipping beer and begging for change. It's canned music and smiling faces about to shatter. It's fear and unpredictability, vastness and people larger than I'd ever believed possible, and others, like the girls I see walking the streets with a cocaine craziness in their eyes, more weathered than any I've ever seen. I wonder, as I take all this in, if there will be a place for me, a small, insignificant space in this huge expanse which is America, but not yet America to me.

Days later, I'm sitting alone in a Cuban café along the ocean front. Trisha is camping out in front of Maharaji's house on North Bay Road, desperate for a glimpse of him. I sip my beer and look around, mesmerised: a bunch of Cuban men in the corner shout, their words jabbing the air like knives. I'm sure they're about to come to blows. On the dance floor, there's a few others with fingers clenched around Heineken bottles and sweat soaking through their Havana shirts. A couple of women writhe up and down against them. I'm not used to such raunchy movement in broad daylight. The song 'Jamblaya' is on the jukebox for the sixth time in a row, but nobody seems to notice, or to care. In walks a Jimi Hendrix lookalike, misplaced in his leather jacket and tight jeans, with a perfectly rounded afro. He takes the seat beside me at the bar and flashes a perfidious grin in my direction. His command of English is woeful, but I remember enough Spanish from my Leaving Cert and a childhood visit to Spain to get the gist of things. His name is Julio. He's two months off the boat from Cuba; escaped from the army, left his mother, brothers, sisters and a two-year-old son behind, boarded a raft with a few mates, sailed through Hurricane David, almost died at sea, made it to Key West, was picked up by a German fishing boat, transported to Miami, stayed in a Catholic hostel, made it over to the beach, works odd jobs, loves music. It's one hell of a story. As he talks, a smile crashes over his face like a breaking wave, then tapers away. His lips quiver. His eyes flicker. His body is rock hard. There's charm to him, but a near-frightening tenacity too. I can't believe such a good-looking man is talking to me.

Half an hour into our distorted conversation, he invites me back to a strange-smelling room on Pennsylvania Avenue and, moments after arrival, suggests, rather forcefully, that I take a shower before slipping into bed beside him. It happens so quickly I don't have to time to question what the hell I'm doing, lying beside a man I've known for all of thirty minutes. Once under the sheets, his hands float effortlessly over my body, slowly, not like most of the men I've known. As he grinds into me I think of comments I heard from naive Dublin girls after they'd dated foreign students: 'Once you go black you never go back.' When his teeth bite into my lower lip, I wonder if this is the way all black men make love: easy and measured, like they've got for ever. Sex has never been a carefree undertaking for me. I was always sure if I'd been better at it, Pat wouldn't have cut me loose. With Julio, for the first time, I let go until my senses flood. I stop thinking. The world disappears. I don't hear the radio, don't care that his room-mate Pedro is stretched out on a bed just three feet across the room. It's just me, my body, and a handsome man bearing down. When we're finished, we lie side by side, quiet, full. Suddenly he's on the move, out of the bed, and through the door.

'Where are you going?' I ask, confused.

'*Un momento* (Just a minute),' he says.

I lie still in the darkness. Pedro approaches the bed. He grunts in a manner which indicates a more than passing interest in copulation. I can't believe it. I've just had the most intense sexual experience of my life, and the guy's vanished and left me in the hands of his moaning flat-mate.

'No, no,' I say, 'bring Julio back.'

Pedro departs. Voices in the hallway. Julio miraculously returns.

I could have walked away then. From the man for whom, in the moment at least, I'm little more than a fresh fuck. And never looked back. Years later, I recognise the decision to stay as one of those moments that turned my world on its head, set me off on a treacherous course with no road back. I know exactly what I'm doing. I just don't know why. Because I'm lost and alone in a foreign country? Because I believe the home I left behind doesn't want me back? Because a few precious moments with a stranger is about as much as I can hope for?

Whatever the reason, next morning when Julio says, '*Trae tus cosas. Te puedes quedar aquí conmigo* (Bring your stuff. You can stay here, with me),' I race back to the tiny room Trisha's sharing with some dreamy English bloke and pick up my belongings. Twenty minutes later I'm at Julio's door.

'*Esto es todo*? (Is that all you have?)' he asks, incredulous. '*Voy a tener que comprarte ropa nueva* (I'm going to have to buy you some new clothes).'

First he has to earn some money.

'*Tengo que hacer un mandado* (I have to run an errand),' he says.

'You don't kill anyone, do you?' I ask. 'It's not like you're a hit man. It's drugs. Only pot, right. Is that what you do? Sell pot? You can tell me. I'm not the police.'

He smiles.

'*No mato a nadie* (I don't kill anyone). *No hago violencia* (I'm not violent). *No te preocupes* (Don't worry).'

As he leaves, he shoves a handful of dollar bills towards me.

'*Vete a comer algo. Te doy más luego.* (Go get yourself something to eat. I'll give you more later.)'

I take to my new surroundings with guarded enthusiasm. Although I'm not sure exactly what it is he does, Julio manages to keep to a schedule of sorts. Off in the mornings to destinations unknown, back in the evenings borne down by brown paper bags filled with rice and beans, malt sodas, cans of condensed milk, slabs of meat and bottles of Heineken which he delivers with enormous pomp. My kitchen skills are lacking, at best, and the culinary madness I concoct out of these items, at first, culls affectionate grimaces that, over time, metamorphose into abusive commands. I have much to learn about Cuban culture, not the least of which involves cooking. I am suspicious about the photos of ancient-looking saints placed in odd corners of the room, the rows of candles lined up in the back of the closet and the foul-smelling herbs I encounter behind the sink cabinet when seeking toothpaste, soap or shampoo. Then there is the matter of Pedro who laughs under his breath when we make love, who insists upon blasting the radio at first light, and who seems not the least bit cheered by my presence in their little world.

None the less, we manage to establish a rhythm: when the sun filters in off the streets, I awaken to a collection of Cuban males, formed in a bizarre human mound in the centre of the room. They appear to be little more than outraged boys who've left behind mothers and wives and kids, but not the memories of decade-long sojourns in jail cells for stealing food, subsisting on their wits, for engaging in the kind of delinquent lifestyles that seemed, according to their account, tantamount to survival. They speak in haunted voices, unintelligible beneath the roar of Latin music from the radio, interrupted every other second by a frantic political diatribe about La Patria. The coffee, more like liquid tar, is put to percolating, the cigarettes smoked, the plans laid, and then they are off.

Left to my own devices, I perform none of the housewifely duties that seem expected of me. No cleaning, no laundry, no shopping or cooking. Instead I go off in search of Trisha. We amble on down to the seawall, load up on Cuban toast and *café con leche* and soak up the sun which blisters my comically white skin. Every so often, Trisha inspects the row of hickeys that line my neck and insists that she has to meet the Lothario who's placed them there. Eventually she does, in Pepe's bar on Fifteenth.

That's where Julio and posse do business, or so we discover in passing. Pepe's is a tiny hole beside an overused Laundromat that doubles as a cigar and liquor store, so dark that you can barely make out any action through the steamed windows. The music, an offbeat medley of Michael Jackson, Donna Summer and Tito Puente, tumbles out into the relentless midday sun, bouncing off the pavement.

'Let's get a beer,' Trisha says, as we pass one morning. 'I'm awful hot.'

'In there?' I ask. 'We'll be ate alive.'

Pepe himself beckons from the doorway, waving at us with this hook-like contraption that extends from his sleeve. He's got a harmless-looking smile so, like obedient little tourists, in we pop. The place is pitch black and takes some adjusting to after the scorching brilliance of the sun, but slowly I make out figures and furtive movements, glasses raised to lips, money passing hands, stealthy action in and out of the bathroom, fingers on skin, marijuana smoke escaping out the back door, and Julio, over in the corner, hidden under the ever-present Hendrix hat, smiling that lethal smile.

He doesn't seem particularly surprised by our sudden arrival, though the rest of the guys launch into overdrive with the '*Ay Mamitas, Que Lindas*' and the penis- and ball-grabbing that invariably accompanies such commentary. In retrospect I suspect that Julio was probably just covering up well.

After a few visits, I discover that he's a big fish at Pepe's: dealer extraordinaire in illegal tender, the kind that rips open minds and swallows them whole. Pills, weed, coke, powders, uppers, downers – you name it, he sells it – all from his vantage point: a corner stool in a room filled with luminous faces and shady grins. Men slap him heartily on the back and thighs. Young girls, beautiful and faint, approach tentatively on wavering limbs, offering promises galore in dismally slurred speech, as they clutch desperately on to the few dollars they press in his direction. I see them pay for the privilege of gradual death night after night as their smiles turn cold and their arms dangle dangerously. There are two fifteen-year-olds from

Boston who arrive at the same time every evening. I catch them sometimes in the toilet with blood dripping from their lips and their eyes turning back into the sockets until only the whites show.

'They'll die,' I tell Julio. 'Don't sell them any more.'

He laughs me off and tells me I'm being neurotic, that they know what they're doing. Neurotic or not, sometimes we hear news of a sudden, brutal loss, and I think of a mother, a father or a young child waiting by a window.

Trisha blends into this surrogate home far better than I do. There's a certain predictability to the chaos. She'd spent her formative years in love with a famous heroin dealer back in Dublin, and the frantic comings and goings, pick-ups and drop-offs are as natural to her as breath. Despite the calmer moments when Julio and I take walks along the beach or visit his friends, gruff Cuban men who ply us with wine and food and stories of how it used to be in the homeland, less than ninety miles across the water, but now so far beyond their reach, I feel like a bewildered innocent thrust into a furnace. Desperate to catch my bearings, to strain from the hype and hustle a trace of reality that I can hold on to, I believe the stories that Julio feeds me – that he doesn't rob, that he'd never hurt anyone, that I won't go to jail – live off them until they displace the brittle version of truth I've been dangling from my whole life. Late at night, back in the room on Pennsylvania Avenue, I tell him I'm scared, that I want a different life. I don't know how to be different. I've spent half of my life in jail, he always says. This is who I am. This is what I do. It's as simple as that for him. As for me, I don't have work papers. I don't know what else I can do.

As the months wear on, I become increasingly concerned by the bevy of hardened Cuban females who seem determined to release Julio from my feeble grasp. One, in particular, with tropically gyrating hips, greedy eyes and a fierce tongue, scares me senseless. Not without reason. I arrive back at Pennsylvania Avenue one afternoon. The door's locked. I don't have my key. I bang loudly. I hear voices. Eventually Julio opens it. She's stretched out on our bed, staring me down as if I'm dirt. He's got this sheepish look on his face, but he doesn't apologise. Doesn't say a damn thing. I walk over to him. I want to slap him. Instead I leave. Fucking women, I guess, is also what he does, who he is. I run off in search of Trisha who manages to calm me down with a savage sequence of expletives before focusing my attention on *dinero* and our lack thereof. We're flat broke.

Employment options for two illegal Irish girls on the lam are minimal. But begging, particularly in the lobby of Miami International Airport, is a reliable if not exactly respectable trade. There's something about the transit from one destination to another that lends itself to munificence and we are only too delighted to relieve the tourist population of their loose change. When the pickings get slim, Trisha makes her way out to the parking lot, to relieve tourists in quite a different fashion. She doesn't elaborate, but she doesn't have to. I always recognise a beaten-down look on her after one of those episodes, no matter how lucrative it's been. When airport security finally spot us and figure out that we've no intention of ever getting on a plane, they boot us out on to the pavement, an act that Trisha protests against rather vocally, at which point they produce a pair of handcuffs which glint like lightning. None too impressed, we trot off, treat ourselves to a slap-up meal on the proceeds of the day and spend the next three months working ourselves into a stupor, cleaning out dirty hotel rooms, begging along the beach and selling hot dogs and ice-creams at the circus.

We travel periodically, to Cancun in Mexico, Cartagena in Colombia for Maharaji programmes, on the money we've raised. It's a haphazard kind of living, roaming from country to country, never knowing when or how we'll get where we want to go, with only the promise of seeing Maharaji to keep us moving. Often we end up on foreign streets, penniless, and have to resort to pan-handling until we have enough for food, for travel and for accom-modation. There's no set strategy to our efforts, though we realise quickly that men are far more approachable than women, and you never stop someone who's in an obvious hurry. I look for smiles, a touch of warmth behind the eyes, and at the clothes, especially the shoes. I'm drawn to the men who dress well, whose feet move with purpose. I seem to be always on the lookout for men who remind me of Pop. During our travels, we eat in hovels where the flies camp out on plates of food (Mexico), sleep in a shack built on thin sticks (Belize), drink wine, smoke mind-numbing grass and wash ourselves with rainwater under a brilliant star-studded sky (Cozumel). When the touring is done, we creep back into Miami airport at dawn and make our way to Pepe's where Julio sits over in his corner, surrounded on both sides, waiting, calm as still water.

Eventually, worn down by the struggle, Trisha opts for home. Trouble is, I have nowhere to go back to, and I've convinced myself and Julio, gyrating *putas* notwithstanding, that we belong together. Using the hazy logic that's taken hold of me, I reason that if we rid ourselves of Pedro's incessant laughing and the Cuban entourage, we'll avoid the drugs and the madness. Despite initial misgivings, I guess Julio figures I'm a useful appendage. I've become adept at warding off pesky police intrusions, ordering food at restaurants, negotiating with landlords, and of course, there's the lovemaking. He says my name over and over in the dark until the image of that naked woman on our bed is wiped from view. I can't imagine how a man who makes love to me the way he does could care a damn about anyone else.

So we walk the ocean front until we're numb, trying to convince those old hotel managers with greying teeth and tattered shirts to rent us a cockroach-infested room. They stare back at us out of vacant, half-lit eyes that don't budge and, assaulted by the notion that a white woman might actually want to live with a black man, swat us away like mosquitoes. In the end, I venture off alone, find a room with a stained Formica table, a single bed and ravaged carpets and, like a thief, sneak Julio in after dark.

The police stick to us like Polygrip, chasing us down in unmarked cars, stopping us on the sidewalks to search our pockets. They even relieve Julio of his wide-brimmed hat a few times and shake it out, right there on the sand: a mini-spectacle for the nose-visor folk, the little old ladies with blue permed hair, and the Hasidic population hiding out under thick black cloth. Master of elusion that he is, the cops never actually find anything on him. As for me, living in a tiny bolthole on the top floor of the Edison on Ocean, the size of the toilet back in Tree Tops, never turns out to be what I expect. The assembly: Angelo, Tico, Pepe and Innocente still group together on the floor like sardines, planning heists, shakedowns, and deals. During the day, I spend a lot of time alone, wandering South Beach, which, without Trisha, is bleak and depressing.

The rest of the Maharaji crew have gone back to their lives, and those who remain have precious little to say to me. I meditate and try to find the quiet, sacred peace that Maharaji promised would be there when I looked, but it fails to register in the teeming underworld I've embraced. Somehow the notion of an alternate universe in which the practical matters of food and lodging, clothing and healthcare feature so unevenly has begun to sour on me. I start to wish that I had more than the breath inside of me to depend on. With increasing frequency, Julio downright disappears. I wait for him often by the window until dark, then trek around the block until I'm followed by some ill-intentioned guy, then circle back to the Edison and look up at 'our' window, with the solitary lamplight flickering down at me. In through the lobby, past the old man at reception, through the elevator doors, down the corridor, ears cocked for signs of life, turn the handle, open the door on to a bare room. I can't sit in my own loneliness. So I make my way back down to the lobby, stand on the sidelines, watching the old folk play chess, or slowly drinking, talking of lives that have run their course and are approaching an uncelebrated close in a dilapidated shell with peeling paint, overlooking a beachfront rife with transgression. Stuck in the place that isn't a place, I drink at the bar until the sun rises. Mornings tell a hell of a story, and I hear them all. Sometimes it's women, sometimes jail. As long as it's not death.

SEVENTEEN

I know what's going on.

I'd have to be comatose not to. There are nights when bullets rattle outside the window. There are stereos and car radios that appear in our room out of nowhere, and a massive TV set, ousted by force from the hotel lobby, that's hoisted up on a pulley of white hotel sheets and placed right in front of our bed until a buyer is found. It takes up half the damn room. There are days in anonymous motels, when we guard entire closets-full of marijuana awaiting shipment, some to my friends in Ireland: pounds of grass stitched into innocent-looking teddy bears dispatched from remote post offices in colourful wrapping paper with no return address. Money, counted and re-counted in brand-new bills, hidden under mattresses, inside socks. Money that pays our rent, buys our food, clothes us, and caters for Julio's nightly dalliances with a steady stream of easy females.

Then there's the shooting.

One afternoon, we're sitting in the shoebox of a room we relocated to in the Clay Youth Hostel after the Edison got too hot. It's small and dark inside. I hear noises from the street below. Julio's playing this sad song about Cuba over and over on the tape deck, singing along to the music.

'I had to shoot some stupid motherfucker today,' he says suddenly. 'He tried to steal my stuffa. Ju know how I am.'

'What are you going to do?'

'Leave, to New York. Angel, ju know, the old man, he give me the money.'

'But what will you do in New York? You don't know anyone there.'

'I know no one here when I come. I can't go back to jail. Will ju come with me?'

I think of his stories: dispatched at six to an orphanage in the country where he grew tall and thin and pale, waiting for his mother. Reclaimed by a distant uncle, deposited in a shack by the sea with some relatives who made him sit in a corner through dinner and wait for leftovers like a dog. He grew hard and cold, and by the time he lived with his mother again, he no longer needed her. Then came the brawls in bars, the petty thefts, desertion from the army. Years in jail. A mad dash across the ocean: Miami.

I look down at the long lashes curving over his eyes, the silky skin, the line of his jaw and the strength of his body. There's an aliveness to him that touches all the hurt places in me. When he holds me, when his body reaches into mine, when a smile spreads out over his face, I go quiet inside. The wounds in me fold back.

'*Bueno*,' he says again, looking straight at me, 'will ju come?'

'I'll come.'

We pick up an envelope stuffed with five-dollar bills, left for us by Angel at the airport post office, board a plane and leave. Julio, decked out in his white polyester suit, bright red shirt and Hendrix wannabe hat, stands out with luminous visibility, drawing stares and gapes as he walks down the aisle to find his seat beside a burly, red-nosed police type. I sit on the opposite side, staring through the window at Miami, the lights of which blink mischievously at me from a distance, wondering how I'll ever survive charging headlong into uncertainty, trying to keep pace with an Afro-Cuban who's spent half of his life in jail, who just that day launched a bullet at some dope-dealing Puerto Rican, and who doesn't know if the man lived or died.

We arrive at La Guardia in the thick of winter with dismally thin jackets framing our shoulders, and just enough in our pockets for a hot coffee and a sandwich. Those first few nights we sleep in hallways, on park benches and in cardboard boxes under the subway. We ride the train back and forth a hundred times over the Brooklyn Bridge through the night until the sun rises and morning releases us. Once or twice we travel through Harlem in the back of a bus, looking out at the bars and clubs, the dim lights, the quiet, frozen streets, the steam rising from the cellars, the rusty stairwells, and the men and women trudging under the weight of cloth.

I beg on street corners. When we have enough money we head to the trick motel on 23rd and Park Avenue, where the whores rent rooms by the hour, and secure a space no larger than a closet for $25 a night. Every day brings with it the challenge of raising enough cash before the snow sets in. On the days we don't, we remain on the park bench. I phone home periodically, always reversing the charges, and tell my father I'm living in a small flat in Manhattan, which is partly true at least some of the time. Every so often I find a letter waiting for me in the hotel lobby, money order enclosed. It is then that I take to the streets that I have come to love, stopping in for a coffee at a local café, buying a second-hand book from the used book store. New York fascinates me. I love its ruggedness, its callous sounds, the thunder of its traffic, the frenzy of its movement. And I think as I wade through its packed pavements that in another time, other circumstances, I could live well there.

One cold morning I'm lying in bed at the trick motel. I hear a shoe hitting the window-sill. A tall, black, rangy body stumbles into the room, head cocked to the side, hair standing on end. A pair of raven eyes impale me to the spot. When I run for the door, the tattered sheet trailing behind me, he pulls me back, shoves me on the bed, and yanks his trousers to his knees. In the moments that follow, everything disappears but the idiotic poster of Peaches and Herb that someone bothered to put up, and I'd never bothered to take down, and a small photo of Guru Maharaji on the nightstand. I pray to that photo, but somewhere deep down, I believe that I deserve to be taken and left to drain.

New York is like that – a series of disconnected mishaps where life meets death inside of me – like the night, a few weeks later, when I follow a red-skinned man with gold-rimmed glasses to his room in Harlem, purportedly to conduct business: the sale of a tiny bag of grass, the proceeds of which will take care of breakfast and one night at the motel for Julio and me. Once inside, he turns the double lock and rapes me. His friends pound at the door. I stare out at a thick black cable that hangs from the roof outside the window. I imagine that if I can just swing from it I'll make it to the tree that stands, solid as a cathedral, a mere ten feet away.

He enters me. Brutally.

I disappear.

He mounts again.

He falls away.

I come back.

A car horn blares on the street.

The battering continues at the door.

He plunges deeper.

He is speaking.

Disconnected, severed fragments.

A vicious wind whistles in the trees.

I fantasise my escape.

He penetrates faster, harder.

I'm flying farther and freer, out into the cold, clear air.

The ceaseless thumping on the door.

I'm back.

My body is pummelled. Into a grotesque shape.

Next morning.

He tells me I'm lucky he didn't allow his friends in for the glorious gangbang they'd intended. As if I should be grateful. On my way out I glance upward to the tiny window, thirty storeys high.

I wouldn't have made it.

I plod back through unfamiliar streets to 'our' park bench, the place that has become as close to a home as I can get. Julio is slumped in sleep, his coat up around his neck, surrounded by a clump of white papers: sloppy, childlike, handwritten notes in fragmented English letting me know he's gone searching for me. Again. And again. And again.

Finally he'd given up.

That night Auntie Lily arrives unexpectedly from Dublin (I suppose she got my address from my father) and leaves a message with André, the Russian transplant who guards the Park Hotel lobby from behind a cage of glass and grilled steel. As instructed, I enter the restaurant of the Waldorf Astoria at seven sharp, pulling my skimpy pink blouse (the best attire I can muster) about me. We dine in elegance, served by a total of ten waiters, drink red wine and pretend that life is normal. In the fine set of her features, the blue of her eyes, the glint of her gold, I find the past I abdicated, meet head-on the sheer wealth I was born to. On this night it clogs the lining of my stomach. I take laboured bites of the delicately poached salmon that sits before me. We chat about the sights, the delightful shops, the theatre and the shows. I omit to mention that I never actually see those shows but rather panhandle outside of them, approaching men and women like the ones I grew up around who attended the bar mitzvahs and the weddings, who ate in our home, whose coats and purses, minks and stoles I carried diligently to my bedroom upstairs, where they hung from the wardrobe door, with their crooked little claws and squashed faces. At the end of the evening, Auntie Lily notices that I have no coat, and that it's snowing outside. She hands me twenty-five dollars, for the cab home, and whatever's left for a sweater. I continue to freeze.

I find a series of jobs: house-cleaning for a famous writer on the Upper East Side, who has the messiest set-up I've ever encountered, and who dispatches me after suspecting that I've stolen a gold locket she's misplaced. (What I'd really wanted to filch, and probably should have, was just one of the twenty or so leather jackets I'd found wasting away in an upstairs cupboard.) I waitress in a doughnut shop, a gig I acquire when I happen to stop two Greek men for spare change in the Village. They part with a few coins.

'You don't look like a poor kid,' the younger one says. 'You want to get off the street. You come to work for me.'

I last all of three months. I'm not fast enough on my feet, they say. Then there's the Italian restaurant, the fancy supper club, and most profitable of all, the simultaneous vending of pot and Mexican pottery in the park opposite the hotel, perpetuated of course by Julio while I make hourly runs to the deli for loaves of French bread, cans of sardines in red sauce and cups of steaming hot coffee. Drug peddling in Central Park during the winter is hardy work.

What the hell keeps me there?

There's an urgency to our love and certainly to our lovemaking. Often Julio says that it's only in my arms that he forgets. The mother, the son, the former wife, the brother and sisters, the father, the music, the food. Especially the son, only two and a half years old when he left, the little boy who used to sleep in his bed and who waited each night for his return. Who waits still. To my mind, Julio has traded one set of hardships for another, and perhaps it was the night he met me in the café along the ocean that the new hardships became palatable. As for me, I need to be needed like that. To make someone's world whole.

It's not all terrible. While Julio sits in the park after dark, pulling his jacket about him, I attend the nightly *satsang* meetings at Maharaji's headquarters in the loft on Washington Square. There I meet Janice whose long black hair, pale skin, dark shades and exotic eyes remind me immediately of my mother. She invites me to dinner sometimes, or to her apartment on the Upper East Side, where we eat bread and cheese, and drink fine wine. She has wit, intelligence, great books and an awesome record collection. And she doesn't ask questions. In her company, I find a net that saves me from the unrelenting rigours of poverty.

The rest of the time Julio and I play out our version of life against a backdrop of hunger and cold: the sound of mice scurrying across the floor of our hotel room, the sight of the grey brick wall that blocks the light outside our window, the awful din of whores wailing through the thin walls and the perverse glances of men who want to see me fuck Julio for a ten-dollar bill. Eventually, I become invisible among the street painters, the skateboarders, the young boys rammed from behind in the parks after dark, the men of the three-card hustle and the old ladies with refined features and intelligent eyes turned mindless who fight over cardboard crates in the park as the snow dissolves into their mottled skin. New York touches me with its desperation, and because it does, in some wayward fashion, it feels like home.

Miami never offered that, not once. But we find our way back anyway. The city that never sleeps proves too cold for Julio, despite the multiple layers of clothing he dons each day: two undershirts, three sweaters, a jacket and a scarf. Nine months into our stay, he is arrested. Sells some of that 'precious herb, guarantee your money back' to the wrong guy, spends an afternoon in jail, manages to talk his way out of it. Then it's time to move on. We borrow a beat-up station wagon and head back to Miami which, as it turns out, isn't nearly as warm as we'd expected. Pepe's has been closed down by the cops, and Julio's buddies don't seem at all thrilled to see him. We spend the first three nights in a fifty-five-dollar-a-week fleapit on the Seventeenth Street Causeway, where we happen upon a few ounces of grass tucked away in a pair of old socks in a drawer. The profits from that keep us in food for a few days, until we secure an abandoned hotel room along the water, cluttered with boxes and crates, cleaning mops and dust, in exchange for which we keep the lobby of the paling complex above par and empty the trash.

He returns to full-time drug-peddling and, as the acting diplomat (my father always said I had a future in international relations), I am called upon to serve as translator on the gringo deals, for even after more than two years in the US Julio still knows little more than the string of incoherent words he lured me with in the first place. In contrast, my Spanish has improved dramatically. Regularly, as we navigate the way home from some seedy spot, him half stoned, me terrified but playing it cool – past the *putas*, the catcalls and the dark-skinned men who slink through alleyways on their way to prison or petty fortunes, the police slam into the pavement and cut us off. Lights flashing, sirens blasting, harsh voices, guns and steel, face to the wall, legs spread, yet Julio always manages to tuck his bags of pills, and even, once or twice, a nine-millimetre gun, into the balloon-like pockets of a silky black jumpsuit I bring out of the closet at night. The fast-talking officers look right past me, setting their sights on the far more interesting target that Julio represents: six foot three and menacing, brown skin, black eyes, gold chains, and a mocking gap between his teeth.

We live like that, off the profits of those deals. But it never feels like I am doing wrong. Life is happening, to me, around me, over and through me, but not in me. In all of it – the wretched and beautiful girls who lose their minds, the desperate boys who give their bodies, the sleep thwarted night after night by images of eyes peeling back in their sockets, smiles that freeze midstream, and the nagging, recurring vision of the old man down the hall, whom Julio and crew relieve of his pension, month after month, his trembling arthritic hands tendering the prize – in all of it, I forget the very thing I've been telling myself since I was a little girl. You pay a price for everything.

EIGHTEEN

—◆—

I'm seven months' pregnant.

A result of one of those afternoons when the biting New York winter kept us indoors, wrapped in blankets, engaged in the one activity that's free in that city. Julio refused to use condoms, and I let it go at that. I wanted to create a little baby of my own.

'Ju crazy,' Julio said. 'I lef' one boy behind before. I know what it's like.'

'Well I'd never leave my baby.'

It's a difficult pregnancy, plagued by a series of urinary infections, one so severe it landed me in the emergency room at Jackson Memorial Hospital where I sat for five hours as everyone in the whole world was attended to while I looked on. When they finally called me in my blood pressure was so high, they kept me there for another two hours trying to bring it down.

'Is there any reason you're so stressed?' the male nurse asked.

'Not really,' I said. Then he questioned me about my life, my diet, my family, my living situation. The answers painted a pretty bleak picture.

'You're twenty-three years old,' he said, 'alone in a foreign country, with this guy who's no saint as your only support. Did you ever think about going back home?'

'No.' And I hadn't. I couldn't see my life through his eyes. To me it was about waking up, dealing with the day's demands. Finding food, making sure we had a place to stay for the night. Reaching from one moment to the next.

We've just moved again, into a hotel room that's rife with roaches and ants. The air conditioning doesn't work. Julio's off with his mates. I feel ill, tired and hungry, have the urinary infection back. Can't make love to him any more because it hurts. Maybe that's why he's gone so often. I stare out the window towards the ocean; the TV sighs in the background. I watch the old ladies rolling past on the sidewalk, with their bags of groceries perched on little makeshift trolleys that they push forward with whatever strength's left in them. Suddenly I want my mother. Want to ask her about babies and childbirth, about bringing up kids and breast milk. I want to tell her that at twenty-three years old, I'm sitting in a soiled hotel room on the edge of the sea. Alone and scared. I think of a Saturday afternoon at Grandma Sarah's, the year she left. We're stuffed into our seats with plates of soggy food set before us. My father announces abruptly that we have to leave.

'And what's the hurry?' inquires Grandma Sarah. 'What about dessert? And the match just starting?'

Rachel and David want to stay for the sweets, Saul for the match, and I for the time away from home, but he hurries us out the door and drives off. When we reach Tree Tops, I notice an unfamiliar white Jaguar parked across the street, and only when we alight and peer through the windows do I recognise my mother, seated on the passenger side, her coat up around her neck, her cigarette breathing smoke into the musty air. Inside the house, we get into position in the study, his territory, my mother to one side, my father in the middle and us children against the wall facing her. The silence builds. She fidgets nervously with her cigarettes. Smokes three in a row. Requests a drink. My father delivers a vodka and tonic. She sips cautiously.

Nobody speaks.

'Could a woman get a bite to eat here?' she asks finally.

'Go make your mother something,' he says.

It is always 'your' mother. I rummage through the fridge and locate the makings of a chicken sandwich which I dutifully convey complete with lace napkin, serviette and fork, touches I think she will appreciate. She picks at the sandwich listlessly. Every attempt at conversation is thwarted by my father's glares. We sit for an hour like that, my mother divided from us on the other side of a toxic space. At one point, the phone rings, loud, blistering, repetitive. I want my father to answer it, to leave us alone, just for a moment, so I can move across the room, hug my mother, but he ignores it, stolid as a plank of wood, and I remain rooted in my seat. There is no crossing the line that day. After the hour is up, my mother leaves in the car that delivered her. The next time I see her is six years later, on her own turf.

I am sixteen by the time I track her down, in her detached home opposite Glasnevin Cemetery. She writes me a letter in her compressed, feminine hand, telling me where she is, but that she can never, *will* never return to Tree Tops. I plan our outing with precision, pick up Saul, Rachel and David from school, find the bus that crosses the Liffey, even though I've never ventured over to the north side. We walk through unfamiliar streets, following her directions, down past the cemetery, until we come upon Camelot, 25 Claremont Court. We are greeted by a solid wrought-iron gate. Marley answers the door, ushers us in through the narrow hall, into the kitchen where she sits, surrounded by children we don't know, our half-brothers and sisters. She feeds us cakes and biscuits on dirty plates, gives us drinks out of lipstick-smudged glasses. She asks us about our lives, about school, about our father and the parade of housekeepers we've endured since she left. She laughs at our responses, that same thick chuckle that's so recognisable. Before we leave, she asks David to sit on her lap. Awkwardly he lumbers across her thin knees and places his head on her chest. She struggles for breath and I notice how gaunt and brittle she is.

We leave then and trudge back past the cemetery as the rains sink through our clothes, me marching forward, lugging Rachel and David behind me. On the way I cry, large, soft tears. I cry until we reach the gates of Tree Tops, and swear that I will go back to see her. And I do.

I look out the window now, searching for someone who reminds me of my mother, a woman with a haggard beauty, a restless defiance, a jaunty step. What I see instead are old, worn-down women, more like my Grandma Sarah, with bodies too large to carry and soft, flabby hearts that will fail them.

Julio appears in the doorway, a huge grin plastered across his face. He's carrying a black plastic bag that swells at the sides.

'*Tenemos buena suerte hoy*, baby (Got some good luck today, baby),' he says.

'What's in the bag?' I ask.

'Stuffa, ju know, *drogas*, Pedro *esta preso. Yo la vendo ahora* (Pedro's been taken to jail. I sell it now).'

He empties the contents on to our little bed in the corner. I've never seen so many drugs in my life, or such variety. Syringes, plastic bags, paraphernalia and hundreds of pills in assorted colours.

'Jesus, Julio, get it out of here. We'll be jailed for life.'

'No, baby, *vamos a ser ricos* (We are going to be rich). Look,' he says, pointing to a collection of small plastic vials, filled with white powder, '*esto es coca.*'

'Great.'

He leaves as briskly as he's arrived. Slowly I hide his stash, in the cabinets underneath the sink, in the bathroom closet, behind the toilet. I don't want to see this gear, much less touch it ever again. Finally, I place the little bags of cocaine inside a jar of some vile-smelling hair product he uses to straighten his rangy afro. I leave the hotel, and head for the beach. Walking is difficult with so much extra weight to carry, but I can't stay in that room, not with all that stuff in there. I edge across the sand, towards the ocean, discard my sandals, and let the water lap against my feet. Daylight inches away. Off in the distance, the sunset, a matted landscape of beautiful colours, folds behind the horizon. In that moment, as it descends, there is peace. Then I see Julio's stringy frame looping towards me. I know his stride by heart, even in the dark.

'Hey Mama, *vamos a nadar* (Let's go for a swim).'

'You can't swim. You'll drown.'

'Baby, I made it here from Cuba. With no swimming.'

He takes off his jeans, throws them on the sand and makes his way out into the water. He travels what seems like a tremendous distance and suddenly I can no longer spot him, just the push and pull of the waves bobbing on the ocean's surface.

He's gone, I think, fucking drowned. Vanished under the expanse of water. Life seems so very thin and incidental to me right then, so easily erased. Frantically, I feel under my breast for the hearty kick of the baby inside me. I start screaming.

'Julio, for God's sake, you fucking idiot, Julio, come back. Where are you?'

The breeze shudders in the palm trees beside me. The beach is bare, no lifeguards, no bodies, just a few mangy dogs sniffing through the sand. The sidewalk looms a mile in the distance with its faint night-lights and the scattered sounds of salsa from passing car windows. I stand in shock, looking out to sea that has turned black. I sit down heavily on the wet sand, defeated. My heart races, my ankles swell and my breath fights to make its way through my mouth. 'Calm down now,' I tell myself, 'calm, you're hyperventilating, your blood pressure, the baby' . . . Suddenly I hear Julio's singular whistle – a reedy, high-pitched singsong – floating through the darkness towards me. He swings his arms as he strides across the sand, then flops down beside me, water dripping from his head, goose bumps covering his skin. His teeth are chattering.

'*Casi me muero alla en el agua* (I almost died out there in the water).' What else could I expect from a man who'd risked his life on a fucking rubber tube, sailed through a torrential storm to a country he didn't know just to get out of Cuba?

'You're crazy,' I tell him. 'A damn lunatic.'

Moments later, we're sauntering along the seawall. He's got his arm around me. His step is jaunty, boyish. The sea agrees with him, I think. He kisses me on the mouth. 'Mamacita,' he says, 'my crazy Irish girl.'

We stand facing the ocean.

'*Es Cuba o Irlanda allá?* (Is it Cuba or Ireland over there?)' he asks, pointing out across the water.

'Don't know, Ireland I think.'

'Ju supposed to be smart. How come ju don't know?'

'It doesn't matter. We're both here. Now.'

He hugs me. I bury my face in his shoulder. For the moment there's hope. That we can get out of the rathole we're living in, have a proper home one day, raise our child right, make some kind of life, as long as we stay together.

'*Te quiero* (I love you),' he says.

A black sports car pulls in beside us. The glass is tinted. A head appears as the window rolls noiselessly down.

'You got anything to sell?' a bearded man asks. I don't like the look of him. Too composed to be buying drugs. Fancy leather jacket, western vibe. I stick my head in through the window and instantly notice his polished cowboy boots. I have a fierce disdain for men who wear pointed footwear. And the woman beside him isn't much better: peroxide blonde with mean eyes and thin lips.

'Why ask us?' I say. 'Do we look like drug dealers?' I point to my protruding belly.

'*Oye, qué dicen?* (What did they say?)' asks Julio.

'No,' I tell him. '*A lo mejor son policias* (Maybe they're the police).'

Julio ignores me, turns to the car, and says, '*Si, Si,*' nodding his head like a damned marionette.

'Hang on now,' says pointy-toes. 'He says you do. You say you don't. Someone's lying here. Do you guys want to make money tonight or not?'

They settle on two bags of coke for $20 each, a deal I have to negotiate, as Julio's English is still pathetic. He races back to the roach-filled room to retrieve the score. I wait by the car. I'm cold now, and still hungry. I want to go home and lie down. I'm not cut out for drug peddling. Never was. While he's gone, they don't talk to me and I don't attempt conversation. I have nothing to say to these people. Julio returns quickly, arms batting the air. His voice is hard when he speaks.

'*Oye, donde conjones pusiste la coca? No la encuentro* (Where the hell did you hide the coke? I can't find it anywhere).'

There's no point explaining, it'd take too damn long, so I march off myself, back up to the room, into the bathroom, feel behind the closet for the jar of stiff hair product and pull it out. It stinks of chemicals. The plastic vials have turned yellow, almost green in spots. Maybe the coke's ruined. I march back up the street, determined now to get this over with. I can see the groceries we'll buy once we're done: plantains, rice, beans, some chicken, good Cuban bread, *café con leche*. I can almost taste them. And the medicines for the infection. I can feel that ease up too and disappear.

'Here you go,' I tell Julio, who hands over the two vials to beardy and accomplice. As soon as those little plastic pouches touch the guy's hand, the blonde gets out of the car, moves around to our side, where we're standing virtually in the middle of the street. I see the glint of handcuffs and suddenly feel cold steel compress against my skin. We've been arrested. They read us that Miranda shit – You have the right to remain silent. Anything you say can and will be used in a court of law – then radio some backup. Within seconds, seven police cars screech to a halt, whereupon an army of cops emerges, demand to know our address, then storm off to search the room. They return shortly, laden down with goods.

'Nice big haul here,' says one. 'That baby of yours will never see the light of day, will never have the benefit of breast milk. Too bad you got caught up with the likes of him' (pointing at Julio). I spot a bicycle stationed over by the low wall that leads to the beach and think, If I can just free myself, I'll scramble away though the dark alleys and escape. But suddenly, they're pushing me into the back of the car. I can't move. My hands are gripped tight, the wrist-bones churning against heavy metal. Julio is flung in beside me.

'*No te preocupes* (Don't worry),' he says. '*Todo esta bien* (Everything's OK).' What the hell is he talking about?

They drop me off at the jail hospital first (given the fact that I'm on the verge of childbirth) where a cursory medical examination reveals that my blood pressure is ludicrously high. None the less they steer me into a frozen cell with a slop bucket in the corner. I sit alone curled in a corner through the night, listening to the hysterical movements of strung-out women being tied down, the rushed sounds of men crashing into walls, officers screaming, prisoners fighting. I hear them, but I can't see them. All I see are steel bars. Every time an officer passes, I ask:

'How long do you think I'll be here? When do you think I'll get out?'

They don't even look at me.

As morning approaches I find it hard to slow my breathing. It races onward, leaving me behind. I can't sit still, but there's no place to move. I want to take a shit, but don't want the guards peering in at me. Eventually I just do it.

How could I have let this happen?

What the hell was I thinking?

I'm going to pay for this for the rest of my life.

Morning refuses to come. I am numb, frozen over, like I'll never move from this spot. This is my end, my sad, unfortunate end, I say to myself. Finally, they open the doors and tell me they're moving me on to the Women's Detention Center.

'Thank God,' I say to the female officer who leads me out to a waiting van. 'I thought I'd never get out of there.'

'Don't you know nothing lasts for ever,' she says, 'not even life.'

NINETEEN

⊷

Terrified, I call my father.

I can't handle the closed-in walls, the microscopic windows, the clanging of doors, the jangling of keys, the child moving in my belly, protruding. The bail is set at $54,000 dollars (my God, what have I done?). The cell is minute. I share it with a blonde from California, in on prostitution charges. There are five other cells on my block, populated by charred females with scars and track marks and tales of brutality and murder, hardened black women who've stabbed their husbands, set fire to their homes or robbed stores at gunpoint. They hang insistently over me, breath in my face, when I use the phone, pressuring me to relinquish my time. Sometimes I call Julio over in the men's jail. We talk for three minutes. 'I love you, *te quiero*, *no te preocupes*, don't worry,' is all he says.

Three times a day we are led from our cells into the long dining hall where we sit in rows on wooden benches. I stare listlessly at my food: grits, potato mix, canned vegetables, the odd piece of meat which the women grab from my plate. I don't protest. Then they lead us back to our block, where I pick at scabs on my hands and arms until they hurt, pull the hair from my head in clumps.

'Another crazy one, always at her head, talks to herself, stupid white bitch.'

They make fun of my belly, follow me from my cell out into the squashed living room where the TV's always at high volume, over to the toilet which sits in full view, back into the cell. They watch. They snicker. There's no peace. The lights go out just after nine. I lie alert on the hard mattress waiting for the deliverance of daylight. I try to veer myself towards an internal calm, to slow my breath to a level pace. Inside, an unbridled turmoil simmers. At 4 a.m. sharp, bright fluorescent beams puncture the darkness. The bell rings. The day starts over. Down to the dining hall, back to the cell, into the living room, over to the toilet, back to the cell. All the while I guard myself against the resolute stares and advances of toughened women who want to invade my body.

From my little cot where there's absolutely nothing to do but think and go crazy, I try to piece it together. Certainly a prison stay never figured too heavily in my naive imaginings of what life might be like in the US. Yet I'd made decisions one after another that had landed me here. With a belly that's becoming increasingly difficult to lug around, and a dose of anxiety that has my blood pressure dangerously high, all I know for sure is that I have to get the hell out. The days pass, all twenty-eight of them, the child in me pressing hard against my insides, swelling its way up towards my heart and into my throat. I try to push it down. My clothes don't fit. My ankles bulge. My heart races. I want to see the sky and breathe fresh air, want to escape from behind these walls, out of the cell, away from these women. It is only in the yard, a tiny space surrounded on all sides by a brick wall, that I feel free. We get fifteen minutes at a stretch. I pace back and forth, as my father had done in the front room back in Tree Tops, talking to myself, until it's time to use the phone, at which point I contact the man far away who no longer has anything to say to me.

'This is what Miami has done to me,' I tell him.

'I don't know you,' he says.

After three weeks of frenzied calls, he relents. Turns out he's read some article in the *Jewish Chronicle* about a Lubavitcher rabbi in Miami who works wonders with Jews just like myself: idiots who've gone and gotten themselves into a pickle. He makes a series of phone calls of his own and one afternoon as I sit in the cell – I think I might actually have been praying because the walls had started to travel towards me – the prison guard calls me out for a visit. I'm greeted in the waiting room by a rotund rabbi sweating under an old felt hat.

'Your fah-der sent me here to see if you're vorth savinkh,' he says. 'I told him that all Jews are vorth savinkh, no matter vat dey've done.'

Grateful in the moment for a brand of philosophy that at any other time would have annoyed me, I say:

'I think I'm worth saving and if I'm not, my baby definitely is.'

At this, he glances down at my bulge, which up to that point, he's miraculously managed to miss.

'Of course, de baby, ven is it due?'

'Any day now.'

That must make some kind of impression, because within hours my father has posted bail and I'm transferred over to the immigration jail where, for a fee, I will be released into the custody of the venerable Rabbi Herschfeld.

Immigration jail proves to be a step upward. It doesn't smell; the rooms are spacious, and there are windows, out of which downtown Miami looks more promising than it ever has. The same streets I'd pounded, penniless and exhausted, months previously now brim with vitality. The clipped Latin voices that once seemed so hostile hit me like cheery salutations. I witness it all from where I sit, behind whitewashed walls, holding on to a Styrofoam cup of lukewarm coffee. Freedom, choice, free will; they stare me down, relentlessly mocking, because standing between me and personal sovereignty is a row of cubby-holes where a bunch of stern men in white shirts and austere ties hold forth: immigration officers; long on rigidity, short on compassion. If you have the misfortune to be taken into one of those rooms and the stupidity, once there, to proffer the wrong answers, you are led into a holding area, and launched, post-haste, back to wherever it is you'd sprung from.

That might have been my best bet. My son would have been raised in Dublin. So what if he'd grown up around kids a few shades lighter than himself? Truth was, my father didn't want me back, especially not with a black baby in tow, and because I sense this, I hold on tight to what I think I do have. Julio has been writing me long, romantic letters (in woefully uneven English) from his jail cell, promising undying love. When Rabbi Herschfeld and his squad of smarmy lawyers inform me that I have to turn Julio in to save myself, I refuse. My father's words drummed against the insides of my head, 'You've made your bed, now lie in it.'

Day three: I'm released to a smart-mouthed, condescending rabbinical disciple who delivers me to the Herschfelds' just in time for Shabbat dinner. I sit before a long table in the same pregnancy clothes I've worn throughout the jail stay, feeling like a bag lady. The scene is oddly reminiscent of a thousand I'd experienced in the dining room back in Tree Tops: the Shabbos candles flickering, shedding an unsteady light across the table, the sweet wine passed in a silver goblet, hand to hand, mouth to mouth. Even the food is identical, but there's no comfort at this table. They, the rabbi, his upstart wife of the manicured nails, Givenchy attire and perfectly coiffed *sheitel*, seem intent on converting me back to what they assume I was once.

'You speak Hebrew so well,' *sheitel* comments, mid-gefilte-fish.

'I did go to Hebrew school,' I tell her.

'But how,' asks the rabbi, 'did you come to be in a jail? Such a smart girl, so vell spoken, from such a gut family, how cud dis have happent?'

'Your father keeps Shabbos, right?' the wife continues.

'After a fashion,' I say. 'I mean he works, turns on the light, drives, but we only eat kosher.'

'Vell,' says rabbi, 'I've heard of vorst, much vorst. Dis shoud not be how you turn out, Nu?'

'Leave her,' *sheitel* intervenes, 'leave her now to enjoy the Shabbat. We can figure this out later, in time.'

Through the night, as they sleep, I make desperate phone calls: to Saul, whose voice sends a warm calm hurtling across the seas towards me, to my friends in Dublin who offer advice, money, a place to stay if I want to go home. When I run out of people to call, I sit on the floor of an extravagantly carpeted hallway in the home of strangers to whom, I imagine, I represent little more than the chance to perform a mitzvah. An anonymous and random opportunity for extra blessings from above.

Next morning, they set me up in the Ocean Spray, a Herschfeld-owned edifice on Collins Avenue (they're well connected, these rabbis). The days are endless and intolerable with only the soap operas on a small black-and-white TV for relief. Occasionally I pop in for a brief chat with an ageing Spanish actress who occupies the room next door. Otherwise I spend my time totally alone, wandering through hallways, riding the creaking elevator up and down to reception to see if anyone has called or written, ambling across the street to the musty hotel café for microwave-heated tea or an insubstantial breakfast. When I'm really at the end of my rope, I embark on a quick walk over to the beach, where I sweat as long as I can before running back to the excruciating solitude of my air-conditioned room. I am invited to the Herschfelds' weekly Friday night extravaganzas and to synagogue on Saturday mornings. I go, out of obligation, out of fear, but more than anything because my father's voice resounds in my temples, nagging and insistent, warning me that I'm very close to falling off the edge of the world.

Julio is released two weeks later to await trial. I meet him in front of the courthouse. He looks awful. His skin is ashen. His eyes are dead. He's wearing stained prison clothes and dirty white sneakers. We take three buses to Little Havana to meet his court-appointed lawyer, some Sanchez guy in a flashy suit.

'What do we do now?' I ask. 'What's the plan? What happens when the trial comes?'

'You do nothing,' Sanchez says with a smile. 'Absolutely nothing, and the trial will probably never come.'

'How so?' I say. Julio is quiet. I don't know what happened to him in jail, but whatever it is, he's carrying it with him.

'It's complicated,' Sanchez goes on, 'but there's a little loophole called the speedy trial law which means that if they don't bring you to trial within 180 days, they forfeit the right to convict you. Let's lie low. Let the 180 days pass, and you're home free.'

'But how do you know they won't bring us in?'

'I don't know for sure but I have a hunch, call it intuition. Now go about your lives and, *por Dios*, stay out of trouble. And,' he adds as we turn to leave, 'you'd better think about getting married. He's safe. They don't send Cubans back, but you're not off the hook with immigration. If you get hitched, they won't deport you.'

He shakes our hands like we're preferred clients and leads us out the door, back into the sunlight. Two days later I'm summoned to defend myself in front of an immigration judge. Before the hearing, we pick up two of Julio drinking buddies, tattered old guys with gold teeth and lopsided grins, and head for the registry office.

'Where are your witnesses?' the magistrate inquires.

I point to Tico and Emilio sitting on a bench in the hallway with their plastic shades and flowery polyester shirts.

'Do they speak any English?'

'Not much,' I say, 'but I'll translate.'

It's as simple as that, our wedding: two signatures; two

witnesses. It lasts all of ten minutes. The immigration judge grants me temporary resident status. I can't work legally, but I can stay. For the moment.

I'm days away from giving birth so Herschfeld arranges for a doctor and a hospital room with money my father sends. My son arrives a week later. The labour is punishing. Ten hours into the contractions, Julio swings in through the doors of North Shore Hospital breathless, just in time for the final thrusts. He lets out a gasp when he sees a little black head clenched between my legs, trying to work its way out. But the baby won't come. The cord is wrapped around his neck. Every time he bears down on me his head thrusts against bone. If I push too hard, I'll strangle him. That's what the nurses keep telling me. I dip under the excruciating pain of the contractions. Each time the agony builds and crashes over me, I find, right in front of my eyes, a piercing white light that spreads through me until the pain eases away. I spend hours dipping in and out of that white light and I think about the baby battling his way through my body. 'You're going to be a tough little guy,' I whisper to him. Eventually I shift positions and he finds his way. In the bathroom hours later I see that I'm bruised all the way down the inside of my thighs. When they bring my son to me I feel the hard lump on the side of his head.

'That baby got a head-bashing coming in,' the nurse says.

Later that night when the morphine wears off, I'm in agony. The worst pain I've ever known. Julio slips into the narrow hospital bed beside me and strokes my face.

'Ju did good, mama,' he says, 'bery good. Now, wat we gonna to call that boy, maybe Julio, eh?'

'No, not Julio,' I say, 'one of you is enough. How about Jesse? It means gift from God. You know like the train robber, Jesse James. Or how about Dylan, like the poet?'

'A train robber or a poet. I go with the train robber. Yesse, I like that.'

I smile as I realise Julio will probably never be able to pronounce his son's name.

We return to the Ocean Spray and set about parenting. The Herschfelds arrive with a trunk of baby clothes: blankets, feeding bottles, baby pillows, bathers, stuff I don't even know how to use. The *bris* is held a few days later in an office block on Lincoln Road. After the snipping, Jesse is passed around a room of bearded men while I watch helplessly. Julio waits outside. Platters of food are brought in from the local Jewish deli. The rabbis demolish them in five minutes flat. When the prayers are over, one of the wives hands me a plate of leftovers.

'For the father of the child,' she says. 'He too should get joy from this day.'

Back in our room, we argue about how to change the diapers, about when Jesse should sleep, and where, in the bed, in his crib. When I'm scared, I ring my mother.

'He has a rash, little white bumps on his forehead. What do I do? He keeps vomiting and crying. How do I stop him?'

She laughs and says it's an awful expensive way to learn about your first child. The truth is I don't know anyone else with babies except for a few hard-boiled Cuban women.

'*Aguantalo asi* (Hold him like that),' one of them says, when I stop by.

'*No asi* (Not this way),' another one shouts. '*Asi* (This way),' as she pulls Jesse from my arms to demonstrate. One tells me to breast-feed. The other says give him condensed milk. One says lift him over your shoulder, the other says lay him flat. Then they forget all about me, sitting there holding my baby, and launch into a heightened debate about child-bearing, child-rearing, childhood, about Cuba and Miami and the nine kids they've left behind. In the end, of course, it's left up to me.

I'd like to say that the shenanigans and the drug dealing cease, that I learned my lesson and became a good girl. But that would be lying and if there's anything at all of value to be had from facing and retracing the unbearable, it comes about only in the most earnest quest for honesty. So, instead, I will say that the show goes on. The room at the Ocean Spray with the twin beds, the hotplate, the tiny refrigerator, the bathtub filled with baby clothes and the little white wooden crib in which Jesse sleeps intermittently, becomes a manic hotbed of criminal activity. I want no part of it. In the end I go out and find myself a job, in an Indian restaurant on Forty-first, where they dress me up in a sari, paint a dot on my forehead and give me a list of unpronounceable dishes to remember. Other than an enduring taste for spicy food, the job offers little, but I relish the time away from Room 601 at the Ocean Spray which has begun to squeeze the life out of me. I need the time away from Jesse so that I can love him again when I return. More than anything we need the money. Drug dealing yields are unpredictable, at best.

It is during this period that my father and Adele present themselves in Miami for a visit. I usher them into the tiny sixth-floor room moments after I've ushered Julio out, and invite them to sit on the twin bed over in the corner. They watch Jesse as he sleeps, marvelling at the golden tones of his skin, the crop of black curly hair on his head. When he awakens, I cradle him, then unbutton my blouse and feed him from my breast. I see in my father's face a tenderness. Hope travels on the silence that passes between us, the kind that's capable of blurring animosity and dampening bitterness. I imagine then the story that fills my father's head as he watches: the story of a mother who holds her child gently, who feeds him from her breast and who wants more than anything to keep him close. I think I see, too, a shade of respect, of pride for the daughter who has learned how to mother all by herself. When they leave the hotel room, he presses a wad of bills into my hand, then hugs me quickly and walks away. Soon after, I'm informed by rabbi and son that our tenure at the Ocean Spray is up.

In our final weeks there I beg Julio to stop dealing and to get a job. He tries for a few but the pay is pathetic, the conditions appalling. Soon he's back doing what he does best. I live in constant fear, for something in Jesse's face, a peculiar hue that casts a strange and resolute shadow over my world, makes me see it differently. Suddenly life is no longer simply happening to me. Jesse's presence seems to me an act of insistence, an unyielding claim that I do better, be better. I recognise it then, but act upon it with only hesitant resolve, with the wavering determination of one who is gravely alone. For there are times, so many they merge in my mind, when I am left behind, nights I march from one end of the beach to the other, pushing that baby carriage forward, to track Julio down. Sometimes I find him sitting on a wall drinking rum, surrounded by men, telling tall tales, or smiling casually as he runs his fingers delicately through a young girl's hair. Most times I don't find him at all and I make my way four miles back up the beach, talking up a storm to a six-month-old baby who vacillates between sleep and waking. There's such trust in his little black eyes when he looks up at me, a terrifyingly reliant expectation that forces me to glance away. I see it in his hands too, tiny brown fingers that reach up and grab the air. So many nights I endure alone, with nothing but the sound of Jesse's cries to fasten me to the ground.

TWENTY

We find an apartment eventually.

Stay there for a few months until we falter on the rent and we're on the move. When I discover I'm pregnant again, we settle in the Riviera Gardens, an unkempt set of rooms on the tip of North Beach. Months later I give birth to Daniel in the state ward of Jackson Memorial with all the other penniless mothers. The first night I sleep on a cot in a corridor beside an overflowing trash-can and feel my blood pressure rise. The doctors are rushed and abrupt, the nurses frazzled. They keep talking about toxaemia, protein deposits in my urine and the possibility of a stroke. I'm carted from one lobby to another on a little trolley with a frayed hospital gown around my shoulders, needles sticking into my veins and a drip rolling behind me. They check my blood so often, they run out of veins, so they move down into my feet, then my hands.

'Don't you have someone to stay with you?' the doctor asks.

I don't want to tell them that I couldn't find Julio when the pains started, that I have left Jesse with a neighbour I barely know. I get through it the way I get through everything, cursing and fighting and gritting my teeth, hanging on for dear life to that small, clamped space inside, the knot of survival that holds it all together. When my baby is born I hold him. He's a shining angel of a child with a face so sweet, it makes me cry. I promise him as he sleeps in my arms that I will do better this time, that I'll learn how to be a proper mother.

The Riviera Gardens is a dirty, dishevelled vacuum of a place with only one bed, on to which we pile carelessly at night, Daniel always close to my right breast. When Julio is home, he's fixing up the grounds, plastering and painting around the complex, in return for which we get a break on the rent. I make friends. With Carmen, the elderly Cuban lady who lives at the end of the block and who appears every afternoon in my doorway, laden down with bowls of black beans, rice, marinated pork loin or mounds of roast chicken.

'Yo te enseño (I'll show you),' she says. 'Al Cubano le encanta su comida (The Cuban man loves his food).' But I never learn, though I diligently attempt a variety of culinary concoctions on the little hotplate in the foul-smelling kitchen. I just keep on accepting those dishes she brings to the front door. I meet Debbie too, a Jewish hippie type with a son and daughter, whose home is almost as dismally equipped as mine, and Nicki, a lovely blonde woman with a beast of a husband, whose daughter spends much of her time sequestered in the back of my jumbled closet with Daniel. Janice, the one from New York who reminds me of my mother, has relocated to Miami and arrives often to squire me off to dinner, sometimes a show, away to a world to which I no longer have a point of entry. There's Margaret too, a Londoner I met during my first weeks in Miami, via Maharaji, and who still phones and visits with regularity six years on.

It's a life.

For a while, the drug dealing recedes into the background. When Julio isn't off tending the gardens or remodelling faded apartments, he's at the golf course across the street where he drives rich Jewish men with questionable backgrounds around in little carts. When he's not doing that, he's on the driving range himself, sending golf balls hurtling through the tepid air. Turns out he has a knack for it.

'Too bad he didn't come here when he was a kid,' the old men say, 'he coudda been a pro.'

Julio tires of this domestic life rather quickly. Too often he gets this awful pinched look around the eyes, like it's hard to keep them open. After he's played with the kids for a while at night, which he always does, flinging them up on his shoulders and carting them around the room, or dancing in a circle with small, jutting steps to Bob Marley records, he lays them to sleep. Then he starts into the ritual massaging of his temples that says life is too much. He gets angry about nothing, about everything. There are women too, in particular the Cuban whore/cokehead across the courtyard. He comes home with the smell of her cheap cologne clinging to his clothing at least once a week. I'm sure it's hers because it's the same pungent smell I get when I cross her path on the way to the garbage dumpsters that sit gathering flies at the edge of the building. There are others, too, faceless women, whose existence eats into my world in the smallest ways: a scent, a piece of paper, a rumpled shirt, a stray hair.

I spend a lot of time walking, to the shops, to the garbage dump, to Debbie's house and around my own apartment, to the kitchen, to the toilet, to the window. Walking off the despair. Or I write, sitting at the desk in the corner, in front of the ancient typewriter I've carted from one apartment to the next. I write about Julio and me, and my sons, about waking up to dread, about being raped in New York and leaving my family behind. But no matter how I spend my time, invariably, as the sun begins its descent, I find myself sitting on the threadbare couch, one leg flung over the arm, staring straight ahead. Jesse and Daniel play in the closet, building things up and knocking them down. They laugh and fight, run wild and eventually sleep as I watch the days fade into darkness. The Budweisers are the only thing that take the edge away. I develop panic attacks, at first only moments long, then hours, then days. I sit on the couch, Bud in hand, watching as my sons seek me out. I have no faith, only fear, and I am alone. When Julio comes home from his nightly dalliances, the *arroz con pollo* is thrown again in the garbage. He tosses my tranquillisers away too and rages all around me as I hang tight to some sacred place inside that is becoming increasingly difficult to find. I borrow money to buy him pot because that's the only way I can tolerate him, and I drink more because that's the only way I can allow him to touch me.

When the rent is due, again I call my father in desperation. Finally, he sends $5,000, once and for all, he says, to buy a truck and set Julio up in a painting business. We get cards made and walk door to door in the fancy neighbourhoods. He studies for his contractor's licence and passes. Secures a few jobs and does them well. Golf is not the only thing he has a knack for. He's a decorating genius, the clients say, and cheap too. But life doesn't change, not perceptibly, not enough. He's still rubbing those damn temples of his, still staring at me from odd corners of the room with a kind of menace I've seen before. And I always end up in the same place at night: on the sardine can of a bed in a box of a room beside my sons as the torment crashes through me. The doctor tells me my blood pressure is on overload, the psychologist says I suffer from agitated depression, the psychiatrist wants to give me lithium, but I flush it down the toilet, and nobody understands that I just want to matter enough to someone once and for all for them not to walk away.

Julio is not that person.

One night I'm perched on the couch. The hours pass. The discarded cans of Bud swell at my feet. By the time I hear him fumbling nervously at the front door it's almost morning.

'Ju want to cach me off gard, heh!' he says as soon as he spots me through the darkness. 'Look Shivaun, I tired. Ju know sick and tired. I don't want hear your mouth. *Esta bien?*'

'It's fucking five in the morning, Julio. You've been hanging out with that stupid Pepillo guy with the gold chains and the coke, fucking women. Are you ever coming back? You know, you, me, the kids . . . a family.'

'Oh, ju so good at the nice talk, the *filosofia*. But what about this house, the way we live' (pointing to the clothes, toys and books carelessly scattered throughout the room). 'I tell you I'm tired. That's why I left Cuba because everything came on top of me. I couldn't breathe. Now with ju, the kids, this place, work. I don't want it. Ju understand.'

He leaves the next morning, the day before Daniel's third birthday, his long legs crushed into the back of a shiny sports car with Pepillo at the wheel.

We wait for him throughout the day and into the night. Jesse starts asking questions. He's used to his father's disappearances, but there's something different about this one. Even he, in his seven-year-old body, senses it.

'I'm not going to bed until we know where he is,' he says.

Who to call? The police, the hospitals, the women? I phone the police first. Bingo. Arrested for drug trafficking, $250,000 bail. Are they insane? The collateral alone will be $25,000. I think of the shabby white van out in the parking lot, the one my father got us, his tools, the few appliances we have in the house, the telescope my father bought Jesse for his last birthday. Total: $4,000 at best. I call Sanchez, the only lawyer I know in Miami, who informs me he needs $5,000 to even take the case, and that without him, they'll lock that fool of a husband of mine in jail and throw away the key. 'It's a fifteen-year mandatory sentence, for Christ's sake.' His exact words.

The lessons we metabolise in childhood stay a lifetime, and I find as I face this latest hurdle that I am adept at handling a crisis. Within hours, I've made contact with everyone I've ever known, even the most cursory and passing of acquaintances, most of whom graciously pledge their support, if not actual cash. Mid-afternoon Carmen appears at the door, fragrant dish in hand, and pulls a roll of dollar bills from her pocket.

'I've been saving some money,' she says, 'and I can't help myself, I love that crazy Cuban, and *los niñitos*, here take it.' When she leaves I count out one hundred dollars. Each day brings with it a new infusion of cash; a handsome cheque from my brother in Ireland, twenties and fifties gleaned from neighbours and friends. None from Julio's crew. Not a dime. By the end of the first week, I've amassed a petty fortune which I count and re-count in little piles on the hardwood floor, right down to the dimes, the nickels and the pennies. The kids get excited at the sight of it.

'We're rich, Mommy,' Jesse says.

'No,' interrupts Daniel, in his three-year-old lisp, 'that's for Daddy, silly. He's in Cuba, and we have to get him back.'

And that's what Julio has told them, when he talked to them late at night, with the sounds of harsh male voices and steel doors slamming behind him: that he was in Cuba taking care of his sick mother, that he'd be back soon.

On Saturday morning, I set up a yard sale, dragging the contents of our modest home out on to the lawn: lamps, end-tables, a microwave, some framed pictures, my old typewriter, tools and a few cans of paint. Passers-by slow to a standstill in their cars, emerge, rifle through the goods, picking them up and flinging them back down as we stand and watch.

'How much for de telescope?' an old Jewish man inquires.

'Fifty dollars,' I say, 'it's still in the box, brand new, the child never even had a chance to play with it.'

'Ten dollars. I give you ten.'

Moments later he's toddling off down the street, the box in his arms.

'Why did you sell my present?' Jesse asks, close to tears. 'That was my favourite toy. Grandpa gave me that.'

'But you never used it,' I say, 'and your daddy needs the money to get back.'

'I didn't use it because I couldn't see the stars. They never came out when I was looking.'

I feel awful, like a thief pilfering from my own sons. Damn you Julio, I think, damn you for putting us in this mess. Damn you!

Suddenly I see Jesse coming towards me. Daniel's behind him, his short bandy legs buckling under the strain of keeping up. In their arms, they're carrying every toy they've ever owned, which they deposit on the ground before me. I want to cry.

A car pulls up. Cielito, a Columbian lesbian Julio befriended on some job a few years back, bails out. She empties the contents of the car on to the sidewalk; clocks, toasters, heating pads, electric toothbrushes, you name it, it's there. Looks like she's robbed a K-Mart.

'*No preguntes* (Don't ask),' she says with a smile. 'You don't want to know.'

Throughout the afternoon we sell it all, plus our TV set, our couch, the dining table, and Julio's collection of tools. He was always bringing home broken objects, filling up our closets with crap and fixing them up to sell. By nightfall, the kids are in bed, exhausted. Cielito and I are sitting on the porch knocking back the Budweisers. The money is counted, safely tucked away in a huge brown envelope. All six thousand dollars. We've done it. I look into the envelope periodically, see all those bills and coins pressed neatly together. I could leave now, I think, walk out of here, back to Dublin with the boys, but then I think of Julio, growing old and tired and stale, and of his sons, my sons, growing bitter and sad. A bunch of bills in a brown envelope just doesn't hold enough promise.

The phone rings.

'*Dónde estabas*? (Where were you?)'

'Making money. Julio, I have it all, six thousand for the lawyer. Cielo helped me.'

'*Esta tortillera* (That dyke). Suppose you fucking her now. Ju no good, ju hear me, eh . . . no good.'

'Julio I've been out selling everything we own . . .'

'Go to hell.'

It is in that precise moment that he loses me. The humiliation, the other women, the fear, the lies, the years of waiting, all of it collects inside me. The cord that ties me to him dissolves. I give up. I stop fighting, for him, for his love, for our life together. I know then for the first time that I will survive without him.

I stand in front of the judge the next morning as they lead him in, proud, beautiful, his back straight, eyes clear as black steel balls. I try to imagine what it would feel like to pack our bags and get on a plane. To leave him behind and forget. I think of Jesse and Daniel, how they would grow into manhood without knowing their father, without ever again laying eyes on him. I just can't do it. In the corridor of the courthouse, I meet the lawyer and hand over the money, down to the last penny.

'Get him out,' I say. 'Do whatever you have to do, but get him out of there.'

TWENTY-ONE

⟶

My marriage is over.

In those first weeks after the arrest, I notice how tired and worn down I look. But I notice too a fresh and conspicuous freedom around the house. In response, I become a new woman, putting on make-up, dressing up like I have somewhere to go even though I don't, smiling at strangers as I walk down the street. Then disaster hits. The phone gets shut off, the electric is about to go next and the landlady delivers an eviction notice. Within a matter of days, I'm donned out in a ruffled white shirt and a pair of black suit pants I get at the thrift store, working the Passover stint at Tower Forty-One, a Jewish emporium of unparalleled proportions.

My first night there, I swing through the kitchen doors with a tray of steaming matzo ball soups hovering hazardously on my shoulders. Bernard, the Tower Forty-One don, complete with over-sized belly, tufted moustache and flirty grin, screams at me from behind.

'Get a move on there, this isn't a funeral procession.' God knows how I make it to the tables without decapitating or scalding any-one. When I arrive, I lay down the bowls (virtually empty; there's more soup on the tray than anywhere) in front of a large party of confused customers. The men are antique, grey-skinned with mummified *yarmulkes* plastered to sweating scalps and tight-fitted waistcoats corseting shrivelled bodies into place. The women, with an almost neon blend of frosted pink and blue hair, permed high up on their heads, are dressed in bright tacky outfits that stretch over their bulges.

'Vere's de gefilte fish?' demands one clearly agitated woman when I approach.

'Ve've been vaiting over an hour, and der's no seltzer vater and only one bottle of Manishevitz for twenty people. Do they expect us to drink from a timble?'

'I'll get to it,' I answer urgently. Where the fuck is that Bernard when you need him?

'And the pickles,' she adds. 'Five to a table. Dey tink we eat like birds.'

'OK,' I say, 'I'll find more pickles, more wine, more seltzer.' Find being the operative word.

'Well,' I ask, 'can I take your dinner orders?'

'Do I eat flanken,' ancient husband asks highly charged wife, 'or would I rather the chicken?'

'He'll have the steak,' the wife says, at which he grimaces in quiet defeat.

Back in the kitchen it's chaos. Half the wine has disappeared. The meat is undercooked. The soup has run out, and there are not enough tables. Some folks haven't even seen an appetiser and the rabbi is late, or missing, or knocking back the Manishevitz in the cloakroom. The other waiters and waitresses, who actually know how to hold the damn trays, file through the swishing doors, barking orders at disgruntled bus boys, retrieving bottles of wine and juice from hidden corners for their tables. I haven't a clue what's going on. My customers, en masse, launch a tirade in my direction every time I poke my head from behind the door. I corral Bernard in a corner. 'Get me wine before they lynch me.'

'Fine,' he says and embarks on a military foray through the dining room, plucking half-filled bottles from under the noses of unsuspecting guests.

'You want wine. Here, you have wine.'

Suddenly, I'm first in line at the food station. It's hot. I feel faint. I forget what I need: five flankens, six chickens, the steak. I'm blank.

'What the fuck do you want, Irish?' the Puerto Rican chef demands (he looks more like a drug trafficker with the flaming bandana tied around his head). 'No time for messing me around. We got two hundred starving Jews out there.'

'You need a hand?' a voice asks.

It's a cinematic moment, right out of *Lady Sings the Blues*, one of my all-time-favourite films when Billy Dee Williams stretches out his hand filled with dollar bills to Diana Ross and says in that drawling, oh so sexy voice, 'You want my arm to fall off?' The man in front of me is tall, black and extremely handsome, with an unnerving sensuality around the mouth.

I get through the night with the help of Mr Swanson who, as it turns out, is an elementary school teacher, working the Passover gig to get a few extra bucks to help his mother out. By midnight, I'm sprawled across a plastic bench, deflated. My legs are numb, my brain shot. I don't think I've ever worked this hard, and I can't find a way home. No taxis. I'm on the verge of tears, thinking that maybe I can just snatch a few hours' sleep on a bed of tablecloths in the corner before the morning shift. This is a three-meal gig, and I've to be back at six anyway. But then I realise that won't work because the babysitter, a fourteen-year-old from across the complex, will have to get home. Finally, Mr Swanson ushers me out to a sleek midnight-blue Caddy and, as we ease through tree-lined streets towards the Riviera Gardens, he talks to me, slow and measured like he's had a whole lot of practice. When we reach the complex, I don't want to get out. It feels safe in his car with the

Commodores doing their easy morning thing over the radio, the tangy scent of him gripping me, a red-hot magic riding the air between us. He leans his head back, closes his eyes and we sit there, quiet, stilled, like the insides of that car are the whole wide world.

We do this every night for the remainder of the Passover stint: drive, sit, talk. He offers only fragments: lives with his mom; had a drink problem; no longer drinks; grew up in Oakland; was a wild boy; got tame; went to college; drifted; had a wife; she left; ended up in Miami, by default like most people, and never got out. His voice swells over me. I forget my sons, forget Julio, forget just about everything except the way my body feels when he talks.

Two weeks later we're out on our first official date. I put enormous effort into this, borrowing a silk blouse, doing my hair up, slapping on the make-up, slipping on the heels, the whole nine yards. He's dressed like a model out of *GQ*. We end up at a sprawling restaurant overlooking Miami Bay with the lights of the boats blinking off in the distance. I drink vodka. He orders Coke. Away from the shelter of his Caddy, he's a different man, jumpy, on edge. And for the first time, I notice his laugh, a big booming guffaw like Eddie Murphy's. We're misplaced in this restaurant filled with quiet white couples.

'So what do you get up to when you're not teaching, or serving matzo ball soup?' I ask after an awfully long silence.

'Oh, not much. I do a lot of driving, on my own mostly, going through the city. Or I walk my dog, Tyson (the laugh). How do you like that? I'm Mike. He's Tyson. It's an awesome combination.'

'What kind of dog is he?' I ask.

'A pit bull. Now don't go telling everyone you met this guy Mike with a pit. It's illegal, you know, if you don't have a special licence. But I breed them. He's got some jaw on him that dog. I walk him a lot, round the lake at the back of my house. Or I watch wrestling. Ever been into wrestling?'

'God no,' I say, stumped. A pit bull, WWF, my worst nightmare sitting in front of me. But somehow I don't see that. What I see is a beautiful man, with protruding lips that curve with scary precision. An anxious, hurt man with his arms clasped awkwardly around his knees, whose body leans into mine. He's talking. I see his mouth move. I don't hear the words. I want to kiss his lips.

Somehow, over the next few days, I get the kids to school, somehow I bring them home, make them food, dress and undress them, put them to bed at night, wake them in the mornings. But I'm floating, barely able to touch ground. I can think of nothing but him, when he'll arrive, where we'll go. In my absence Jesse and Daniel are sent back and forth to an array of minders, Debbie at the complex, the fourteen-year-old, an old friend, basically to anyone who'll have them. I'm on autopilot, except when I'm with him, and I rarely stop to ask myself what I'm up to. When I do, I tell myself that it's the fact that Julio's locked away with little hope of release that's making me act like this. And me not used to being alone. I do have the boys, but kids can't hold you at night and make you forget. They, with their sad, wondering eyes, their spirits fastened on to some kind of desperate hope, their huge questions, to which I can offer no plausible response, remind me of my aloneness all the more. And it's M too, how he carries himself, what he touches in me. I don't want it to end.

A few weeks into this, we find ourselves on the beach. M flops down on the sand beside me. I want to feel his warmth, to tuck myself deep into the folds of his body, but when I inch closer, he backs away.

'There's something I've been meaning to ask you since the first time we met,' he says finally. 'Do you think you have space in your life for me right now? I mean, what's gonna happen when your husband gets out? Are you going to take him back?'

'He might be there for a long time,' I say, 'but even if he came home tomorrow, I wouldn't want to stop seeing you.' I look over at him. His face is bright, shining through the darkness, his eyes alive with wanting.

Hours later we sit in silence under the streetlamp across from my apartment. Suddenly, he leans over, puts his tongue in my mouth, a cool, sweet tongue. He unbuttons my shirt, releases my breasts from my bra and buries his head between them. I raise my hand to his face, uncertain whether or not to touch. At last, I run my fingers along the lines and edges, like a blind person, groping towards recognition. He remains so still, locked into place. I watch the rise and fall of his chest, take his hands in mine and hold them to my lips. He looks across at me baffled, and I know then that no one has ever touched him like that before.

The following night he takes me to the Ponderosa on his side of town. It's a run-down bar where the patrons, a collection of wizened men and curvaceous women, purchase their liquor by the bottle and drink in a back room until dawn. The jukebox is playing some bump-and-grind number. Everyone's dancing, even M. He moves well, like a stallion, with his head thrown back, his eyes closed.

'C'mon,' he says, 'get in there. I'll teach you.'

'I don't dance,' I say, 'but I love watching.' We sit in the corner after that, him with his gin (just for tonight, he says), me with my vodka, our knees touching under the table. I can't stop looking at him. And I know that no matter who this guy is, no matter what he does, I won't be able to walk away.

Suddenly he's on his feet, in a hurry.

'Have to get something from the car,' he says. 'Be back in a sec.'

I sit alone with my vodka. I'm the only white woman in the place. Thirty minutes pass. It's stifling hot. I'm getting drunk. I feel exposed. I want him to come back. Finally, I head out to the parking lot and walk over to his shining blue Caddy. The windows are rolled tight, fogged with smoke. I tap on the glass. He opens the door. Immediately, I'm assailed by the force of a thick pungent odour.

'Get in quick,' he says.

He's sucking on a small pipe, inhaling massive mouthfuls of smoke, holding it tight in his lungs, then releasing it in long, slow breaths. His eyes are wild. Beads of sweat form along his forehead. His jaw darts in and out. His beautiful suit is crushed. He draws in the last breath of smoke, looks around like a trapped animal, then searches the floor for minuscule white boulders of crack, picking up bits of fluff, inspecting them like they're gold dust, then letting them drop.

'I know I have more, I couldn't have smoked it all,' he mutters to himself. He doesn't even know I'm there. He rifles through the ashtray, pokes under the little carpet, gets out, searches under his seat. Through it all, his jaw keeps jerking like he can't control it, his eyes are close to popping.

'You're a crack addict,' I say finally.

'Yeah,' he says. 'That's me. Teacher/preacher by day, crack addict by night.'

'Take me home. Just take me home.'

I know I should walk away, but I don't. Not then, and not during the year that follows when he moves into our new place, with its high ceilings and intricate fireplace. Not when he barks orders with a vengeance, plays vicious games with the boys that leave purple patches on their golden brown skin. Not when he mocks and belittles me, spanks my sons with his belt, makes them rise at dawn and shoves unwanted food down their throats.

Not even after the fight.

I land a job as a reviewer with an entertainment mag. I'm supposed to go places – restaurants, clubs, hotels – and write about them. So I book us a room (on the expense account) at one of those new art deco suites right on the ocean, the kind Julio and I were evicted from when South Beach was full of Cuban criminals. We stop at a quaint Italian restaurant for dinner (also on account), then at a New Orleans bar for drinks. By the time we get to the hotel room, we're quarrelling. I've misplaced $100. I accuse him of taking it for crack. He claims he didn't. I don't believe him. The manager, a short Latin fellow, knocks on the door and asks us to keep it down. I'm embarrassed. I flop on to the bed, defeated. I'd wanted this night to turn out well.

'You're a fucking nagging bitch. I can't stand you. Worst mistake of my life getting involved with you,' M shouts.

I look up at him, confused, and suddenly feel the thrust of his fist against my face. He grabs my arms. I try to get away, dragging myself across the room. He pulls me back. He pounds into my head. Then, as suddenly as he started, he stops. I gather my clothes in a little plastic bag and walk out the door. I have no money so I hitch a lift to Deb's house. It's 7 a.m. The moment she sees me, standing on her porch, my clothes in my hands, she shrieks:

'What happened to you, honey? Oh my God, who did this to you? It's that bastard, isn't it? That fucking bastard.'

She applies ice to my bruises. My lips are cracked. There's a gash along my eyes. Jesse and Daniel, who've spent the night, step into the living room, bleary-eyed, still half in sleep. They run towards me, then sit beside me on the couch and pat my head with their little hands.

'You can't stay with him, Shiv,' Deb says. 'If you can't do it for yourself, do it for those boys there, but you have to leave him.' If I could answer her I would tell her that for me love and pain are fused. I can't imagine one without the other. Instead I say nothing.

The house is empty when we return. We set off in my Chevrolet that travels at a maximum of twenty miles an hour, down to the Belle Glade Correctional Facility. Jesse and Daniel chatter as we pass insipid landscapes on our way to the prison. We arrive early and wait in line behind the gates, along with all the others: wives, children, uncles, grandparents, dressed in their Sunday bests, batting off flies and giant mosquitoes, flapping fans against the unrelenting sun.

The sound of the gates opening always startles me. Jesse and Daniel cling to my legs as we watch the men on the other side of the barbed-wire fence. Julio is always the last to emerge, resplendent in glittering prison whites. We hand him gifts: toys the boys made at home, cards with messages in their best handwriting. The visit is conducted on the grass, out in the open. He takes the boys on his knees and bounces them up and down. He points to my face which, even through the make-up, shows evidence of a beating.

'Don't ask,' I say. 'It's nothing.'

He shakes his head.

When the hour is up, we say our goodbyes.

Jesse doesn't want to leave.

'I don't mind it here,' he tells his dad. 'I'll stay with you. Mom and Daniel can get me next month.'

'Ya, ya, *muchachito*,' Julio says. 'The men are mean here. They no like little boys. Too rough for ju and Danielito. I be home soon.'

Every month he says the same thing, and every month tears stream across my son's cheeks as he catches the last glimpse of his father being herded around a corner and out of sight.

The boys are quiet on the three-hour drive home. We stop at Mario's and order the same thing as always: two pepperoni pizzas and garlic bread. They get Cokes. I drink beer. We return late in the evening to a house filled with its own kind of dread. This time M's asleep. I slip into bed beside him. He grunts and turns towards me, encircling me in his arms, the way he always does. I lie still, my body pressed against his, wondering when I will ever find the courage to walk away.

On the Fourth of July, M and I are in bed. It's early afternoon and we're supposed to be taking the boys to the park. He steers my head under the covers. I know what he wants. But suddenly I get the unmistakable whiff of woman's pussy. I stop mid-motion.

'Is there any reason your penis smells like it's been inside a woman?' I ask.

He doesn't respond.

'Well, is there?'

I know the answer.

He doesn't respond.

I ask the kids.

'Have you seen M with any other women?' (just like my damn father!)

They're quiet. Then Daniel blurts out in his small voice:

'When we went to the beach this morning, he brought me into a house, and he went to the bathroom with a blonde lady.'

'What did you do while he was in there?'

'Nothing. I sat on the floor in the hallway.'

'How long for?'

'I don't know. A long time.'

'Well, an hour, thirty minutes?'

'I don't know, Mommy.'

He's upset now, close to tears.

I stop.

I approach M in the bedroom.

'I know about the blonde.'

'So?'

'Do you love her?'

'Love her? She's an aerobics instructor with a great body. She gives good head.'

'Good fucking head,' I scream. 'That's what matters to you, jaw movements?'

Within minutes we're embroiled in an all-out battle, at the height of which he hurls a pot of boiling water in my direction, which misses me and destroys my computer. I call the police, who arrive on the doorstep in their shining blue to inform me that in the absence of markings (scars and bruises) and a witness (children don't count), there is precious little they can do.

We patch it up.

Hours later we're at the beach. Daniel and I sit by the water's edge. Jesse and M play football.

'Don't be a fucking wimp, get in there,' I hear M booming across at Jesse, who stands to the side, dwarfed by hard black bodies with muscles that glisten in the sunlight. Daniel sits by me, playing quietly with a sea roach that scampers across the sand.

'Mom, can I take this little guy home?' he asks.

'No. It's just an insect.'

'But I've always wanted a pet. He's playing with me.'

'Don't be silly,' I tell him. 'Maybe we can get a puppy instead.'

'Promise?'

He knows I won't get the puppy. Knows that I'll forget, like I forget everything, that the words will get drowned out by beer, or by the heat. When we leave, he gathers up his bucket and pail.

'Mom, this is the very best day of my life.'

At home, I remove his shirt to put him into his pyjamas. His back is blistered, every inch of skin covered in raw, red welts.

'Too much sun,' I say.

That night, I drink even more than usual, sitting there on the same old sofa, in a different house, and I can't get the image of the sores out of my mind.

TWENTY-TWO

—◅—

M's at the wheel.

We're supposed to be going out for dinner. He's in one of those jittery bipolar moods, laughing at things that make no sense, running red lights like it's going out of fashion, slapping the kids on their backs with a force that jolts them out of their seats. Then he gets all serious and morose out of nowhere, talking about God and shit. I've come to recognise these behaviours as the precursors to serious crack indulgence, but I'm praying as we speed through the streets that this won't be another of those nights, like the last time he ripped off Jesse's piggy bank. He smashed it on to the floor, snatched a handful of bills, and disappeared for two days. Three years, Jesse had been saving. Or the time I'd come home all pleased with myself because I'd finally sold some ads for the entertainment rag. Had a stash of $400 tucked safely into my bra as I lay in bed.

'That'll show those bastards,' I thought to myself, 'I'm not some flake who can't produce. I can bring in the bacon along with the rest of them.' Next morning, even before opening my eyes, I felt under my bra. Nothing. Not a single dollar bill. The bed beside me was empty.

Anyhow, here we are, off for a nice dinner, I convince myself, even though he seems to be driving in the wrong direction. Turns out, he knows exactly where he's headed.

'Not again,' I scream, 'come on, you promised we were going to take the kids out. Please, not tonight. We have wine at home. Let's just eat . . .' Oblivious, he steers forward, with that gritty, no-nonsense look that says right then and there that he's not about to be swayed.

We land outside the crack den with the pushers swarming by the windows. The kids cower in fear as M gets out to score. I jump behind the wheel. I'm about to take off when he points a gun in my direction, wielding it like a crazy man. Jesse and Daniel start to cry, and in the eerie light of the moon I catch in their eyes something so very familiar. For the first time, perhaps ever, I see who they are, and I remember the little girl who used to sit under the stairs in terror waiting to be claimed by her mother's fists. I drive away, careening through the streets, the image of M's distorted face spurring me forward. Back at the apartment, I put the kids to bed. Alone in the dark, making my way slowly through the bottle of expensive red wine I'd bought, I remember suddenly the man against whom I have measured all others, the one who, despite his blindness, recognised me always.

Sitting, waiting for M, I am returned to the front bedroom of Tree Tops, the space I shared with Pop until he died. I think of M, getting high still, or getting his dick sucked by some five-dollar crack whore. I visualise us, hours earlier, as we lay on the bed, like two slabs in a morgue, close enough to touch, yet dead to each other. He'd stretched out his hand, and run it along my back. I'd felt myself suddenly spring to life, igniting inside, and I'd wished in that moment, with everything in me, that I could dissolve into his caress and lay my heart open in it. But I knew better, knew instinctively that his hands were cruel, uncaring, capable only of destruction. How had I gotten things so wrong, so messed up?

*

Where are you now, Pop of the two-pack-a-day Players unfiltered habit, honed senses of sound to replace your lack of sight, silver-rimmed glasses, voted best-dressed man in the British Isles, entre-preneur cum gambler, weaver and fabricator of tall tales, chaperone to a child, blessed angel in my life. Do you remember the night you watched us while Mummy and Daddy strayed, how you fed little Saul from the bottle, and became indignant at his relentless cries until I pointed out that you were aiming the teat at his ear? How you comforted my sobs after I'd been pummelled? Did you wonder how a daughter of yours could mangle her child so? Do you remember that you held me the night Mummy left for good, soft, clean hands finding wounded flesh? I always wanted to tell you that she arrived at your funeral in a sexy black miniskirt, fishnet stockings and a wide-brimmed hat. They laughed in her face, those facackta old Jewish women from their low shiva stools, and she crumbled at their feet. As for me, they wouldn't let me come, said I was too young, so I stayed locked in the room we'd shared, surrounded by the echoes of your hacking cough, the cancerous one that eventually killed you, courtesy of ten thousand smokes, and I promised you I'd become the 'beautiful bandit' you always claimed I was. I often wonder how you, in your blindness, saw me this way while I, with my sight, saw only your empty shadow.

I have two sons, you know, with lips and eyes that speak of you, and wisdom too. They entered the world, latched to a turbulent stream, a chaotic current of my making. You see, I looked for a man like you, Pop, with neatly creased pants and expensive cologne, a man with a flashing smile and a charm that danced all over my memories. But my sight was blinded, my heart obstructed, and I found instead a man who could offer me a little black baby doll like the one I'd got from Mommy as a present that Christmas before she left. Only he beat me like Mummy had, dismissed me as Daddy had done. And you were not there to hold me. So I cradled my little black baby boys instead, through that, and my subsequent drinking, the constant moves from street to street, apartment to apartment, room to room, job to job, pay cheque to pay cheque, fight to fight, sorrow to sorrow. They grew beautiful and proud, new angels in my life, and I looked for you constantly in their eyes.

By the time M finally appears, I'm curled in a foetal position on the couch, locked in a wine-induced slumber.

TWENTY-THREE

—◆—

Next morning.

I'm sitting numbly behind my desk at the PR office, where I get to write all the press releases and receive none of the credit. Fighting off the typical hangover, I try to muster a semblance of creativity, an infinitely challenging undertaking when the object of your endeavours is the Radisson Hotel in some bleak east of Jesus town that needs a whole lot more than a few well-coined phrases to set it alight. Anyhow, this particular morning as I plough my way through an Alpine Lace cheese sandwich, the stench of which makes my cohorts dive for cover, I answer the phone to find an authentic Irish voice at the other end: a woman from California responding to one of those media blurbs about free airline tickets. I ascertain within seconds where she was born and how long she's been away from home. Then she asks:

'What did you say your name was?'

'I didn't, but it's Woolfson.'

'My gracious,' she says. 'My best pal in school married a Woolfson, Solomon, I don't suppose you'd know him.'

'That's my father.'

'What a small world. Your mum and I were best friends. Her parents owned a hotel on Grosvenor Place. I'd go there every day after school. Your mum was such a beautiful girl. All the fellows were after her. Then she met your dad. What a catch, we all thought. And your grandad, Ike. A lovely man, but your grand-mother, well she was something else entirely.'

'What do you mean?'

She pauses, unsure of how to proceed.

'Well, first of all, she was an imposing woman; the very sight of her scared me, but there was a cruelty to her. I remember one day I was there and she had a packet of chewing gum. Now this was years ago, when it was a delicacy. She offered me a piece and I took it. Your mum was standing there all excited with her hand out, waiting, and your grandma goes and takes the last stick out and pops it into her own mouth. I don't know to this day why that made such a strong impression on me; it was the look on your mother's face, I think, like she'd been hit from behind, and that awful mean sneer your grandma gave her. I'll never forget it.'

Something takes place inside of me as she speaks. I see my mother then as a timid little girl, full of promise, with the strapless red satin dress and the flashing eyes, the rotating hips and the deep guttural laugh. I see how she had toppled steadily towards insanity, how she had never, in all her life, been able to turn away from that bitter, cruel stare on her mother's face. I vow then that the cycle will stop, that the wheels of evasion and outright neglect that my mother had been turning her whole life will come to a halt in me. I will leave. No matter what it takes. I close the door to my room, light a candle and sit quietly on the floor. I call out to my Pop for a long time, and ask him why I can't trust myself, why I've journeyed so very far from the bright-eyed, wise child he believed in and loved. In the darkness a sound emerges – the cadence of his soft, calm voice.

'Do you remember when you were six years old,' he asks, 'and we used to walk together, how you held on to me, and when we reached a kerb or a crossing, you pressed my arm, one tug for up, two for down? I put my life in your hands, Shivaun, when you were just a child.'

Two weeks later I ask M to leave, and when he calls I do not take him back.

TWENTY-FOUR

I decide to throw myself into work.

But to do that I need a new job. I've had enough of the PR office. I think they've had enough of my Alpine Lace cheese. I hand in my notice on Monday morning, leaving myself exactly one month to find something better. I want to earn my living by writing. A ridiculous notion, my father says when I phone, but I'm determined. I call every publishing company in the Yellow Pages (there's all of six in Miami). Nobody's hiring. Finally I contact *Chai Today*, a Jewish magazine. Rabbi Lozenik, the owner, answers.

'Don't I know you?' he asks, after my long-winded spiel about what an asset I'd be.

'Maybe. I used to go to *shul* with Rabbi Herschfeld.'

'Of course, Shivaun, the Jewish girl from Dublin. It's *besheret* (God's will) that you should call today. Fraydee and I were just saying how we need a person.'

I meet him and his wife next morning in their offices on Lincoln, the same building where Jesse's *bris* was held. Two days later I'm set up at my own desk, as editor at large. It sounds good. Over the next few months I interview mystics, healers, a black man turned Hasid, a cosmetics magnate cured of cancer by the Rebbe and an expert on Jewish sexuality. I send my father a leatherbound collection of

Chai Today magazines for his birthday, hoping he will be proud.

Business picks up. Fraydee tells me we need an assistant. I approach Deb, my friend from the Riviera.

'C'mon Blonnie,' (she has quirky names for everyone) 'can you see me in an office, with paperwork and files?'

Actually, I can't. She makes her living in homecare and spends most of her nights caring for terminally ill Jews whose families can't afford the time. Her kids, Joy and Michael, sleep over at my house when she works, and she arrives in the morning, tired, her unruly head of hair spiking in all directions, to rush them off to school. With that and her aromatherapies, healings, cleansings and astrology readings, she has more than enough on her plate.

'What about my niece, Cece?' she asks. 'She's brilliant that girl. Only eighteen. Living on her own. At university and working in a preschool. I'm sure she'd love to make more money.'

I remember Cece. I met her first in Deb's mismatched apartment at the Riviera when she was fourteen, babysitting her niece and nephew. I think of a big, bold girl, with beautiful eyes, long flowing hair, a phenomenal backside and a disturbing propensity for cutting into her own skin.

'See if she's interested,' I tell Deb.

Two days later Cece's installed. I continue with the writing and editing. She does the accounts, the marketing and the graphic design. Deb's right: she is brilliant and, as I discover, also a forthright lesbian, with a girlfriend. That intrigues me.

Most afternoons, as Lozenik and his wife Fraydee attempt to lure the big boys with advertising sales, Cece and I find our way to Rancho Grande, a tiny Mexican dive. The waiters, compact, dark-skinned men, who hang on our every word, communicate to each other via high-tech headset devices that look like something out of *True Lies*, and the entire restaurant isn't more than four feet wide. But the chips and salsa are great. When we're not there, we camp out in her studio apartment, also about four feet wide, where she pores over my writings and laughs at my jokes.

I see Cece on our days off too, usually for traditional Jewish dinners at Deb's house. She and her girlfriend Patri always arrive late, slumping in under the weight of obvious discord which surfaces through dinner in the form of terse remarks lobbed back and forth across the table. They fight often and loudly in Spanish. We all wonder why they can't seem to let each other go.

Cece moves on after a year to a job at the Coconut Grove Playhouse. Without her, the *Chai Today* office is a friendless place. I miss her laughter, the raunchy music from her portable CD player, the outings to Rancho Grande. Most of all, I miss having someone to talk to. Fraydee and Michoel battle to keep the magazine afloat. Advertising sales droop. The Hasid's cheques continue to bounce. Eventually, they cut my hours.

TWENTY-FIVE

It's 1991, eleven years since I last set foot in Ireland.

I haven't laid eyes on my mother for over a decade. My father visits Miami twice a year, but the reunions are thwarted by Adele's foul moods; each stay is shorter than the last. Saul, Rachel and David have come for holidays but are tired of the oppressive heat and don't want to return. Looking at my life through their eyes makes me sad. What they see is a woman approaching middle age. Alone.

'You need to get out of that wasteland,' Saul often says. 'It's no good for you. You have nervous attacks. You've put on weight. You're only thirty-three for God's sake, on your own with the kids all the time. Why don't you come home once and for all?'

The truth is I want my family near. I need help. I miss my first city. I've never found a way into my second. I can't connect with its faux finishes and neon lights, its pretence and its faulty promise. I want out. But how do you walk out of your own life? And if you stay, how do you quiet the nagging inside your head?

After all these years, Miami is still, to me, a demon city that seduces then systematically dismantles you, so that in the end, there's not enough left of you to get out. There are too many cultures and not enough culture, so many languages but so little communication, so many people, so few connections. I see it as a slip of land on the edge of the world where crumpled old men who were once doctors and lawyers in Cuba hold court on street corners, reliving the past, where psychologists and midwives from the Caribbean care for embittered old Jewish ladies in dark, musty rooms for minimum wage.

Miami does not give hope.

It drowns out dreams.

I have none left.

I yearn to walk through the streets I grew up in, to feel Dublin's rain lash over me, to hear the sounds of that city, the voices, the music, the buses down O'Connell Street. I try to fill the holes with trips to Irish pubs, by reading every new Irish book on the market, by making a point of picking up the *Irish Times*, by living on tree-lined streets that remind me of where I grew up.

The tactics rarely work.

Apprehensive, I phone my father. Every time I've suggested coming home with the boys, he counters with the Israel bit, talking about how much better off I'd be there with my two dark sons and what wonderful opportunities that country offers for people like me. This conversation is no different.

'You're being ridiculous,' he says when I approach the matter.

'Well I want to come for a visit at least. I haven't been back for twelve years. I haven't seen Mummy since I was a child.'

'Not on my steam, you won't be coming for any visit, and your mother, who in their right mind would want to see her?'

The phone goes dead in my hand.

I hatch a plan. I'll raise the money for the trip myself, and there's nothing he can say or do about it. It's a novel idea: I can accomplish something without his help. Saul, Rachel and David pool resources and come up with $500 for our stay.

'All you have to do, Shiv, is get yourself here,' Saul says. 'We'll take care of the rest.'

I find a freelance job: typing a six-hundred-page report on the mating patterns of shrimp for a biologist. I can't believe how many varieties of shrimp there are. Night after night, after Fraydee and Michoel have left, I sit in the office punching away at the keyboard. Around eight, the cleaners arrive. At ten they leave. I get lost in the work. Often it's after midnight when I make my way down to the car.

A month later, I have the money. Now I need a visa. When Julio got arrested, my case was put on pending status which amounts to this: I sit still, maybe for a lifetime, waiting for an outcome. Meanwhile, if I leave I can't come back. The only way around it is to apply for a temporary visa. But first I have to prove that one of my parents is on the verge of death. I convince a Dublin friend to slip into her employer's office (he's a surgeon) and swipe a few sheets of headed notepaper. When I get them in the post a week later, I type up a very convincing letter about my mother's terminal condition and sign it. The next afternoon, I sit in the office of the Immigration and Naturalisation Service (the same one I was detained in) and wait. Finally, one of those stiff INS types calls me over. It takes for ever for him to hand me my passport.

Granted: twenty-eight days.

TWENTY-SIX

We arrive in Dublin at dawn.

Moments later we pile into Saul's scruffy car. The city looks so small and peculiar. Known, yet unknown, at the same time. But its smells, its sounds are so safe to me – the part of me that's been missing.

'The cars are on the wrong side,' Daniel says.

'And the streets are so tiny,' adds Jesse.

'Typical American boys,' Saul mutters. 'I suppose you'll be asking for a Big Mac next.'

Our second morning, Saul and David drive us down Orwell Road. I've always wanted to show Jesse and Daniel Tree Tops. We park outside the front gate. The house looks different; the transparent window-panes have been replaced by tinted criss-crossed glass. The walls are painted brown, not white. The garden is trimmed and most of the trees we used to climb have been cut down.

'Let's knock on the door and see if they'll let us look around,' I say.

'That's crazy, Mom,' says Daniel (always wary of the unfamiliar). 'We can see from here.'

'It's not the same,' I say. 'I want to show you my room, the little one at the back. Maybe they won't mind.' I get out of the car, march up to the front door and ring the bell. I don't recognise the sound. A middle-aged lady in a headscarf answers. She's holding on to a Hoover.

I explain the situation, pointing to the car where they're all sitting like prisoners waiting for a verdict.

'It's not a great time for guests really,' she says, pointing to the vacuum cleaner. 'But have a walk around the back if you want.'

We spend five minutes traipsing through the gardens. There's nothing about these manicured lawns and neat flower-beds that reminds me of home.

Over the next few days, I meet every friend I ever had (Jesse and Daniel are amazed at the number of people I know). I track down Moira, who nobody's seen for years, like she just evaporated. Turns out she's living in the country with a disagreeable husband. She travels to Dublin and we spend two wonderful nights with her, singing Irish songs the way we did in the old kitchen in Tree Tops. Auntie Lily stages a lunch for us in her immaculate townhouse with all the living relatives in attendance.

'It's a miracle,' Lily says, 'an absolute miracle that you're back. Would you not think about staying? America is too hard a country for you.'

'I know,' I say, 'but Daddy has other ideas.'

'Your father, where is he, off on some trip?'

'Actually he's in Israel, left the day I arrived.'

'So will you get to see him at all?'

'I don't know. He didn't say.'

She shrugs at that and pulls me behind her towards her daughter, Janice, my Auntie Sylvia, cousin Fraya, and all the others.

'An editor she is now, for a Jewish paper. Doesn't she look gorgeous? The spitting image of her mother.'

'How is your ma?' asks Sylvia, who's well into her eighties.

'I'll know tomorrow. I haven't seen her yet.'

'An awful shame,' Lily mutters, 'what happened to that woman. I always thought maybe we could have been kinder, more understanding and she wouldn't have gone and left you all. I was very fond of your mother, you know.'

'I know.'

Next morning Saul drops me at 25 Claremont Court on his way to work. He doesn't want to come in. I stand holding my breath in front of the same wrought-iron gate that greeted me almost twenty years previously.

I ring the bell.

A long wait.

She opens the door.

Nothing in me was prepared for this.

She's stooped over like a broken bird.

Her body is emaciated.

Her face is a caked mask.

I can barely find her eyes.

I hug her and feel the crunch of bones.

'Hello darling,' she says and smiles. We walk back towards the kitchen, slowly, because her legs don't gather much momentum. Marley's standing by the sink, fussing over a pot of tea and a plate of sandwiches.

'Doesn't your mother look marvellous?'

I pause.

I can't look at her.

'Yes,' I say, 'yes she does.'

As Marley and I eat, my mother picks at a plate of lettuce, breaking the leaves into little pieces and placing them one by one in her mouth, just like she used to with toast. I wonder if she's anorexic. Afterwards we sit in the garden for a while. She's opposite me on a plastic chair. The sunlight catches the shades in her hair: a deep magenta at the roots, burnt orange around the edges. She notices me looking.

'I did it myself,' she said, 'for your visit.' I try and force my mind away from this moment to the woman she once was. But all I see is that her make-up, which she used to pride herself on, has gone astray: the lipstick is smudged over the edges of her lips and the eyeliner has veered off-course and is streaked across her cheeks. She looks almost spooky. She's straining to see me even though I'm only a foot away.

I realise she's almost blind.

We sit in silence for a long time.

'I forgive you, Mummy. I forgive you for everything.'

'Do you, darling? Because I don't really forgive myself. I love you very much, you know that, don't you?'

I leave around dusk, her image fading behind me in the doorway. As I walk back past the cemetery I think of her stuck in the dank back room that she'll never leave.

The next evening Saul, Rachel, David, myself and the boys meet my father and Adele in the Jury's Hotel restaurant. He has an hour to spare. For fifty minutes we talk about their cat, the most recent trip to Israel and the hotel food, which they claim isn't as good as last time. Then they excuse themselves for an important dinner date with Elissa's in-laws. Before he leaves, my father motions for the waiter.

'Add the dessert and coffees to my account.'

'Of course, Mr Woolfson.'

Two days later Saul drops me at my father's factory in Naas on the way to the airport. I wait outside his office for an hour until his agitated secretary ushers me in. I wait another forty minutes as he takes five phone calls back to back. I gaze at the walls. There are no photos of my sons, only one photo of Saul, Rachel, David and I, turned sideways on a cabinet. The rest are of Adele and her daughter. Finally, he's ready for me.

'I wanted to find out your plans,' he says.

'I want to come home.'

'That's not a plan. I won't help you make that happen.'

'Then I'll do it by myself.'

'Since when in your whole life have you ever managed anything on your own? The only thing you manage is to get into trouble. I've said it before and I'll say it again. You get sorted out in Miami, you go to Israel or you can count me out.'

I leave Dublin feeling like I have a deep hole where my heart should be.

TWENTY-SEVEN

—◂—

Two months later my father visits me in Miami.

He's on his way to a conference in San Diego and has three days to spare. We meet in a Bal Harbor restaurant. Alone. Adele's shopping in Sachs; the boys are at baseball practice. Halfway through the second bottle of wine, I realise there's more to this meeting than dinner. He wants to set things straight.

He's decided to buy me a house, in his name of course, but left in trust to me and the boys: Contact the estate agents.

He wants Jesse to have a bar mitzvah, it's all been arranged with Rabbi Herschfeld: Start lessons immediately.

He's ready to take care of my debts, whatever they are, once and for all: Fax him a list.

He's found some new hotshot immigration lawyer, recommended by Herschfeld: Set up an appointment.

Then he asks, 'What's it going to take, Shivaun, for you to get your life on track? All the opportunities you've had, all the intelligence. What is stopping you?'

It's the very thing I'd asked of myself so often and come up empty.

'I don't know how to live like other people,' I say finally.

'What do you mean "live like other people"? You've had more chances than most.'

'True, but I've had more challenges too. It wasn't easy growing up in our house.'

'Easy, you're telling me it wasn't easy. Wasn't I the one who took care of you after your mother left? It was harder on me than any of you, I can assure you.'

'What happened?' I ask then. 'I mean what really happened to her? Was it because of Roberta, because she died during the operation?'

His face loses form, collapses in on itself. He looks away like he's about to cry.

'She didn't die in the operation.'

His voice is so low I can barely hear him.

'Then how?'

'Your mother beat Roberta so I sent her away to stay with the nuns in England. It was supposed to just be until your mother got better. Roberta got pneumonia. And she died. We went over on the plane to collect her body and buried her in Dolphin's Barn. She's with the family now.'

'How come you never told us?'

'What was the point? Would it have brought her back?'

'No, I guess not.'

He sips on his wine. He seems so small and fragile, hunched in the chair. It's been a long time since I've seen my father like this. I wonder how many awful secrets he holds and what they've done to his heart. But I'm angry: that he let it happen once, then again, that he failed to protect me from my mother, that he'd allowed his children to suffer at the hands of the women he'd chosen, and he didn't know how to stop it. And I realise that I'm angry at myself too for following his example, for letting M beat and belittle my sons, for not having the courage, the strength or the fucking guts to stop him. I had wanted to be so different from my parents, and I'd ended up the same. A weak woman who let life happen to her, who rationalised every gross misstep with images of her own beleaguered story.

'She beat me too,' I say.

'I never knew that.'

All the way home I think about what I've just heard. I'm not surprised or shocked. Just frozen inside. I remember a photograph of Roberta, unframed with torn edges, that sat on the mantelpiece in Tree Tops. I see her sweet cherub face, her bright eyes, the black curly hair, and I think of her passing away, alone, feverish, probably cold, a three-year-old child cast out so that her own mother wouldn't destroy her. I wonder how my father has lived with this. I have another memory too: I'm in the sitting room, in my favourite spot – perched on the window-sill looking out at the garden. My mother and Teresa are in the kitchen, as usual, smoking Rothmans and drinking coffee. The floor is littered with white sheets. I'm listening to the hum of their voices. The talk suddenly turns to Roberta.

'How come I don't remember her?' I ask through the hatch.

'Because you were so young when she died,' my mother says.

'Was I nice to her?' I ask then.

'Very nice,' my mother says. 'I used to bathe you together and you used to make her laugh and stroke her face. You were a very good sister.' I search for the memory and while I can't capture it in pictures, I can hear the faint sounds of her laughter, can feel her face break open in gladness.

Driving over the Causeway now I call out to Roberta. I strain to feel her small spirit. I wonder where she is, if she's come back as someone else. If I could, I would tell her that I'm lost without my sister. If I could, I would still stroke her precious face.

TWENTY-EIGHT

The next time I see my father we're signing the deeds to my new home.

A double-fronted, peach-coloured house with a long, tree-filled garden that Jesse spotted on an unbearably hot Miami afternoon.

'This is it, Mom. This is the house for us,' he shouted as we drove past. 'We don't have to look any more.'

Three weeks later we move in.

Daniel goes to a new school.

Jesse starts bar mitzvah lessons.

I begin therapy.

'Put your experience to good use,' Evelyna, my feisty Puerto Rican counsellor says about three months into our sessions. 'You've healed, now help others.'

I don't exactly feel healed, more like put back together. I start to see what she's talking about the day she compares me to a vase, a delicate piece of china that's been smashed on the ground. We can pick up the pieces, she says, get some glue, and put it back together. It won't look as nice, but it can still hold flowers. So that's what I do, start picking up pieces and reconstructing myself. That means using my brain, something I've let putrefy. My secret regret was not finishing the degree at Trinity. Since then I'd free-floated from one job to the next and ended up with an existence that bore little resemblance to the life I'd so often imagined for myself as a child. If I couldn't have the writing life that I'd envisioned, I could at least find something that stirred my heart.

I enrol for a degree in social work at Union Institute, which I acquire long-distance, in a record eighteen months. This prepares me for my new position: program director at a youth centre in Allapattah. What my new boss, a former priest from the west of Ireland, doesn't tell me at the interview is that we don't actually have a centre yet or the money to open one.

'That's why we picked you,' he says. 'With your writing skills and gutsy attitude, we should have one in no time.'

That first afternoon he drives me through a bankrupt industrial triangle on the edge of the Miami river. Run-down warehouses and shopping strips line its sidewalks. Dead animals and refuse populate the uneven streets. The stench of the river swells the air. Gardens double as illegal dumping sites and the rows of brick shells its residents occupy bear large red Xs marking gang territory. I find myself oddly at home in this disenfranchised borderland, surrounded by the hulking remains of a generation gone berserk. I notice kids languishing outside storefronts, shooting hoops on steamy tarmac in the park: boys and girls with the faces of angels who'd burn down homes and laugh as the inhabitants caught fire, young guys who'd gangbang unsuspecting girls and grin as their terrified victims fought to stay among the living. I recognise these kids because I'm not all that different. I've travelled recklessly close to the edge often enough to know that you don't always get a second chance. I want to give them one.

'Well, what do you think?' Mr Brown, the former priest, asks back at his office.

'Can you make a difference here?'

'Damn straight, I can.'

'That's what I thought. Now all we need is your work papers and we're set.'

Work papers. Shit. What I have is a faded non-renewable permit that's about to expire. My case has been pending for years. The laws are tightening. I'm convinced I'll be rejected. And once you're denied there's no appealing the decision.

'No problem,' I say. 'I have it here.'

He leads me into a dark office to meet Antonio, accountant, human resources person, budget manager. He's got a lot on his plate, Antonio, which may be why he accepts my paperwork without question.

'Of course, you have to go through a security check, like everyone else.'

'Of course,' I say.

I wait all evening for the phone to ring. For a voice on the other end to tell me I've been found out: drug arrest, wavering legal status. Nobody calls.

Over the next nine months I put every hustling tactic I ever learned on the streets with Julio to powerful use. I apply for grants and raise thousands of dollars. I find an abandoned mechanics shop. The floors are covered in grease and debris. The toilets don't function. The windows are slashed. I organise a team of volunteers, arrange for donations of paint, wood, floor tiles, plumbing and electrical supplies. We work every day including weekends until we're done. On the 1st of September 1993, I and my staff, Colin, a soft-spoken social worker from the north of Ireland, and Catherimarty, a vivacious twenty-two-year-old who was raised in the area, stand in the doorway. The transformation is almost miraculous. The building is divided into classrooms, an office and a community area. The walls are painted in vibrant art deco colours. There are couches and desks, cabinets, bookcases and lamps. Even the gardens, formerly one of those illegal dumpsites, have been cleared. All we have to do is make sure we have enough students to justify our existence. Shouldn't be too hard, I tell Colin and Cathy. It's a known fact that Allapattah has higher drop-out and poverty rates than almost anywhere else. We contact judges, schools, government agencies, prepare information packages, deliver workshops, and then we take our recruiting to the streets.

First stop is the park off Twenty-second Avenue. When we arrive, there's a bunch of teenagers running around with a football. Cathy and I sit down on a broken bench.

'Wassup?' asks Pepe, an eighteen-year-old drug dealer, who's been stopping by the centre to help out.

'Who you talking to with your wassup?' says Cathy.

'Sorry, Ms, street talk. How can we help you? Is that better?'

A crowd gathers. They're a motley crew with baggy pants hanging below their buttocks, baseball caps turned backwards, Nike sneakers covering their feet. Some have shaved heads. Others have dangling dreads, or knotted rigid hair that reaches upwards in unlikely configurations. And the stance. It's near frightening. They stare us down, challenging, relentless, everything that's ever happened to them ensnared in a moment.

'We're here to help you,' I say finally.

'Help us how?' demands Tito, an apparent ringleader.

'We're opening a school next week, up there on Twenty-seventh, for guys like you.'

'Whaddya mean guys like us?'

'Oh c'mon,' interrupts the only white kid in the bunch, 'dope dealers, gang kids, poor kids, with no school. Guys like us, just like the lady said.'

Suddenly, talk ceases. A dread-like calm clamps itself over the group. Their heads turn, en masse, to follow a white van with dark windows driving along the edges of the park. The van slows, stops. The windows roll down. It moves on again.

'CAP,' says Billy, the white kid.

'A gang?' I ask.

'Yeah, Central American Posse, there was a fight last night, someone got shot. They're out for revenge.'

'Gotta hide out,' Tito shouts as they scatter. 'See you at the Centre next week.'

The van circles the park a few more times, then disappears.

A week later we open our doors to fourteen students, half the park crew included. We hold classes in the mornings, English, maths, social science, for the equivalency exams; art, woodwork, photography, landscaping and performance poetry in the afternoons. We're in the newspapers constantly, even get a feature in the Living Arts section of the *Miami Herald*. We're cited as a national model, visited by dignitaries from Eastern Europe and the subject of a Washington report. The irony of it all is chilling: here I am with no papers, working for a programme funded by the Government.

Guests to the Centre are impressed, particularly with our morning meditation sessions, when we sit quietly in a circle and breathe to the sounds of Colin's classical music. They're fascinated too that the students arrive early and stay late. And it's not surprising, considering the homes they come from. Few have parents. Some of the girls are prostitutes, or drug runners. Many are raped by older brothers or uncles. Some of the guys are homeless or in foster care. They all live by their wits. Each morning they bring us tales of shootings and stabbings, of friends who die in their arms in deserted parking lots. We get used to these stories and to seeing wounds in their flesh, bruises across their faces and a vagueness in their eyes. Not all their wounds are so visible. We watch for other signs too: pencil-thin scars on wrists, disturbing speech patterns, a persistent lethargy. A fifteen-year-old boy puts needles under everyone's seat before meditation one morning. We find out later that his father has been taken to jail and his mother is in the hospital dying of cancer. He doesn't cry. Another kid puts matches up a kitten's ass. We expel him for a week, then learn that he's been raped every night for months.

At the end of the first year we hold a graduation ceremony with catered food (donated), flowers and awards. A local department store contributes a dozen white shirts and ties. Wild Mango, a knockout Latin band from San Francisco, read about us in the newspapers and offer to play at the reception. The Archbishop and the Mayor attend. The students sing 'I Believe I Can Fly' by R. Kelly to a packed house. We have a burning candle in the centre of the room. One by one they stand in front of it and cite their dreams: Mikki wants to play pro baseball, Billy wants to go into the Marines, Tito wants to be a good father. Not all their dreams come true, but three make it to university, one goes on to the Army and a few get local jobs. The rest go to jail or worse.

Nine months on, we're sitting in a circle for morning meditation. Colin has left for Ireland, and I'm having a hard week. This new batch of kids is wilder, angrier. For the first time, I'm afraid. I've been robbed, threatened, and had my car windows smashed.

'Let's just close our eyes for a moment, take a deep breath, focus on our hopes for the day. Breathe in all the positive, release all the negative, everything standing in our way.' The words sound empty coming out of my mouth. I don't believe them today.

'We have special guests,' I continue.

'Oh, so we have to perform for you again,' blurts Fausto, the kid I have the hardest time with, 'behave like little goody-goodies so that you get to look like you it.'

'We're going to have a seminar,' I continue, nonplussed, 'on non-violence using the methods of Dr Martin Luther King. Anybody know who he was?'

'Yeah, that fool who got shot,' says Carlos.

'Who you calling a fool, fool?' demands Ernest, one of the few African Americans in the group.

'My bad, my bad, he was one of the good guys,' amends Carlos.

As if on cue our guests arrive in a black County-tagged limo, cellular phones in hand. Rachel, head of the Community Relations Board breezes in, perfume hitting the air, a chic Anne Taylor number concealing a svelte frame. She is followed by two government types and a lieutenant, all certified in the Kingian method of non-violence. It takes me and the staff twenty minutes to get the crew logistically placed in the classroom, another ten to set up the projector, and then we're ready, save for the din that's erupted. I ask for some respect for our guests as they attempt to launch into what promises to be a most enlightening presentation. They start talking. Fausto and his brother lob chalk across the room. Another kid starts screaming. Two girls get into a fight.

'Stop, stop,' Rachel says. 'This is exactly what we're trying to teach here. Now, what exactly is the problem between you two young women?'

'That bitch stole my man,' says Chantela, a striking fourteen-year-old with a scar down the left side of her face.

'Did not fucking steal yo' man. If you had him, I wouldna been able to take him,' counters Lil Bit, a diminutive Puerto Rican who takes no shit. Rachel and her Kingian crew draw diagrams, pass out leaflets, organise games, making valiant stabs at outlining the causes of violence, internal and external, its roots and manifestations. They talk to, at, and with the kids, who respond with an onslaught of verbal abuse. Finally, I leave the room and escape to the quiet of my office. I sit down, exhausted. It occurs to me then that I was so desperate to create for these kids a sacred space in a society constructed with their obliteration in mind that I had forgotten to guard my own space. What I had actually fashioned was a war zone. I think of all the sixty-hour weeks I've logged, the endless miles I've driven across the city, the receipts in my purse that will never be paid. And in the moment, it doesn't seem worth it. That day I leave used up and very, very tired.

On the way home I stop at the bistro and drink a bottle of wine, slowly. This is time that belongs to me, not the Centre, not my sons. Quietly, inside my head, I conjure a life in which my heart is filled and the world falls effortlessly into place around me. When darkness settles, I make my way home to the boys who wait for their dinner and who will wonder why I am drunk again.

Later that night I stand in Jesse's doorway. He is sprawled on the floor, his eyes fixed on the TV set for the college baseball game. His sports psychology manuals are on his desk. Beside him on the bed is the notebook filled with his brand of beat poetry and his most recent list of goals and objectives, neatly typed on computer paper. I register his activity then move quietly back into the hallway.

'Why are you always walking away?' he demands. 'Why can't you just sit down?'

I gather myself and make my way to the edge of his bed where I sit with him like I used to when he was a little boy. In a faltering voice, halfway between infancy and manhood, he sets out his inchoate dreams, and asks me over and over if I believe in him, if he'll make it to the pros. I place my finger at the centre of his brow and rub it like I did when he was a baby. I tell him that I have faith in him, that he can do anything, be anyone, that he is master of his own destiny. I shrivel inside as I speak, because I know that he knows I let mine slip away.

'I love you, Mom,' he whispers. And then, 'Can you give me a hug?' When I reach down, his muscular, 220lb frame melts into me. I press my face against his stubble and feel the wetness of his tears. . . .

Daniel's door is ajar. He sits brooding, stubborn, in the centre of the room, surrounded by neighbourhood boys, a compound of faces, creamy and dark. Over in the closet his clothes are ordered to the point of obsession on neat hangers. On his desk lie his paintings: vibrant, exotic images that scream up at me. When the boys are gone, he calls to me in a voice hardened by injury, wanting me to tend to him yet not wanting me to know that he needs it. I make my way precariously over the cords and plugs and video systems and try to find a space on his bed. He pushes against me, almost forcing me away. But I sit firm, running my fingers up and down his golden back. And I remember the Halloween I sent him off to school in a pink bunny suit with hard ears that stood up. Sent him off through streets he didn't know, and told him I'd be along later. I never made it to that party or to the little gathering the teacher held a few months later on his fourth birthday. Instead I walked three miles in the heat to the seashore where I stood and watched M make out with the blonde aerobics instructor under a brutal sun.

I stay with Daniel for a long time and as I feel him finally and gently relax into my touch, I am assaulted by images of M taunting and jeering, crudely mocking and belittling my son for holding on to my hand as we walk, for jumping into my lap at home, calling him Mommie's Boy, MB for short. I see the stain of tears on Daniel's face, a stain that I can't remove no matter how I scrub. I see myself, lifting yet another can of Budweiser to my lips, smoking yet another cigarette, taking my leave at midnight. Chasing M down, running, always running from the terrified eyes peering though a second-storey window. And I see Daniel, hiding under tables, clutching little toys, making up worlds, concealing himself behind his own version of sanity. There's nowhere on this earth that I can hide from those sights, no safe space that screens them out. I swallow them and keep on rubbing my son's back.

TWENTY-NINE

I will throw myself into motherhood.

The game of baseball takes on a significance of enormously large proportions in our home. Most evenings are given over to driving Jesse and Daniel to and from practices, after which we spend the remainder of the night focusing on Jesse's batting stance, his swing, his throwing arm, which has begun to look rather crooked. Baseball is his obsession. And it becomes mine. I'm quickly classified as the team mother from hell, the pit bull of a woman who sits on the bleachers through practices, who screams during games, 'Bend your back, straighten your arm,' and who has minimal regard for the authority of coaches. Jesse and Daniel become accustomed to the sight of me hovering by the dugout with cold drinks in my hand, taking my place alongside the field with the other fathers.

Although their own father was recently released from jail after a five-year stint he has no time for his sons. He promises a lot but delivers precious little. He makes it to a few games but always leaves early on the pretext of some very important job he has to do, even though we all know that the job has two legs and a pussy. We joke with him though, call him the hardest-working man in Miami. The title fits.

I don't manage home-cooked meals, but we do eat well and often. I'm not quite the mother I want to be, but I'm not my own mother either. We live in our own house in a quiet residential street that reminds me ever so vaguely of Tree Tops. We have a garden, a car, a life. I'm trying to do it right. Yet I feel always like I'm running on empty, like I just don't have enough energy to power me through my days. Often, at night, when I finally reach the quiet of my room, I realise just how exhausted I am, but I can't seem to ever settle into peaceful silence. I become brittle, as breakable as the delicate china dolls that had adorned the mantel back at Tree Tops, the ones we were never allowed to touch. Which is perhaps why I let Jose, the Jerrycurl king, Bush supporter, Santeria (witchcraft) practising stalker who happens to dial my number by mistake, enter my world in the first place.

I'm sitting in the kitchen one evening with a cup of tea. The phone rings. A man's voice asks for Merta. No such person here I tell him. He apologises, but doesn't get off the phone. Next thing we're having a conversation. He's in real estate. I tell him I'm a social worker but that I really want to be a writer. This fascinates him.

'What's your accent?' he asks.

'What do you think it is?'

'God, can't say, New York?'

'That's what everyone tells me. But I'm from Dublin originally. Just have that New York attitude, even over the phone I guess.'

'Yes, you do.'

It goes on for forty minutes. Finally, he says, 'I'd better be going now. I've taken up enough of your time, but do you think I could call you again? I've really enjoyed talking to you.'

'Sure,' I say. 'Call me whenever.'

For a whole year, we communicate like that. I never know when he's going to call. I forget that he even exists, and suddenly he's on

the other end of the line. We argue constantly: about blacks (he's
an Afro-Cuban racist), about gays (homophobe), about the dis-
advantaged (screw 'em), about AIDS (you can get it from kissing),
and about the military (bomb 'em). It isn't even much of a mental
workout, but something happens as we embark on our second year
of telecommunicative combat. It's June the 3rd 1994, the night of
my thirty-sixth birthday. It's also the night he tells me that he cried
when Bush was ousted from office. I don't know whether to laugh
or cry myself at that piece of information. As we chat, sounds drift
from the living room where a bunch of my friends have gathered
with a small cake, candles and an assortment of gifts.

'You sound sad,' he says. I think for a second and realise that I
am, and lonely too. I miss my home, my family. I've managed to
lock myself into a self-imposed exile. I can't go back again. The
work permit has finally run out and wasn't renewed. The new
immigration lawyers my father found are not hopeful. I'm stuck at
the Centre, can't change jobs even if I want to. I live like a fugitive,
knowing that the immigration authorities can knock on the door at
any moment and cart me away. And I've developed a contentious
relationship with the ground beneath me. I hate all that Miami is,
with its torpid heat and fast lingo, its shallow beauties and ruthless
promise. But I can't leave.

'How about I take you out and cheer you up for your birthday?'
he says then.

'That would be nice. Tell you what, I have my family coming
over for my son's bar mitzvah in a few weeks. So it's kind of manic
round here, but after that I'll be free.'

Two weeks later I collect Saul, Rachel and David, Saul's wife
Aisling, Auntie Lily and two distant relatives from the airport. My
father's footing the bill for the lot. My brothers and sister and I
spend a week shopping, at the beach, in restaurants, laughing,
drinking wine. Saul and David take the boys to the park, to the

movies, and for slap-up Cuban breakfasts each morning. We stay up late and get up early, packing what living we can into this short time we have together. The night before the bar mitzvah my father and Adele host a party at the Sea View Hotel. It's the first time we've gathered as a family since I left Ireland. My father is gracious. Adele smiles. Her daughter's there with the husband. Her in-laws too. I look around me and marvel at what I see. Saul and David are prematurely bald. Rachel is a ringer for my mother. Their lives have moved on without me. Saul is a lawyer and works with my father, has Aisling and a daughter. David has a girlfriend and is studying classics at Trinity. Rachel has a partner and lives in London. Yet, to me, we are still the wild, motherless kids who clustered together in the back room. With them I feel safe. And I know as I watch them that I will crumple when they leave.

The next morning there's pandemonium: Saul spills coffee over his brand-new mustard-coloured suit five minutes before we're due at the synagogue. We wash it, then can't find a way to dry it. Auntie Lily gets locked in her room. We lose the table plan for lunch. But we walk into the extravagant synagogue on Ninety-fourth and Collins, a proud, well-dressed family. Herschfeld delivers a moving address in which he refers to me as a Jewish princess who went astray and came back. As he says those words, I spot my father through the *mechitza*, a thin white film of fabric that divides men from women in an orthodox synagogue. For a second, his face thaws and a wave of forgiveness washes over it. Then he's up at the *bimah*, reciting his prayers, pledging money, the patriarch about to call upon his first grandson. Jesse strides forwards, clutching his notes in his hand. In them are the 180 lines of his *Haftarah*, the phonetic English version. Rabbi Dalfin, his young, bright-eyed teacher, is smiling. Jesse glances in my direction for a second then takes his place at the centre of the *bimah*, and begins. *Boruchu es adonol Hamivorah*. I know every word by heart. He doesn't falter, not once.

Five days later I drive my brothers and sister back to the airport and wait at the window of the departure lounge, waving as they board the plane. An awful heaviness descends over me as I walk out to the car. I am tired of goodbyes.

'There's a message for you,' Daniel says the moment I step through the front door. 'Some guy with a deep voice, named Jose. Said he'd call back in an hour.'

'OK,' I say, walking towards the bedroom.

'Mom, it's not going to be like M, right, you're not going to let him move in, are you?'

'I don't even know the guy yet.'

'Michael moved in after a few weeks. You didn't know him well either.'

'This is different, Dan, I'm different.'

'If you say so.' He doesn't look convinced. The truth is I haven't a notion what the guy looks like or what his life is made of. For all I know he might be a serial dialler of wrong numbers, but the sound of his voice has inched its way steadily into my psyche, and if I know nothing else, I am sure at least that one faceless man out there thinks I'm worth talking to.

We meet a few nights later at one of those mammoth restaurant set-ups on the water, so typical of Miami. I watch the boats float by for about an hour, then step indoors in case he's missed me. I'm about to pack it in altogether when I bump into this tall guy smack in the centre of the lobby.

'Shivaun,' he mutters in surprise. 'Are you Shivaun?' I recognise the voice immediately, but everything else is way off base. First of all, he's in a time warp: seems he loaded up on Jerrycurl sheen after seeing that movie *Coming to America* and never looked back. His jeans are so tight that he must be inflicting some serious damage on his privates, which I imagine will result in bodily dysfunction, sooner or later. He looks like something straight out of the Mod

Squad. But he smiles at me so eagerly. We take a table overlooking the water and talk for hours. About what, I wonder now. He's enthralled, has never met anyone like me, he says, tells me things he's never told anyone before: veiled family secrets about a brother in a mental home and black magic his family practises with sacrificed chickens and hollowed-out coconuts. When we finally say goodnight, at four in the morning, he comes right up to me, kisses me and asks,

'Do you think you'd like to do this again? If not, I understand, but I'd really like to know.' There's something so earnest, almost endearing in the way he says that.

'I'd like to,' I tell him.

THIRTY

I'm all dressed up, ready to roll.

Waiting for Jose, again. He's always late and by this stage I've consumed so many Godiva chocolates, been treated to so many extravagant dinners, that I'm not about to be seduced. We fight all the time. My friends make fun of him and his distorted patriarchal logic. I'm questioning with increasing frequency why the hell I still see him. He seems to like my kids, takes them fishing at some God-forsaken hour on Sunday mornings even though all he's managed to get his hooks into thus far is Daniel's silk windbreaker, in addition to losing three knives, and a bunch of lures. We've gone horseback riding a few times, and the sight of him, bareback on a wild stallion, puffing on a cigarette like the original Marlboro man, seems to excite everyone but me. In bed at night, I get scared. There's a part of him that's sweet and cuddly, affectionate even, but there's that other side that wants to ram me from behind till it hurts, that talks non-stop about tying me to the bedpost and covering my mouth with duct tape. In the mornings, when he tries to cover me with sloppy, wet kisses, I feel ashamed. Every time I let him enter me, another piece of me goes missing. I tell myself I'm imagining things, that really he's a decent guy. After all, he spends a fortune trying to impress me, always calls when he says he will and seems to want to be with me at every available opportunity. Perhaps, it's the Cuban witchcraft business that's messing with my head, I think, and the fact that he refused to bring me to his house for months, said there were dead chickens everywhere, things I wouldn't understand.

One night I spot a bag of white bones hidden under old blankets in the trunk of his car and he alludes to some bizarre ceremony but never actually explains it. Then there's his mother, an old black lady with no teeth who he claims perpetrates spells and hexes on unsuspecting neighbours, and his twin brother who he finally introduces me to one Sunday afternoon at the homeless shelter on Collins. He turns out to be a carcass of a man who speaks in the jumbled dialect of the insane and gobbles his food like an animal. When Jose and the mother are at the counter paying for lunch, he pulls me aside and begs me to buy him a case of beer.

After ten months I decide I've had enough. I can no longer stand myself in the morning after a night with him. He starts drinking, and the sordid late night phone calls begin.

'I drove by your house tonight,' he tells me one time, 'and I just had this vision of you walking out on to the street and being hammered by a truck.' I block his number and he goes to a payphone. I block that too and he finds another until I feel like I've blocked every public telephone in North Miami. I call his mother and tell her to get control of her son, warn her that I'll contact the police if he doesn't stop driving by my house and making threatening calls, during the last of which he assures me that he's going to inform Immigration of my whereabouts. I pray for him to disappear, to just ease back into the shadows from whence he emerged. Finally, in desperation, I ask Josie, a New Age friend, to conduct a ceremony, with sage and candles and lots of 'cleansing energy', which, miracle of miracles, actually seems to work. The calls cease.

Afterwards she tells me, 'I'm not sure who it was, but I felt such a strong presence during the ceremony, an elderly gentleman, with kind eyes; he protects you.' Pop, I acknowledge immediately. I hear from Jose sporadically after that, but he has lost the determination and the ability to instil panic.

THIRTY-ONE

I give up on finding love.

I'd tried too hard, too often. I'd been wooed, brutalised, mocked, betrayed, and wined and dined. I'd been called honey, sweetie, precious, star, bitch, whore and slut. In the end, it all sounded the same. I got tired, very tired, waiting for love to come around. I'd concocted lists outlining the ideal partner, repeated affirmations: I will be loved in this lifetime, I will be cherished in this lifetime, I will find the perfect partner. I'd gone out on dates: with a high-school principal from New York who had expensive white jeans and a soft voice, but he doped himself up on valium before I arrived, talked about sex all through dinner, then invited me back to a threesome in his motel. There was an African musician from Gainesville, seven feet tall, with a beguiling demeanour that nearly masked the rage that festered beneath the soothing sounds that flowed from the odd-looking Nigerian guitar thing he played. He gave himself away when he mentioned that his ex-wife had a restraining order against him and that he wasn't allowed to see his kids. I met an artist in an Irish bar who turned out to be a psychopath, and a stage manager who couldn't get through two sentences without insulting me or someone else. I tried. God knows I tried.

I close up my heart, form a callus around it. I live for two years like that. Unfeeling, dead. Eventually, my world splinters. At work I excel. I sit on committees. I'm always in the newspapers. I consult on innovative projects. I'm an 'ideas person'. I get paid to think. Everyone wants the Woolfson touch. At home, it's a different story. I am lonely, and I wonder too often if I will ever know what it feels like to love, to be loved. I stop thinking about men. I no longer view them with desire.

I start thinking about women instead. I remember the after-noons I'd spent in front of the mirror in my parents' bedroom dressed in one of my father's suits. Some part of me knew even then that I could love my own sex. That petrified me. But the notion of living out my life alone is even more frightening. So I play with the possibilities: I sneak into lesbian bars and watch. I explore the Internet chat rooms and find a young woman from Arizona named Bird 00257 whose online banter sends my heart into a spin. Some days my mind is so crammed with fear and fantasy I can't get any work done. One night I'm sitting on the floor in the boys' room. Daniel's at the mirror checking his abs, as he does every night. Jesse's swinging the bat, back and forth, and the force of it sends a shaft of hot air towards me. I cover my face.

'Stop swinging the bat. You won't be happy till you've beheaded me.'

He laughs.

'Mom, you're such a pussy. It's just air.'

'It's too close. Move back.'

He stops, then flops down beside me on the floor.

'Do you get lonely Mom?'

'All the time,' I say.

'Do you think you'll ever have another boyfriend?'

Right at that moment it hits me. I don't consider myself a lesbian, but there are things I want. I never found them with men. At thirty-eight years of age, I'm on the verge of looking for them in a woman.

'I don't know about men, but I do know that I want love in my life, wherever it comes from.'

'What does that mean?' asks Daniel, turning away from the mirror to face me.

'Well, I don't think gender is that important any more.'

'Oh no, here we go,' says Daniel, and I recognise fear in his face. 'Sons aren't supposed to have to deal with this kind of thing. You're not talking about a woman, are you? Please tell me it's not a woman.'

'I'm not talking about anyone in particular. All I'm saying is I want love in my life.'

We leave it at that.

It's at this juncture that Cece (recently single) and I take up near-permanent residence on Deb's couch with a group of sex-starved women who delight in a kind of perverse physical closeness. It's perverse because it leads nowhere. And while Cece's the only self-identified lesbian among us, the boundaries are blurry. All of us are single, lonely and desperate for human touch. Jesse and Daniel balk at the all too frequent sight of their mother stuffed between two bulky women, her arm being tickled on one side, her back rubbed on the other. I find myself waiting for these sessions. There's something about the way Cece looks at me and strokes my back and runs her fingers up and down my arm that thrills me. I'm not the only one who notices. Often, Deb proclaims,

'She's in love with you, Shiv, just crazy about you.' I reject that notion. I'm afraid of her intensity and the way her face lights up when I enter the room. I pretend it's not happening. Then one night, Cece, Aunt Deb and I are in a funky Chinese eatery, navigating our way through suspicious-looking bowls of sweet and sour soup. The conversation veers towards relationships.

'I don't want anyone even winking at me gratuitously,' I declare adamantly. 'I mean if they're not willing to follow up, why bother?' And out it pops, in broad restaurant light, across the table, a bold flirtatious wink. Cece just slips them into conversation. Only this one is launched in my direction.

'Not that it would do any good,' she says. 'You wouldn't do anything about it anyway, if someone did want to be with you.'

'Why do you assume that?' I respond before I can switch on my self-editing machine.

'This is great soup,' proclaims Deb, oblivious to all but the slimy piece of egg-drop dangling from her spoon. The moment passes, but not before its surge hits me smack in the stomach. Later in my room, Cece on the bed, me on the floor, we talk and talk, steering our way round what's being left conspicuously unsaid, the air becoming pregnant with repressed urgency. Her energy overwhelms me until I can barely breathe. Finally I get up to go to the bathroom. From behind the door, she blurts,

'What did you mean when you responded to my comment like that?'

I emerge to find her perched gingerly on the edge of my bed, heart in her hands, eyes bright with wanting.

'You're a brave girl,' I tell her.

We start negotiations, vacillating inelegantly between sexual innuendo, flirtatious banter and ongoing dialogue regarding the practical ramifications of a possible union. These exchanges are frustrating because her phone battery always expires right at the point of intersection, whereupon she gathers up her quarters, races down to the call box by which time the moment has passed and we're back to a deadlock. She pursues. I resist. But I don't want her to stop.

'Let me take you out on a date,' she says one night. I go into a kind of shock; the notion of a real-life date with a woman, and in particular with Cece, frightens me. I'd witnessed her power over Patri, seen how she'd reduced her to emotional shreds. We're too alike, I offer, too different, have known each other too long, our friendship would suffer. She doesn't give up. Aunt Deb warns me not to hurt her niece, warns Cece that I'm too closed, too scared, too guarded. I convince myself it would never work; Cece's too big (I can't imagine steering my way around a woman's body, and certainly not one as obviously overpowering as Cece's with its ledges and humps, and bundles of flesh), too young (she's twenty-four), too opinionated (she's always right), too forceful. I'm too busy, too driven, too old, too everything. Through it all, Cece maintains a tremulous balance. She derails all my doubt with three simple words:

'I want you.'

Each time she utters these words, my heart flutters, to which I respond internally in typical no-nonsense fashion.

'Stop that shit!'

On Valentine's night we find ourselves at a grimy gay bar on the outskirts of Davie where the women, with their slicked-back hair, tight jeans and cowboy boots, their pool cues and macho swaggers, look more like men than men themselves. Some even pack fake penises, although it's difficult to be certain in the dark. We're listening to a friend play the blues, side by side on bar stools, making sure not to touch. Suddenly I glance over at Cece, look into her eyes and see myself there, whole, not pieces of a self long discarded. I see also, in the dim light, how utterly beautiful she is and for that moment, I don't care what people think or how enormous she is. I feel myself go soft inside, and it's then, precisely then, that her body gently grazes mine. Hours later, in front of my house, we sit in the car. She holds my clenched fist to her mouth, firmly unfolds the fingers and brushes her lips against my palm.

'I'd like to make love to you, Shiv,' she says. I'm speechless, as scared as I've ever been. I don't take my hand away.

We're lying in my bed. It's dark outside. The boys are in their rooms. I see her face, that striking face that I've always thought belongs in another time, through the candlelight. I lie still, afraid to move and afraid not to. Barely breathing.

'I think it would be safer if I slept at the other end,' she says finally, and positions herself at my feet. The silence between us is thick. I want her. Want to feel the heat of her, the rush of her breath.

'Come back,' I say softly.

'Are you sure?' she asks. 'Oh baby.'

I stretch out beside her, terrified. She curls against me, inhales deeply, runs her mouth up and down my arm, like she's breathing me in. She moves her hand across my body, slowly at first then with greater obstinacy. We hold each other under the covers, our fingers twisting together, our whole lives knotted in that grip. We do not sleep, not for a second. The next morning, we're clumsy.

'I'd be open to doing this again,' she whispers as she leaves. I sit on the porch and wave as she blows me a sweet little kiss through the car window. Then she drives away. Once alone, I'm paralysed by ambivalence. I want her yet desperately don't want to want her. She arrives the next afternoon on the pretext of delivering a blow-drier though we both know that my hair does its own thing, and I never use one.

It's dark in the room, very dark. She touches me. I can do this, I think, I can go for this, as long as I lock out the light. My back is turned. It's safer that way. Her hands travel over me dangerously. 'Kiss me,' she murmurs, 'Kiss me.'

I face her.

'I can't. I can't do that yet.'

'Well, I don't think I can go any further with this. I'm not the fuckbuddy type.'

'You're just so cool,' I whisper finally.

And she is. I admire the way she holds back, something about the club that just isn't that sure if they want me as a member. The fear fades.

'Hey you,' I say, turning towards her suddenly. She looks up, her surprise flickering through the dimness. I kiss her then, for the first time. Her lips are so soft. Her skin is so smooth, the little noises she makes so unfamiliar. My breath catches in my chest. Slowly, I find my way around her body. I touch her breasts and feel her nipples go hard. I put my fingers between her legs and explore her wetness.

'Fuck me baby,' she says.

Those words sound so incongruous coming from her lips. Cece, the New Age spiritual goddess who'd lain her hands on me and healed me when I was suffering a gruelling bout of bronchitis, who spoke a language of universes unfolding, spiritual artistry and cosmic manifestations, speaking my words, words that to me mean sex and sweat, and heat and abandon, scratches and bites, and nails digging into skin. In my mind, 'making love' to her means something else.

I panic.

How the fuck do I fuck her?

'I get so turned on turning you on,' she tells me then. Her eyes haze over. I dig my nails into her back until I break skin. She looks up at me, so fervent and vulnerable. In sex, the speech in our bodies becomes aligned. We approach each other with a compulsive hunger, for we both have bankrupt hearts.

THIRTY-TWO

This is how it starts.

Moments snatched out of nowhere: in the back of her car by the railway tracks or parked under the trees on the edge of Biscayne Park. When the local policeman, who coached both my boys in Little League, draws up beside us one night and shines his torch through the car window, we move to an alleyway behind my house. Jesse and Daniel wonder, sometimes out loud, why she visits so often, and even though we've shared my bed on occasion as friends, it doesn't feel right under this new arrangement. I want to tell them, but the memory of Daniel's face that night in his room stops me. So I travel to her studio on the beach, where she waits for me with candles, incense and flowers, with arms and legs and tongue, a body that takes me in, and a heart that's so open it's frightening. I stay late, sometimes till dawn, then drive across the Causeway, up the Boulevard with its hookers and tramps, the radio on, my body tingling. I try not to think as I drive, about consequences, about love, about the boys, about anything, but I can't shake the sense that I'm doing something terribly wrong.

When I reach the house, I slip through the door, remove my boots to avoid the creaking floorboards and slide across the living room. With every step I relive the terror that seized me as I used to tread from the top step on the landing at Tree Tops to my room at the back of the house. To get there I had to pass the door to my father's bedroom. I always woke him. And he always interrogated me with the same fierceness I'd seen him use on my mother. Waiting for me now instead is Jesse, seated in the early-morning light, the contempt on his face highlighted with eerie precision by the streetlamp, his body coiled in the grip of betrayal.

'Where the hell have you been,' he demands, 'out till this hour? Don't you know I was worried sick?' These words and the look of disgust take me back. I slink silently to my room where the shame comes creeping up over me like cool water slipping over stones.

Cece herself proclaims that I live in fear. I can't for the life of me utter those three crucial words. In fact, I can't speak much at all. Oh, I dig into her skin when we make love, bite her neck in just the right place. I listen for her gasps to spill out. They are loud enough to shatter memories, to kill the lonely moment. But it's only a moment. The rest of the time I hide the spoils of our love, describing her as a friend to my colleagues and concealing photos of us together in my closet. I bury her away.

But interred truths have a way of making themselves known, of coming up for air and taking breath. This one surfaces one evening while I'm sitting out on the back porch. I hear the boys in the bedroom, fighting, joking around, and suddenly I want them to know. I'm always pontificating about honour and standing up for who they are and what they believe in, and here I am, hiding behind curbed versions of truth, pretending to others that Cece is just a friend, imagining to myself that it'll end in a week or two. When I know, really know, that I have never been looked at or touched this way before. I march into the bedroom.

Jesse's lying there in his boxer shorts, stretched out across my pillows. Something in the way he looks at me, with those same, round, probing eyes he's always had, makes me speak, though I've no notion of what I'm about to say.

'I have to tell you something important,' I blurt out.

'What, Mom?'

I stall.

'Cece and I are together.'

He doesn't answer, at least not in words, but his eyes fill with tears. He looks so disappointed, and there's nothing I can say to make it right. Daniel emerges from the bathroom, dripping wet with a towel wrapped around his body.

'What's up?' he asks nervously.

'Mom's gay, with Cece,' Jesse tells him. Daniel chuckles, with the awkward laughter of kids who've just found out someone has died. That night I dream of faceless brown-skinned boys cowering in corners. Two days later Jesse hands me a sheet of paper:

Where to Go, What to Be, I'm Not Quite Sure, but I Know This Is Me

A stained rose lays on the ground
Leaves flap at the wind's demand
Due South the next gust shouts
But the petals flee and run about
Where to go, what to be, I'm not quite sure, but I know this
    is me.
I have to be true to the path I take
there have been so many breezes this almost feels fake
the thorn at my side, the base at my stem
without these two, I would come to an end
but I do need to choose a path to take
for without a step forward I would surely break
I'd look all right on a summer's day

but then when the nights got cold I'd be in dismay
and my thorns and my stem
where would they go?
I built them from the bottom so I could watch them grow
Would they go?
Would they shed?
Could my choices leave them dead?
Huh?
Where to go, what to be, I'm not quite sure, but I know this
    is me.

Leave them dead. Leave them dead. Huh?

Daniel wants Cece to remove the Rainbow sticker from her car so that his friends won't discover his mother is a lesbian, or at least to park the car backwards so they don't have to see it. She refuses. He takes to getting dropped off by his team-mates after practice on the corner or down the road. A dreadful terror transposes itself over the house. Neighbourhood boys like Prem, Ferdel, Sylvan, who've grown up at my sloppy kitchen table, are now swiftly ferried back and forth. God forbid, anyone should catch me and Cece touching. The night of my fortieth, after she'd gone to all the trouble, with the streamers, the catered dishes, the balloons (too many, this is claustrophobic, I proffered graciously two minutes into my surprise), she pulled me close in the back of Deb's kitchen.

'I love you,' she said and kissed me on the lips. Over her shoulder, in the reflection of the sliding glass doors, I saw Daniel's face, taut, thin, menacing. No one can know the truth about his mother.

THIRTY-THREE

⌐⎯

Three months after the birthday party I start to unravel.

Something untoward happens in the body when you hit forty. That's what Janice tells me. 'The wrinkles appear, the weight stays on, the mind gets sluggish, the energy falters.' For me, it goes deeper. I think about death and can't stop. Why now, when I've finally found a kind of love, I ask myself. Maybe it's because I've found it. On the nights Cece stays over, I wake myself up screaming and stagger from the bed in a stupor. Sometimes I'm so disoriented I circle the room like a spinning top with my heart beating so fast I'm sure it will implode. The first time this happens, Cece wakes up immediately.

'Is it a nightmare, baby?' she asks.

'No, night terrors. I think I'm going to die.'

'You better not be dying,' she says. She pulls me close and strokes my forehead with her fingers. 'You're sweating. Did you take your blood pressure medicine today?'

'I took it. I think it happens when I feel close to you. I just wake up terrified.'

'I'm not leaving you, Shiv, I'll never leave you.'

The tears fall. I can't stop them. I don't trust that I can be loved. I am so sure I will end up alone. Every time she stays the same thing happens.

On the nights she doesn't, I smoke too many cigarettes and drink too much wine. And every morning I face the prospect of loss, as if life itself will take from me the very things it has bestowed. I worry constantly about Jesse and Daniel, even when they run to the corner shop. I am besieged by a series of nagging physical ailments for which the doctors can offer no logical explanation. I agonise about my family back in Ireland and rack up an $800 phone bill just so I can hear their voices. I spend hours in my bedroom watching *Matlock* reruns on TV. I find it hard to manage the most menial of tasks; preparing of dinners, washing of laundry, paying of bills such that the lights get turned off periodically, the phone line interrupted for non-payment, the cars repossessed, the manuscripts deserted midstream, the job ignored, the boys silenced. I no longer have the energy to talk to my sons, or to listen. My body hurts, from over-exertion it seems, yet I can't walk three fucking paces without resting.

I dwell in the realm of the non-living, glancing backward at the thriving, dynamic person I imagine myself to have been, no longer able to grasp or feel her. I ignore the rhythms of my own body, harden and fossilise myself against them, and instead adopt the agency for a kind of compulsive non-action – the picking of scabs and scalp, the pulling of hairs, the fiddling with papers, biting of nails, the repeating of words. And breath by breath my energy siphons itself away, diverted by the wounds of the past. The scars have hardened over and every new stretching motion threatens to pull them apart.

And truthfully, I'm not sure where to begin, just quite how to set the act of living in motion, though I try, desperately. Every other night we embark on an exhausting two-mile walk during which I lag behind Cece as she charges across the Boulevard. The smarting feeling that flutters up and down my limbs hints at the stocky eleven-year-old girl I used to be. An unlikely sports day victor who stormed past the senior champion in the 440-yard dash and who spied as she broke through the finish line a handsome man with honed features, worn down too young. The tails of his dark suit flapped in the breeze as he hurried to greet her. The fact that my father arrived too late to see me triumph drowned out the cheering that came from a row of young children seated on the high brick wall overlooking the Maccabee field – among them the daughters of Teresa O'Brien, our housekeeper, who wore my clothes when I'd grown out of them, who played with the toys I discarded, the girls who piled together five to a bed in a council flat, but who laughed with a heartiness that was as alien to me as a foreign language. Their eyes stayed with me as I crossed the ropes and recognised in me something I could not.

These days as I reach inside for the determination I cannot find, I long for the zest that sent me hurtling around a grassy field that day even though there was no one waiting for me at the other end. More than anything, I want to know where I lost it. Mark out the process, step by step, like a choreographer preparing for a show. I so very much need to come home and to understand the forces that have contributed to the slow-motion collapse of my psyche. Through it all I remember what I felt that first day, stepping off the plane at Miami International. I knew even then that in this city I would become unstitched and more of an outsider than I ever was. In Ireland growing up I was trapped between the Irish and the Jews, then left behind by a mother, misunderstood by a father and rejected by Pat. So I went looking for a place that would take me in. Miami is not that place. Here, I have been stripped not only of the spirit I arrived with but of the wherewithal to create a life. Without work papers, I am invisible. I do not exist. Cece understands this. She's had her own battles: cast out of the family home when she was seventeen, dispatched to the mental hospital, drugged up on pills, and left to rot. She made it out. Alive.

'Have some hope, honey,' she tells me. 'You've got to find hope. Look at all you've done for those gang kids. You give them something to live for. Do it for yourself.'

The truth is, hope is way too scary. It means wanting and believing. I've lost too much already to start that. But without it I crack. So again I reinvent myself, building a life on expectation. With Cece's help. To me, she is like those little girls sitting on the wall at the Maccabee field. She sees what I can't.

I decide to go back to college for a doctoral programme in writing and culture and immerse myself in texts – *Lost in Translation, Letters of Transit, Altogether Elsewhere*; in them I find my own story. I continue at the Centre but hatch a plan to get out.

'I'm going to teach writing,' I tell Cece one evening.

'That's great, Shiv, you'd be amazing. But what about your work papers?'

'Hey, I'm not going to let a little detail like that get in the way. I'll set up the course, find the students and go for it.'

'That's my girl.'

The administrators at the community college accept the faded copy of my social security. Albeit warily. I have 180 days to produce an original – a problem I choose to overlook. Two Saturdays later I'm holding court in a large classroom on the second floor. It's only a part-time gig, and I still run the Centre, but I have five students: a doctor, a stockbroker, a fashion student, a linguist and an Irish woman who runs a bookshop on Miami Beach. In front of them I come alive. I connect. I have hope.

THIRTY-FOUR

Hope needs a back-up.

A few months into this new optimistic incarnation, I wake up determined to get to work on time, to pay the bills and to start that doctoral programme. I need to write and I need something gripping to write about, anything at all that lends itself to the pen. After the obligatory cup of Seven Eleven Decaf, followed by the requisite five Newport cigarettes, I scour the newspapers and find a story about Cuban hunger strikers. Several hours later, work dispensed with, I'm driving out to Krome Detention Center. Cece's with me, camera poised. She has a knack for capturing life on film.

'This will make a really good photo-essay,' I tell her. 'Four old Cuban women on hunger strike to get their sons out of jail.'

'Yeah, great photo-essay,' she says. 'But I'm not so sure you should be getting that close to a detention centre. What if they pick you up, or something?'

'Come on. Everyone thinks I'm Ruby Wax, the accent, the attitude, you know I've got that American thing down pat. Don't be scared.'

None the less, a ghostly shiver passes through me as we head down the Tamiami Trail, a desolate track of tarmac bordered on either side by yellow grass, with only the rare oncoming interstate truck for company. The sun shimmers spookily against the gravel, creating a mirage ahead that we never reach no matter how fast we drive. We are thirsty and very lost, but seeing as I've never once managed to get accurate directions in Miami, from anyone, there's not much point stopping to ask. Usually if I'm told to take the first right, the second left, I do the exact opposite and eventually end up where I need to go. But this Tamiami thing seems to extend for miles and there's no sign of a building. We stop eventually at a roadside café, where a group of men, covered in sweat and dirt, are knocking back beers.

'INS,' I ask, not wanting to utter the words that squeeze lives into knots.

'*Alla* (Up there),' says an old man with crooked teeth and turned-down lips, pointing into the long stretch of road before us. I follow his finger. It's so still and quiet not even a blade of grass shifts.

'I feel like I'm in some Western,' I tell Cece.

'You are,' she says, 'everyone knows Miami is a cowboy town.'

And it is, with its paedophile, drug-peddling school principals, gangster ministers, money-laundering mayors, vote-thieving politicians. I've come to realise that what goes into the making of a place is important, that a city can be only as good as the dreams it's built on, and what are Miami's? Some Mafioso's crude version of paradise, a borderland town where you can get rich quick and move on, build a casino, a hotel, and live off the sun's vapours. The playpen for the rich and famous, the nursing home for the elderly and, more recently, the receptacle for Castro's unwanted. What kind of a life can you build on that? On shifting sands, on land drawn back from the sea? I'm tired of the resignation in the air, of the choking, oppressive smog that clings to buildings and landscape alike. I long for a sense of history, to gaze upon homes, cathedrals and monuments that speak to me of a preserved past, of people engaged in hard work, long ingrained. I don't want to hear any more of those heartbreaking life stories that chart so clearly the hazards of packing in one life and taking on another. Yet here I am, about to meet a group of people who almost died trying to get here, and whose lives, in this very moment, ebb slowly towards obliteration.

We drive on for another ten miles or so.

'There they are,' proclaims Cece, 'up there on the right.' And through the flickering haze, I can just about make them out, a small group settled under a cloth tarp on the roadside in front of the detention centre. Four women and a man, worn down by hunger and heat, lie out on a few wobbly cots. They are surrounded by wilting bouquets of flowers, posters denouncing Janet Reno and the American Government, an old TV set, tattered American and Cuban flags and a bunch of supporters including a Santeria priest garbed in white, a gay cabaret singer wearing far too many clothes for such a hot day, and an elderly doctor who tends the strikers free of charge. I stand aside and listen as they repeat their stories: a son arrested for domestic violence who has spent nine years behind bars, another caught in a robbery still held captive two years after completing his sentence, and yet another with a drug problem detained in Louisiana for possession. All are held without hope of release. Lovingly, the strikers hold up photos of children and grandchildren, families torn asunder by a system that does not view them as human. I sit beside them on their little makeshift beds and listen. Two have been hospitalised during the strike. One, who raises her dress to reveal a livid pus-filled wound, had to stop altogether.

'The doctor told me I don't have long to live,' she says, 'so I need to spend whatever time I have left with my son. *Él es mi vida* (He is my life).'

I steady myself. I am touched by their pain, and have nothing to offer. Marta, who started the whole thing, sits back out of the sun's glare in a wheelchair and begins to paint her nails. '*Que color más bonito* (What a lovely colour),' remarks the overdressed cabaret singer.

'*Claro que sí*,' she says, '*Quiero lucir bien cuando salga mi hijo* (I want to look good when my son gets out).'

'You have to eat something,' overdressed continues, 'you know *calditos, sopitas*, nothing heavy.'

'Ay,' says Marta, 'they tried to kill me at the hospital, with a big plate of rice and beans, thought they'd do me in with food.' The strikers laugh. God knows where they find the heart to joke, and the fact that they do, forty-seven days into a fast, and can then talk about sons who've lost their *fundios* (asses), trips they've taken to Louisiana by bus, only to get there and be turned back without a visit, hours they've waited for phone calls, for answers, for a sign, anything that will let them know this torture is close to an end – hits me the hardest of all. It's their resilience that moves me, but also how they're throwing their hearts and their lives on to a sizzling sidewalk that holds such little promise. I can't imagine anyone considering me worth that.

'Hope, *la esperanza*, keeps us alive,' said Myrea Cortes, the one who, to me, looks closest to death, 'because *no veo nada*, I see nothing from the other side, they treat them like *cierdos*, keep them locked up twenty-four hours a day, no windows, no books, no TV. And if I don't hear something positive on Thursday, if they don't let my son out, I'm going to stop drinking water too.'

This is so unjust, I think as I listen. Miami's full of former criminals, who've done their time, and moved on. I want to feel sorry for them, but I know that in yielding to compassion, I will also be pardoning my own past, the mistakes, the defective reasoning, all of it. In endorsing their plight, I will somehow rationalise my own criminality. I'm not at all sure that the boys behind bars deserve their mothers' efforts, or are worth their lives.

Most likely, I think, they'll get out and go right back to what put them there in the first place. I can't move beyond that thought. So I roam from cot to cot, striker to striker, from one set of worn-down, despairing eyes to another. I fill twenty pages of scribbled notes, with Cece trailing behind me, flashing tentatively. I walk away finally, their words reverberating in my head, the distraction on their faces clinging to me. All the way home I am nagged by an ugly feeling in the base of my stomach. Their stories echo the ones I've been telling myself all along; that I am hard done by, unfairly victimised and excluded, and I've always found a way to demonise the system. Outrage protected me from the truth. I'd relived my own story so many times, it had become a fairy tale, the moral of which had been obliterated by repetition.

Later that afternoon we visit Patri, Cece's ex, and her new love, Chelala. To spark conversation, but also because the strikers' faces are festering in the back of my mind and I need to rid myself of them, I mention where we spent the afternoon. This prompts a debate of epic proportions.

'Who the hell do they think they are coming to this country and committing crimes? They don't deserve to be here,' Chelala rants. 'I know what it's like back in Cuba. I visited last year. The walls in my mother's house are peeling. She has no food and no water, no medicine for her blood pressure. Don't dare to tell me about inhumane conditions. And what did they do with their chances? Rob, cheat, steal, beat their women. Send them back so that Castro can have his way with them.'

'Well, what about me?' I ask finally. 'What do I deserve?'

'You,' says Patri, 'you were plain stupid, to get hooked up with that low-life husband of yours, but you didn't commit any crime, right?' Cece looks across, waiting for me to answer.

Suddenly I am overwhelmed.

The façade falls apart.

They see a woman who writes and teaches and mothers, who keeps appointments and attends baseball games and graduations.

I know something different.

I practise deception.

I haven't paid taxes in years.

I feverishly dispatch invoices to my father – for construction work on my house, medical and dental services, computer parts, school fees for my kids – sharp professional documents, fashioned on my home computer, that reach his desk in manila envelopes, statements he signs off on and returns, cheque enclosed. I've become adept at yanking dollars from dirt, via complicated little banking schemes that allow me to pilfer from my own tomorrow. I make up stories to tell my employees about important meetings that don't exist, phoney grants that I have to write, doctor's appointments that I'll never attend, so that I can walk out of my office, every bit as truant as the delinquent kids I'm supposed to serve. I leave behind the real world of responsibility, the world in which my word is supposed to mean something, to enter one in which I am nothing but a middle-aged woman on the heavy side who orders too much wine at lunch, who looks too sad behind the smile and who speaks too freely to the cute waiter who doesn't give a goddamn about the new writing course she's teaching. Ever on a hustle, forced to stay one step ahead of my own life, I can never rest. But subterfuge endures only so long before it spins you around, grabs you by the neck and slams you to a wall.

The room has gone silent. They are waiting for me to speak.

'I'm no angel,' I say finally.

'We know that, sweetie,' says Chelala with a chuckle.

The afternoon wears on: food, drinks, music. In the bathroom alone I trace the curves of my life and realise that in much the same manner that I scorned fellow Jews in Dublin for attending synagogue, having marriages and children, joining social clubs, buying suburban homes, today I hold in contempt an entire generation of Americans and a whole city simply because I cannot belong. And this has licensed me, in my own mind, to live outside its laws, to disregard its values and to diminish its intentions. I imagine that's part of what allowed me to keep on loving Julio. There was something so cruel and unfair about a world that was capable of perpetrating such grievous damage on his soul. And no matter how he hurt me, what I chose to see was a small spindly boy, with protruding bones, who clutched on to a faded photo of his mother as he waited by an orphanage window. What I saw was a six-year-old trying to be a man, bathing a dying uncle, washing his scabs, listening to his stories, holding his hand as he passed away. And because I saw only that, I defied that world on his behalf and swore that I would never succumb to its conventions. My life has been an act of revenge, one of getting back at the universe for exacting such high tolls, for being so brutal and unflinching, for just not giving a shit. It occurs to me suddenly that I may as well be talking about my own mother. And everyone who followed her into my heart. Julio included.

He is no longer part of my life. By the time he got out, he'd forgotten the few elements of fatherhood he once knew. Too often, he brushed me off when I really needed help with the kids. Too many nights they fell asleep waiting for him, hunched on chairs in their best clothes. It's been so long since I've thought of him as that sad little boy. What I see instead is a selfish man, who cannot love. Yet something in the strikers' stories brought me back to what we once had: an attachment cemented by the careless tyrannies that had cast us aside. I remember him telling me that after leaving his mother and his two-year-old son in Cuba, nothing would ever hurt again. He lived like that, as a man who thought of himself as beyond hurt, someone for whom life was a series of transient opportunities. Wives, mothers, children – all were dispensable. But how had I lived? Like a reckless orphan who trashes a foster home because it will never be hers. Memories of who I was, Dublin memories, have been suffused by the heat of the tropics. I got on a plane and crossed an ocean, simple as that. I arrived with an open, broken heart that gave way to circumstance. Yet, even after two decades, my internal rhythms remain calibrated to the land of my birth, to its sense of time, its language and its sounds. All the attempts I've made to bend and shape myself to the place I now live have melted my spirit, ironed it out with a red-hot heat and changed it for ever from what it once was. I have tried to speak the language of this city, but words don't mean the same things here. Words, in fact, don't mean much at all, and words are my most precious currency. I have tried to immerse myself in its culture, to listen hard to its cadence, but my ears catch only the still, silent sound of loss.

The myth that Ireland represents continues to ground me, and latched to nothing but a fiction, I flounder, for I belong neither here nor there. And those who dwell in the in-between lose capacity for compassion for the ground that stands beneath them, find it very hard to approach their lives with love. But there has to be another story, one in which loss and desperation don't convert into wrongdoing, but instead form the foundation out of which a life is carved.

I hear that story later in the evening when Cece, Patri, Chelala and I sit in the Coconut Grove Playhouse listening to the Cuban singer Willy Chirino. I hadn't expected to be moved. But in song after song, Chirino recounts the story of exile, his own, his family's, his people's. He sings of the Cuban *pasaje*, its beauty and its splendour. He sings of Havana's beaches, its prostitutes and street vendors. In the end, he chants, '*Nuestro Dia (Ya Viene Llegando)* (Our Day Is Coming)', the cry of a usurped people. A perfumed crowd of exiles, dressed to the nines, join him:

Apenas siendo un nino alla en las antilla
mi padre me vistio de marinero
tuve que navegar 90 millas
y comenzar mi vida de extranjero.

When I was just a child on the island,
my father dressed me as a sailor.
I had to navigate 90 miles,
and begin my life as a stranger.

The theatre throbs. In that moment, I want to stop living the outsider life.

I had considered my victimhood so unique. But I see now that I am just one of many, part of the very crew I've derided so vehemently; the Cubans with their sad stories and manipulative ways who jerk off on America's promise, and the starving mothers who sit under a tarp on a dusty highway, waiting for word from Washington as their lives sway towards extinction. They are all as split as I am. I think of my Grandpa Willie who left Russia during the pogroms and arrived on Irish shores with nothing but a small suitcase. I think of his struggle to make good, and I wonder how he'd left behind one land, and claimed another. How had he managed to open his heart? Where had he wrapped his memories? He lived to be eighty-six years old, and I'd never thought to ask him, not once, about his mother, his father, about the little corner of the Lithuanian landscape that had been his. I look around me. Sheltered in the dark, people are crying, for mothers, for fathers, for brothers, sons and daughters, for the feel of the land they were born to. How, I need to know, did they survive the transplant? How do they endure, day after day, without being eaten alive by loss?

Outside, under the harsh streetlights, I see Ana, a middle-aged woman I met briefly before the show. Her eyes are damp behind her glasses.

'I love America,' she says, 'I really love this country. I love how big it is, how open, how it received me when I came as a young girl without my mother or father. But I miss Cuba. I miss *mi gente, mi patria.'*

'I know,' I answer, 'I really know,' because I recognise in her the gaping hole I've found in myself so often. Yet there's a difference between the history she lives by, the story my grandpa would have told, had I asked him, and mine. They had to leave, forced out by poverty, hunger and politics. I could have stayed. Because I didn't, I'd walked myself into a borderland far more rigid and unforgiving than anything they'd known.

On the drive home, I am quiet. Cece's beside me, lost, I imagine, in her own thoughts. The strikers, perishing under a brutal sun, have provoked in me a need to make peace with the country that has claimed half my life. This land is not and will never be home. But the foolhardy girl who arrived two decades ago with an old suitcase and a heart that brimmed with hope has been transformed into a cantankerous, determined woman. And no matter how I've railed against it, American culture has formed me, breath by breath, with the insistence of water dripping on rock. There is a part of me now that belongs here, a part that no longer fits there. If I don't accept it, I forfeit my hold on life.

Willy Chirino sang,

> *Paso lo que tenia que pasar*
> *de mi nueva ciudad tome su abrigo*
> *pues la resignación es fiel amigo*
> *del hombre cuando tiene que emigrar.*

It happened how it was meant to happen,

from my new city, I took its coat,
for resignation is a loyal friend
to the man who has to emigrate.

I've never worn a coat in Miami, not even in winter.

Through the night, Cece and I cling together in the dark of my
bedroom.

'It's OK, baby, it's OK,' Cece says as I cry. 'You won't always be
so far away from your family. And you have beautiful sons, a good
life. You have me.'

'I know,' I say finally, 'I know all that, but I still feel so empty
inside, like I'll never get it right. I'm just not good at this living
business.'

'Yeah, but there are some things you're good at,' she says.

Even in the dark I feel her smile, the raunchy wink. I take hold of
her, not kindly, not gently, but with terror.

THIRTY-FIVE

She moves in.

Carrying the boxes and crates that make up her life on those strong shoulders. Within days, she's reorganised my closet, cleaned the kitchen floor (which hasn't seen a mop in months), emptied out my study (cluttered, in my estimation, beyond restoration) and transformed the bedroom (a drab structure) with flowers and candles, pictures, soft quilts and pillows. The boys balk sporadically, and tensions run high, in particular, regarding bathroom activities. She can't understand how they consistently manage to shower the toilet seat with a steady yellow stream. The fact that they have to walk through 'our' bedroom to reach the only working john doesn't help matters, or that it's common for them to sit on my bed and chat before sleep or, even worse, lay on the bed when we aren't there to watch movies, then proceed to cover it with candy wrappers and potato chip bags that they never retrieve. Ignorant entirely of the nuances of functional home management, they cannot comprehend why she gets so worked up over what she terms the 'locker-room' odour that permeates 'our space' after even a hasty visit from the boys. As for me, locker-room odours are the norm.

She loves baseball though. Finally, I have someone to sit beside me on the bleachers, in the soft evening light, someone to cheer

Jesse on when he stands at the plate, bat in hand, and twitches those hips of his, knocking the ball into the next field. She shouts almost as much as I do, 'C'mon number eighteen, get in there, you can do it. C'mon Jesse, remember your breathing, it's all fun. Remember that. Follow your joy.'

But it's not all fun, 'cause Litman his Naziesque coach hurls abuse like it's going out of style.

'What the fuck are you doing, eighteen, get your head out of your ass. Motherfucker, goddamn stupid kid' (under his breath). I watch the maniac marching up and down by the railings, banging his head against the dugout walls, crushing soda cans in his fist. I see his face turn purple with rage. I hear him calling my son a pussy, a faggot, a wimp, a coward. I see him spit words into the dirt.

Then I watch Jesse walk back to the dugout with his head down after a strikeout.

'Don't worry, girlie,' Cece says, 'It's OK. Ignore that asshole, don't give him space in your head.'

She comes to Daniel's games too. Cheers him on when he pitches and scoops balls up from the dirt, like he's got a suction pump on his glove.

'That's my boy,' she proclaims proudly. 'I love that kid.'

Then we all head off to Chili's or Gusto's or Friday's or whatever's the restaurant *du jour* and talk about the game, move by move, complain about Litman, word by word. Baseball is what binds us.

And despite the acclimatisation difficulties, and there are many, living with her soothes me. I begin to feel almost safe, in a city that has never once offered sanctuary. Over time, cursory dots on the bland landscape – the Laundromat, the Publix supermarket, Borders bookstore at Aventura, Paquito's Mexican restaurant – transfigure themselves from the abstract to the tangible, becoming the map on which I can pinpoint my existence.

Life gradually changes: pre Cece, shopping was a facile affair that called upon me to make repeated trips on any given day to the Seven Eleven on the corner, for milk, butter, cheese, and other staples, the obscene prices of which horrify her; actual meals I purchased, at even more exorbitant cost, ready-made from local restaurants. Under her guidance, I grow to embrace the practice of food inventory, a process which, I discover (albeit rather late in life), involves actual lists, trips to the supermarket, where we march hand in hand up and down the aisles, giggling at how totally clueless I am. Laundry is something I had paid others to do. With her, I fold towels and sheets, make piles for whites and colours. Late at night, when the boys are asleep, I sit in the bathtub for hours, calmed by the water, the candlelight and her presence. Then I lie quietly in bed as she reads to me in her soft, flowing voice, and the general hardship of managing my life, of dealing with my sons, and making decisions on their behalf, recedes off into some distant place. Slowly, though not ever completely, Miami starts to make sense. The night terrors stop.

There are times in the beginning when I think again about making love to men, when I crave the almost violent assault of a penis. She senses that.

'You're just like a man,' she tells me when I fail to deliver the kind of loving expression she seems to need so desperately.

'Say something, speak to me,' she says often. 'Tell me what I mean to you.' The responses hang heavily in my throat, incapable of movement.

'I love you,' I want to tell her. 'I want you. I adore you.' In the end, I answer her with silence. Then there's her insecurities that spring to life every time one of my exes is mentioned, every time Julio visits the kids (which isn't often) or M or Jose phone (even less often).

'You still like the sound of their voices, or what?' she demands.

'Tell them to go to hell. Tell them you have a girlfriend now.'

'You're not my father,' I shout. 'You can't tell me what to do.' And I remember the nights he stood in the doorway of my bedroom, arms raised to block me as I pushed past him out into the world. Every time I made it through, a little less of me came back. In my own home, standing squarely in front of Cece, a quarter of a century later, I feel the pressure of his arms. At these moments, when I look at her, sitting cross-legged on my bed, her beauty and sadness are lost on me.

THIRTY-SIX

Is that why I entertain thoughts of Steven?

No other reason to explain why I go falling for a moody, long-haired, existentialist with a penis.

The day before Valentine's, our second anniversary, I set off for the Fort Lauderdale Hilton, where I'll be ensconced for the best part of two weeks for the doctoral colloquium. No visitors allowed.

'What are these people thinking?' Cece asks as I leave. 'Don't they believe in romance? You'll be gone for a week and a half. What am I supposed to do?'

'Maybe I can sneak you in later in the week,' I say flatly.

I arrive at the Hilton (two hours late even though I'm the only graduate student who actually lives in Florida) and immediately notice Steven. He has the kind of dense sexual energy I've always been drawn to: deep voice, concentrated movements, and a penetrating gaze that I find impossible to ignore. After the initial meeting, we descend into the bar, a freezer-like chamber more suited to meat storage than avid conversation. None the less, we end up talking and drinking (Cece hates it when I drink). For hours we sit facing each other. Occasionally his knee rubs against mine. He's flirting, deliberately, even though I broadcast, in front of the entire group that very morning, that I was bisexual and involved with a woman.

'When you walked in I thought you were a non-approachable lesbian,' he announces, the second night in the bar.

'And now?' I inquire.

'Now I think you're an approachable lesbian,' he says and laughs. We establish a routine after that. Every night, when the sessions are done, we migrate to the meat locker and sit amid the businessmen (one night), the romance writers, decked out in floral prints, straw hats and shawls (the next night), the gay contingent, drag queens, transvestites (the night after that). Within days, the rest of the group have labelled us the Bobbsey Twins. And the truth of it is he unnerves me. On one of those nights, after too many drinks, we kiss in the elevator. It's an innocuous moment, with lips momentarily grazing cheeks, but alone in bed later, I think about fucking him, about having him inside me. When Cece arrives the next evening, for that clandestine visit, I usher her in and out like she's contaminated. It's not just the Steven thing. I want to do this doctoral bit on my own, without her surveillance, without her slant. And she knows it.

At the end of the week, when Steven and I say goodbye, we hug a moment in the lobby. I look into his eyes and think I see the beginnings of tears. I find myself wanting to cry too. Suddenly I feel like I'm losing something very precious.

Days later, back at home, Cece watches me scramble to the computer.

'Are you having an Internet fling or something,' she asks, 'with someone you met at the doctoral programme?'

My cheeks go hot.

I look away.

'I just met someone I feel close to,' I say finally. 'Like a brother, we had a connection, you know, a heart thing.'

'Are you attracted to him?'

'I guess. But I'd never be with him, with anyone. I'm not the unfaithful type.'

'How can I possibly compete with that? I just don't have a "best seat in the house",' she mutters later in bed, referring bleakly to an irreverent and, given the circumstances, foolish comment I made back in the beginning. She makes me promise not to email him. I promise, then break it. She finds a way into my passcode. We fight. She's determined that if I really loved her I'd just get rid of him, and I'm equally determined that no one is ever again going to tell me who to spend my time with.

'I'm forty-one years old, godammit,' I tell her, 'and I'll do what I want, talk to whomever I want. No one is going to tell me what to do.'

In December I visit New York to defend my thesis, to meet my doctoral committee and Steven. She begs me not to see him at all, then not to see him alone, and finally to let her come with me. The answer is a firm No on all counts. By then, it has very little to do with Steven. I've already recognised him for what he is: an abominable flirt who wants the undivided attention of every woman on the planet, including non-approachable lesbians. I'm not about to let her go for that, but a carte blanche submission to her demands is not an option either. It feels to me like a renunciation of the spirit I've worked so hard to ignite.

'If you cared about me at all . . . if you considered me at all you'd let him go, get him out of our bed, out of our lives,' she cries the night before I depart. 'You'll see,' she threatens, 'I'll cultivate an attraction of my own, then you'll know what it feels like on this end.' We fall quiet eventually, into the kind of beleaguered sleep that makes you wish morning was just a breath away.

I do meet Steven during that trip. Alone. Well, the rest of the doctoral candidates are there, but his girlfriend, it seems, comes down with the flu and can't join us, so we end up sitting side by side in one of those nifty New York eateries. Suddenly I feel the warmth of his arm draped across my back. His head is turned into mine, his breath close. I glance over at the door, and in my mind's eye, I see Cece walking through it. I catch for a second the look of total horror on her face as she registers the scene. I shift away from Steven quickly, internally conceding that I myself am probably up to no kind of good. If I want her, I realise then, I'll have to work for it. All the way home on the plane, I think about running into her arms and staying there. When I see her standing in the lobby, exhausted, anxious, but putting on the good front anyway, I know that if I never make love to anyone again for the rest of my life, I will be fine.

THIRTY-SEVEN

Some things come too little, too late.

This is one of them.

I notice the changes at first in small ways. Cece becomes irritated by things she once found endearing: my peculiar dietary habits (an unrelenting need for piping hot tea which waiters invariably return to me lukewarm even after the third try, the simultaneous ingestion of Coke, water and wine); my capacity for always managing to get the wrong order at Burger King, McDonalds and Wendy's, which usually prompts a minimum of two if not three return trips and a heated exchange; my lack of banking knowledge, which has fucked up her account more than once; my innate ability to screw up the computer and my equally innate ignorance as to how to fix it; my penchant for farting and burping (loudly) in cinemas, restaurants, basically anywhere at all, regardless of who is present.

For a long time, Cece took care of me, catered to the nutty-professor-type qualities that I had worked at developing. They made her laugh and, at times, I believe she thought I was brilliant. But in these weeks, a sharpness creeps into her voice, a hardness to her eyes and, when I touch her, she freezes. There are reasons, of course, I tell myself: my enduring facility for running hot and cold, for loving her one minute, ignoring and dismissing her the next, my penchant for what she terms 'intermittent reinforcement', giving her just enough to keep her there. And then there were the times I wished she'd talk lower, laugh less, the times I looked at her body and wished it were smaller, felt her intensity, her passion, and wanted to stamp it out.

The residual guilt lingers and because it does I accept that she comes home later and later from work, goes out on her own more often, joins yet another dance class. Her legs are closed to me far more than they are open. Lovemaking occurs only within a rigidly scant time frame, moments plucked from her busy schedule, and if I don't make it to the bedroom at precisely the right instant, proffering precisely the right quotient of loving ardour, I'm stumped. When we do get the timing down, and steer our way back to that 'us' place, even then, we can't quite find each other.

And then there's the small matter of the 'attraction' she'd threatened to develop. A damn singer. It's fun at first following south Florida's blonde darling, DW, from club to club. She wears her pain like skin. There's a catch in her voice that makes you look away, but lets you know you're alive too. We often find ourselves back at Partners, the dyke dive in Davie we started off in, staring up at the stage, mouthing the words to her songs. Sometimes we even dance, over to the side, in the dark, slow and pressed together, nothing, not even air, between us. One night, Cece's on the dance floor alone, sashaying her way through Madonna's 'Erotica', with that behind of hers spinning up a storm, the way only it can. Even I have to admit it's an inspired performance. Obviously I'm not the only one who sees it that way. I sidle up to the bar to get a drink, and DW blurts out,

'Hey, your girlfriend is so fucking sexy.'

'You think so?' I respond.

'Hell yeah,' she says.

That's how it starts.

Fool that I am, I march right over to Cece with a big old smile and tell her just how sexy DW thinks she is.

As for me, the woman who can't find the words to tell her how sexy I think she is, I start to get jittery. I don't like this new, independent Cece, not at all. I'm losing my grip, I can feel it. And DW is fast becoming a fixture. The next time we see her, Cece executes another of those erotic routines, this time to 'I'm Thirty-Two Flavours and Then Some!' On our way out of the club, DW comes right up to her and says,

'Hey, if you get any sweatier I'll have to take you home myself.'

'What was that about?' I ask as we walk to the car.

'"I'm forty-one years old, and I'll do what I want." That's what that's about,' she says. 'Quit writing to Steven and I'll tell her to cut it the hell out. Keep it up and . . .'

'That's fucking emotional blackmail, just like my father used to pull. "Do this or I'll cut you off." Steven is a non-issue, I don't care about him. What does it matter if I email him? I'd never cheat on you. Don't you get it?'

'Obviously not,' she says.

We leave it at that.

Why don't I just cut him off? Because I don't want to be told what to do? The emails are sporadic and not all that interesting. Even so, when he rings a few weeks later and tells me he's coming in for a conference, I arrange to meet him. I think perhaps this will snuff the suspicions once and for all. Cece'll see us together, realise there's nothing going on, his girlfriend will be there and we'll all be back to normal. Except the girlfriend doesn't show, again. During the meal, he pins me to my seat with his eyes. I stare him down. I want him to stop. He doesn't. Him and Cece launch into a duel, batting verbiage back and forth. She's talking louder and faster than usual with her 'me and Shiv this', 'Shiv and I that', 'right honey', 'yes sweetie', her arm around my shoulder, her hand on my head.

Twice when I laugh at something he says, she kicks me hard under the table. I can't wait to get out of the place. We don't talk on the way home.

Something has to give. We're slipping fast like a train that's about to run out of track. We'll move, I think, abandon 585 and its locker-room odours, get a new place, any new place. A brighter day, a softer, kinder tomorrow. I'm always headed for somewhere else, towards a future that presents itself in fragments, tiny spots of time which speak of hope. The trouble is, hope always vanishes. This time I want it to last.

After a bout of highly contentious negotiations I convince my father to sell 585, not that he understands my reasoning. What can I tell him? That my lady lover and I need a new start? What I do say is that the neighbourhood has gone down, prices are dropping, the plumbing is rotten. It's time for a change. The For Sale sign goes up, and we wait. Next off, I leave the Centre and its pack of disturbed gang kids, because I'm too tired to keep on fighting. I take a full-time job at the university teaching undergrads. I'm amazed that I get the position at all, given that my degree is in social work, not English, that I'm only halfway through the doctoral programme and have no work papers and not a hope in hell of getting any. I agonise for weeks, then, in desperation, give Julio $150 to get me a false social security card. I'd made it this far with the faded copy but I have a notion my luck's about to run out. In order to work, I have to turn criminal again. Smear the edges of fact and create a working document that entitles me to legal status. At least on paper.

I wait weeks for Julio to deliver the damn thing, and when he finally hands it over with some long-winded explanation of how it was manufactured out in California and that all the illegals are using them successfully, I have to laugh. It looks like it's been fabricated on a toy printing set. All the numbers and symbols are lopsided. I call my lawyer. What the hell can I do, I demand, I can't work, I don't have papers, I can't leave. I'm stuck. Yes you are, is all he says. So off I venture, over to the campus, with the torn-up, faded copy of my social that I've been carrying in my wallet for close to twenty years. The lady who greets me in the admin office is distracted.

'Oh, you only have a copy. We usually ask for the original.'

'I can get it,' I tell her, 'but I'm supposed to start this week.' Next thing you know she's signing affidavits, filling out forms and handing me a contract. I run out of the building into the midday sun. Life is good. Life works. I can work.

That week Jesse starts at University of Miami, on a $22,000 baseball scholarship. Cece convinces me to invade Target Super-stores and purchase this enormous black crate which we dutifully fill at considerable expense with toothpaste, shorts, blankets, towels, tissues, contact lens solution, all the things he'll need, she explains. 'Everyone does it.' I'd have preferred to get him books, a set of African beads, some designer shoes. But I listen to her, and am sorry I do when I see the confused look on his face as he fumbles through the shampoos and conditioners, the socks and boxer shorts. It's sad sitting with him that night on his bed. He's close to crying, and he's scared. He'd had surgery that year, to replace a torn ligament in his elbow, hadn't played for ten months and had never found his way back to form. But this was his chance, his big chance, part of the reason I couldn't leave Miami. It's sadder still driving him out to Coral Gables where we wade through a throng of anxious parents and their eager offspring under a gruelling sun, then help put his stuff away in the tiny dorm and make polite conversation with his room-mate's parents. We leave him there and drive off, Cece and me in the front, Daniel in the back, and a huge gaping silence between us. Jesse has always taken up a lot of space.

We're greeted at home by a frantic message from the real estate agent. The contract is signed. The house is sold. We have less than a month to find a new place. During the night as we sleep, the toilet, as if affirming that we've outstayed our welcome, floods, and we awaken to a thick layer of wet sticky gunge that has seeped under the door, into our room, across the carpet. Then Jesse calls.

'I have to leave here today, Mom. I can't play on the team. Some mix-up with my maths in high school. I took the wrong course. They won't let me play and if I attend even one class, I'll have to sit out two years. I need to find another school. They said they'll try and get me into Broward, the community college.'

'Jesse, this is ridiculous. You can't just leave like that. What about the scholarship? I have to go and teach five classes today, a hundred and twenty-five students, I can't get there.'

'Well, send Cece. I have to leave. Now.'

She flashes through traffic in her little burgundy Toyota to retrieve him. I head off for my first day of teaching. Jesse's big opportunity, his golden moment, has lasted all of twenty-four hours. We have three weeks to find a place to live. I scan the newspapers, contact agents, set appointments, and every last house I find has a problem: my father doesn't think it's a good area (what the hell does he know all the way over there in Dublin), too expensive, already under contract, leaking roof, uneven floors, too claustrophobic, bad lighting. Cece and I can't come to an agreement about any of them. Is the universe trying to tell us something, she asks me. Fuck the universe I say. I'll find us a house.

And I do, while she's visiting her family in Atlanta on Labor Day weekend. It's only a temporary rental and my father's footing the bill, again. For six months he says, that's it. And if I haven't found a place to buy by then, I'm on my own. But it's a beautiful old edifice with a balcony, a writing room, polished wooden floors, a bedroom each and two functional bathrooms. I can't wait to pick Cece up at the airport and take her there. But she hates the place the minute she sees it. Bad energies, she says, too many negative vibes.

'I hate the colour of the walls,' she tells me the day we move in, and truth be told it's one of the worst faux jobs I've ever seen. I have them repainted.

'I hate my room,' she says then, 'it's like a dungeon, hate, hate, hate it. I don't belong here. This just doesn't feel like my home. And you better tell your boys that our room is off limits, I mean off limits. No sitting on beds, no camping out and watching TV. Period.'

I say nothing.

I buy lamps and end-tables, adorn the place with cute glass ornaments, candle-holders, framed photos and pictures for the walls. I position gifts thoughtfully on her side of the bed to surprise her when she returns home. I send her flowers at work. I want her to settle in, to throw down some roots, so that I can uncoil into the cradle of a shared life, but her boxes remained packed, stretched like cobwebs across the hallway, eating up space, her books untouched in crates, her personal belongings stored in closed suitcases. I want simply to come home to her. Instead, I have to content myself with watching her entries and exits, to feel her only as a spectral, shadowy presence. There are moments, once or twice when we make love, when we return again to that tender place. I want them to last; they sizzle briefly like firecrackers and then burn out.

Our second week there, Julio shows up to see the kids for the first time in over a month. He hands me the child support.

'This is only a hundred dollars. What happened to the rest? I was expecting three times that.'

'Rest, what rest? This is what I have. I got my little daughter Yennifer' (another child whose name he can't pronounce). 'I work three yobs. Ju take it. Ju leave it.'

'Hey Dad, I'll take it,' says Daniel (that Capricorn thing for money).

Julio walks through the house, obviously impressed.

'This a nice place,' he says, 'but ju done shit to it. Ju no know how to paint. Who ju get to do the work, Haitians?'

'No,' I say, 'an expensive guy. Some pro.'

'He no do it like I do it.'

He smiles. The boys laugh. This is so typical of him, to tell me how to live my life, how to paint my house. To me, it's just Julio being Julio, insinuating himself where he doesn't belong. I listen to him as if from a great distance and think as he speaks what I've always thought, that his words are like toilet paper, good for nothing but wiping ass.

'Don't worry about the paint job,' I say. 'Concentrate on taking care of your sons. Just because you have a new daughter doesn't mean you forget them.'

'I no forget nobody. I here no?'

They drive off in his new jeep, and I know that they will return in less than two hours, angry. They always do.

As soon as they leave the fight starts.

'How can you let that good-for-nothing piece of trash come in here and take his dick out and piss all over our territory?' Cece demands.

'I didn't. That's just the way he is. Ignore him.'

'You don't seem able to ignore him. You kowtow. You take his side over mine. It's as if I don't exist.'

An hour later we're still at it. I try to see things from her perspective. I sit by her on the bed and hold her hand. I tell her that I love her not him, that he has long since ceased to be any kind of threat to her. In the end it doesn't matter. She hates me for having loved him, having fucked him. I can't reach beyond her revulsion of me – 'you'd suck your daddy's dick for a dime,' she says. And I am taken back once again to Tree Tops, and my father, to the look of repulsion that flooded his face whenever he mentioned Pat, the

Boomtown Rat. I become again, in the wake of Cece's fury, my father's whore, the slut who is just like her mother, who will never amount to anything, whose love is only good for reprehensible trash.

'You can't talk to me like that,' I tell her finally. 'I can't take it.'

'Poor little victim you,' she answers bitterly. 'This is who I am and where I'm at. Deal with it 'cause it doesn't look like it's about to change any time soon.'

I stay in the pale blue room writing for a long time. When I approach the bedroom Cece turns towards me. Through the half-light, her eyes fill with a brutish hue – dark, distant, cruel. I look at her face and find everything I know. In bed, she turns away from me, and as I lie beside her I feel like a small child, left behind. Panic sets in, the low seething quiet of insanity.

THIRTY-EIGHT

We're at the club again.

Why do we keep going back? Because there's not much for lesbians to do in south Florida? Because I'm a brave girl and can take the pressure? Because I don't believe that Cece will ever leave? Whatever the reason, I'm sitting in that bar in hyper-vigilant mode, watching Cece watching DW, checking every gesture just like I used to monitor my mother's every move at the breakfast table to make sure I knew when the slap was coming. We're side by side on stools facing the stage, like always. Cece's eyes widen as she watches. I notice in them a type of awe, and I recognise suddenly where I've seen it before. It was when she looked at me as we sat on the couch in Aunt Deb's living room before we got together. There it is, right before me, glimmering under the dim lights, parting the smoke, finding its way towards its target on stage. I see it and it frightens me.

Then there's the hug.

She even checks with me first.

'Should we just leave,' she asks, 'or should I go say goodbye?'

'Say your goodbyes,' I tell her. I try to force myself to glance away, but with the same kind of morbid curiosity that draws your attention to the scene of an accident, I catch sight of them in the light. They're clinging to each other. And what I sense jerks me back to a restless, anxious place I never wanted to return to. It reminds me with burning clarity of the day I'd gone to search for M at the hotel he'd moved into. Found my way to his door, stood outside, and listened. Two voices, a man and a woman, laughing and groaning. I'd kneeled down, pressed my face to the crack under the door and caught sight of a pair of women's shoes, a bra and panties. I knocked on the door hard. Stood there for twenty minutes, the most humiliating twenty minutes I'd ever lived through, before I finally walked away.

On the way home I question Cece:

'That was an intense hug. What was going on there?'

'Nothing,' she says. 'We always hug goodbye.'

'Not like that.'

Back at home, in bed, I ask again.

Finally she says: 'OK. I feel something for her, all right. The way she looks at me makes me feel wanted. When she holds me like that, something happens inside. She responds to me.'

'Feel what?' I ask.

A sweet, dreamy smile washes over Cece's face as she relives the moment.

I feel sick.

'The way she responds to me is the closest to the kind of love I want that I've experienced in a long time.'

Babbling, I say, 'But don't you see she's just flirting with you? She had six beers; you won't even let me touch you after one. She plays with you right in front of me. I hug you. I tell you I love you.'

'Not the way she does, not like you mean it. With you it's always a concession, something I have to beg for. She just gives it to me, no holding back.'

'She's got nothing to lose,' I say, 'nothing to risk. I don't see her hugging her own girlfriend like that. She barely holds her hand.'

'It doesn't matter,' Cece says. 'It's contrast for me, that's all, a point of contrast.'

I don't know it then but Cece is already gone. I hang on, digging my nails in, trying to claw my way back into her heart.

THIRTY-NINE

＾

She tells me she's leaving.

Two nights after that club incident, sitting there on the edge of our bed, normal as you please, with me still curled in sleep, the sun fading in against the walls. My eyes are slits, barely able to greet the light.

'I just can't do this any more,' she says.

I'm flummoxed, wedged between words. Me, the one who never finds quiet in her head or outside it, silenced. I start to open my mouth, but the look on her face – that jaded, I'm giving up for good this time, gaze of hers – halts me. I sit up and take a deep breath. My heart clutches into a knot the size of a penny. Stricken, I glance around the room, to the window and the walls, the bookshelves, the mirror, to the rows of candles placed on her side, the butt-infested ashtray on mine, then back at her.

'You can't give up on me now,' I tell her.

'Why the hell not?'

'I'll change. I'll do whatever you want. Stop drinking, stop writing to Steven. I'll be nicer, more considerate, compassionate, loving, caring. Whatever you want. I'll do it. I promise.'

I realise this sounds an awful lot like begging.

'It's no good, Shiv,' she says finally. 'I'm done. It's too late.'

A total of six weeks after we'd moved into the house, she picks up her belongings, packs them into a suitcase and walks away. I'm left on the bed in the 'dungeon' of a room we'd shared, surrounded by her boxes, the remainder of her clothes, her books, her vitamin bottles, her photos and the scent of her perfume. I can't move, can't make it to the bathroom, can't wash myself, or prepare myself something to eat. The world whirls around me. Faintly, I hear the trains rushing along the tracks, the chirping of the birds outside my window, the croaking of that manic rooster next door, and the chatter of my sons below, but I am flattened on that bed, not an ounce of life left in me. I have entered a dead space. Eventually I manage to get up, walk to the bathroom, back to the bedroom, down to the kitchen, and into the pale blue writing room.

I force myself to sit at the computer. I will my hands across the keys. I have nowhere to put this grief. I have to write it out. The blank paper can hold it. I feel so raw, so broken, and I don't know how to get whole again. So I sit in front of that screen for seven hours and I write. About my mother and my sister Roberta, about my body and all the places that hurt and all the things I've lost. When I'm done I print out thirteen pages. It feels like that's all that's left of me. Words.

I read them over and over. The house is quiet, almost ghost-like. Dreadful images fill my head: me dead, me alone, me frozen. A memory comes: I am sitting in the middle of a large room with high ceilings. The floor beneath me is cold. The room is empty and the door is locked. I am waiting for my mother. I sit for a long time, without moving. I am not afraid because I know she will come to get me. But she doesn't come, and the light outside the windows fades to dusk, then to black. I begin to cry. I think to myself: If I am a good girl, if I stay put in this spot as I was told, she will rescue me . . . I'm not sure how I ever got out of that room. Not all of me did;

a part of me remains there, paralysed by fear, determined to be brave and not to cry, resolved to never move.

Tears fall blindly down my face as I remember this. I wish my mother was here to hold me. Or my Pop, or Mr Walsh, or even Teresa. Someone who could make this pain stop. I sit still in the chair. My hand moves across my body and settles in the hollow underneath my breast where all my losses live. I feel the heat of my fingers piercing through my shirt and the icy chill of the space beneath them. Every part of me is screaming, a violent, besieged scream that makes no sound. I focus on my breath, inhaling long, even shafts of air, and try to force myself back into my own body, to power my breath back into my flesh and make it stay. For a moment, I am calm, grounded. Then I look up and see that the room has grown dark, too lonely. I cannot sit in it. I move through the corridors, looking, waiting. I can't stand the sight of her things or the scent of her that lingers in the air. And I can't block the memories. Finally, I rush out to the car, drive down the street, buy cigarettes, smoke a pack, enter a restaurant, can't order, order, can't eat, leave, then drive past Janice's house where Cece's staying, supposedly to cat sit, even though she hates cats. See her car in the driveway, stop, cry, drive on, back to the house, lie in bed, hold myself, cry again, try to stop my thoughts, to fill that goddamn hole, to pack the crater shut. I'm going to die, I think, right here, of a broken fucking heart.

The phone rings, and I wait to hear her voice on the other end. A bill collector. I see vaguely through my grief, my sons, on the edge of the wall that divides me from the world, standing, watching, their eyes filled with a fear I haven't witnessed since the M days.

'Get up, Mom,' Jesse says, from the doorway. 'You can't fall apart on us now. You've got to be strong, like you taught us.' I try to listen, but words don't reach me. Nothing does. I go to class the next morning, stand in front of the students, wade my way through a particularly difficult passage of literature, but feel so close to crying that a voice over in the corner blurts out:

'Are you OK, Professor Woolfson?' It's David, the New Yorker who insists on staying every day after class to show me his poems. He walks me to my car, carrying my books in his arms. The look on his face, a kind of love, sends me hurtling from the room. Throughout the day I keep the mobile phone on, something I never do when I'm teaching, just in case she calls. She doesn't.

At night, the hell starts over. The pacing back and forth, smoking cigarettes, driving to nowhere. I arrive home shattered. I can't sleep. I try her at Janice's. The answering machine. I dial until my fingers ache. I lie in bed, and the words of that old Elvis Costello song, 'I'd Rather Be Anywhere Else Than Here Today', repeat themselves in my head like a mantra. But there's nowhere to run to. Anywhere I go, I know I'll walk smack into the same God-awful loneliness. My body hurts, literally aches. I lie in the darkness and think about holding her, making love to her, think so hard that I imagine I can conjure her up. I feel her presence beside me, and dip periodically into a dreamy blur in which she magically appears. I stroke her hair, kiss her face, hold tight to her hand, then realise there is nothing beside me but a pillow. I wonder why she left, why now, when my heart is wide open. 'Please, please, God, please bring her back,' I cry into the darkness. 'Please girlie, please come home. Just come home.'

A car pulls up outside. I race to the balcony, knocking over the nightstand. Under a gentle sky I stand and witness the neighbour, the one I've never spoken to, emerge silently and slip behind closed doors.

I'm waiting. Standing on a balcony, watching water dribble from the heavens. Water that covers my face, my shoulders, my back. I feel it drop softly against my body. I'm waiting for the woman who left.

I have been here before.

FORTY

⸻

God knows how I survive the next few weeks.

Blasted, interminable patches of time, every moment of which I spend in heartbreak, like a zombie mooching around the periphery of my own existence, driving through streets without recognising them, digesting food without tasting it, talking without thinking, teaching without connecting. I start behaving like a stalker. Wherever she is, whatever she's doing, I know about it. There's a false comfort in tailing her, as if she can't slip away from me really, not for good, if I can somehow keep up. It's not that difficult. When her tenure with the cats ends, she transfers over to her Aunt Deb's mismatched apartment which is much like the eight or so previous apartments she's inhabited since I've known her. Deb has always lived in places that smell of week-old spaghetti, with kitchens that overflow with garbage and couches that harbour, in addition to cushions, socks, food particles, toys and electrical equipment. But wherever she's lived, I've found a spot on the sofa (amidst the rubble) that I could retreat to when I felt like I had nowhere else to go. Which was often. So I call Deb every morning as I've always done, and she tells me, 'Cece's doing well', or 'Cece was upset last night', or 'She just left', or 'She'll be home in an hour, she went off to meet this one or that one'. I keep track. Vigilantly. Until the night she doesn't show.

'I can't imagine where she could have gone to,' Deb says when I clock in for the fifth time in an hour. I can. I check the gig listings, find out where the singer's playing, call the club, describe Cece to the polite barmaid, have her take off on a reconnaissance mission and sure enough, within seconds, she's back, at the other end of the phone, describing a woman that matches Cece perfectly, right down to the little black jacket she's developed a fondness for since she lost the weight. She's at a table in the corner the barmaid informs me. I sit on the edge of the bed cradling the receiver until that awful monotone beep starts. I see it all: she's there, right in front of that singer, nothing between them to melt the wanting. Cece'll probably be swaying that big undulating behind of hers, shimmying up and down like a lap dancer, and that singer will be tracking every move with her lusty eyes, raunchy hand gestures and sly, flirtatious comments. Who knows what might happen, and they're two hours' drive away, and that's if I do eighty. I can't erase the image. My head starts to throb.

Got to keep moving. That's what I tell myself. Keep pushing forward. Leave the torment behind. I pull on my jeans and head for the car. I drive, by rote, past the places we inhabited together: the Bella Donna on Biscayne where we had what we referred to at the time as 'our first real date', which meant that we sat across from each other in a candlelit room and ate precious little of the over-priced food. It was thrilling, so deliciously naughty. I stop at the traffic lights at the West Dixie intersection, where Cece used to make a point of kissing me in broad daylight, and I remember how terrified I was that the neighbours, or my kids, or even worse, their friends, would catch me with my tongue in a woman's mouth. At each juncture, I am tugged to awareness of a kind of geographic binding that came about as I metabolised her presence into my life. But there is tremendous danger in setting your markers, your tags of connection to a place in another person. Without Cece, I travel through these streets a stranger, unhinged from what was keeping me here.

Without realising it, I arrive at 585, the last house we truly shared. I stall in the driveway and remember the Valentine's night when we sat together in her car. I remember feeling then the beginnings of hope and a tentative belief that I could last in Miami another while. It seems so long ago now. Without her, there is nothing to anchor me to this city, this country. I struggle now to come upon the truth: why had I put the brakes on loving and sent her away?

Sitting alone, in the fading light, memories flood through me: I am three years old, wavy brown hair, a wide smiling face, eyes so large they take in too much of the world at a glance. I'm holding my mother's hand, tight. She's walking fast; my little legs can't keep apace. I gaze up at her as we swing through the doors of Newells Children's Wear on Grafton Street. She lets me sit on top of the toy pony in the centre of the shop. I try on outfits, one after another, until I'm exhausted, stand before the mirror as she appraises me. 'Makes you look too fat, too short, the hem's not right, that one's pretty.' She purchases six in total. Six new dresses. I hate dresses. I'm a tomboy, she says. The elderly shop assistants with their frosty grey hair, painted fingernails and grandmother faces, tell her what a lovely daughter she has. She smiles that sensual smile, ruffles my hair, kisses my cheek. It's the kind of moment I live for. All the way home, I stare up at her with devotion. But when we reach the house, she turns. I say something wrong – that I'm tired, that I don't like some of the dresses – and she drags me up the stairs. The carpet hair cuts into my back. When we reach the top, she pushes me back down. I cling to the banisters and count the steps as I tumble forward. The bottom seems so far away. Sometimes making love to Cece, I felt again like I was plummeting head first down those stairs with nothing to break my fall.

Before the shock treatments, my mother found joy in her body. I saw this when she'd call me into the sitting room, turn on the gramophone, and just dance, with a raw wantonness that radiated across the room. She'd rumba, samba, foxtrot, twist, tango, all for my benefit, with her head thrown back, her eyes wild, and her feet manoeuvring in bewitching motion. I loved to watch her, but when, at her behest, I tried to imitate her, I'd stumble over myself and she'd laugh or sneer. Years later, I stood on the sidelines at the club watching Cece, like I did that last night, watching others watching Cece. She beckoned to me, sidled up to me, rubbed up and down against me, and though every cell in my body wanted to answer her, I remained completely still. I had learned too well that responding is dangerous.

I make these connections only now that I am alone. And I wonder when precisely it was that I stopped allowing the world to enter me, what the cut-off point was. And then I recognise something essential: I have lived my life waiting for the moment when I would again be flung down a staircase, or tickled until I wet my pants and beaten when I actually did. I have expected always that the hand that caressed me would become the hand that couldn't help but strike me, that the lips that claimed they loved me would before long diminish and mock. This is what I carry in me.

FORTY-ONE

I look around me.

Daylight has been washed away. Outside the air is still, thick. A light goes on in my old living room; the door opens and a figure approaches the car.

'*Ola, chica, como estas?* (Hey girl, how are you?)'

'*Bien, bien, sentada aqui mirando la casa* (Good, good, just sitting here looking at the house).' I can lie in Spanish too!

'*Entra, quiero enseñarte lo que hemos hecho* (Come on in. I want to show you what we've done).'

I can't refuse. After all, she bought the crumbling place. I can see already that they've managed to rid themselves of the overgrown bushes, the weeds, the overflowing garbage cans, the wild mess of gardenias that used to populate the flower-beds under the window, which bloomed for two full days in summer and blocked out the light the remainder of the year. The house is barren, my life there drained out, excised, along with the debris. Suddenly Nelda is beckoning for her husband, her daughter, her son, her aunt, her uncle, her dog, all of whom have taken up residence where I used to live. The puppy flaps amiably at my heels, taking an immediate fancy to one leg in particular. The daughter is smiling, gracious. I follow them inside. Instantly I am struck by order. Vanished are the litter of paper wrappers, Burger King bags and assorted oddities (photographs, artefacts, family heirlooms, passports, Hebrew prayer books) that covered all available floor space; the array of old and unused vitamin bottles that adorned the dusty counter, the towering stacks of unpaid bills, gone. I notice, too, cracks in the wall sealed, taps fixed, peeling paint retouched.

I sit awkwardly on the slender couch, tentatively balancing a scalding cup of *café con leche* that Nelda has deposited in my hands. Voices float through the air: the uncle, a carpenter, the husband, a plumber, the son, a Godknowswhat, all talking. The paint, the wallpaper, the tubes, the pipes, the leaks, the foul electrics, the faulty alarms, the dismally fractured windows and swollen doors. I've landed in Do-It-Yourself hell. A cracked smile is plastered across my face. It's hurting my cheeks. Looking around me, I can't help wondering why it has been so hard for me to build a durable container for life, why it was that my friends seemed capable of creating homes, with potted plants and charming *chatzkas*, with functional kitchens and dogs that behaved, and I instead had fashioned a bunker existence. Walls, floorboards, ceilings, a bed. That is how I have lived. Always.

'*El cuarto tuyo, tienes que ver lo,*' says Nelda with pride, 'you jus' haf to see it.' I don't want to see the bed where Cece and I made love. But they're behind me, the whole troop, pressing forward, proud of the transformational powers that have turned my crumbling tenement walls into such a delightful habitat. They bear down on me with bright, proud, insistent faces. First off, I spot the gargantuan dresser, the monstrous oddity that a friend dropped off in my bedroom one night, and that stayed in the closet for ten years, drawers empty, because I just couldn't get it out. Now repainted, it sits to one side, elegant. The broken ceiling fan that hung precariously on a live wire for the duration of my stay (I don't know how many nights I dreamed that it knocked me dead in my sleep) has also been replaced. Then I see the bed, perched on the black wrought-iron frame I'd left behind.

'*Qué te parece?* (What do you think?)' inquires Nelda, smiling broadly.

What do I think?

I stare at the bed. The purple comforter is gone. The pillows, hers flowered and fluffy, mine, a thick grey sickbed cushion, gone. I can no longer shield myself from the bare and simple fact: this is not my home, this is not my bed and Cece is not my partner. Any more. There's a faint noise, the shallow breaths of Nelda and Co. stationed behind me, waiting for me to speak. I can't. Nelda leaves the room. I hear the opening and closing of drawers, the brisk rustling of papers. She returns and hands me a large stack of envelopes, mostly bills.

'*Se ven importantes, no?*' (They look important?) she says. Her hand is outstretched. Her eyes are soft. Perhaps she knows what I have left behind. I take the papers and kiss her on both cheeks. It seems like the obvious thing to do.

Outside in the car, I turn on the engine, and glance at my watch. I have been inside for fifty minutes. My father is arriving in a few hours, on one of his biannual whistle-stop tours. I'm supposed to meet him in the lobby of the Sea View at seven. Meeting him is taxing at the best of times, when I'm fully intact, and virtually untenable when I'm falling apart. I take a deep breath and head for home, where hopefully my sons will be waiting, decked out in their best, ready for our tryst with their grandfather and his wife.

The drive over the Broad Causeway to meet him is the same as always – swift stop to valet the car which, less than three years after he purchased it for me in 1995 looks like a dirt carriage from the Stone Age with an acute aversion to water, followed by rapid make-up application at every traffic light until we reach the hotel, with a few additional dabs of lipstick and perfume mid-motion. Tonight I can't seem to mask the sadness, no matter how much make-up I apply. The gnawing in my stomach sharpens with every passing mile. I'm afraid that my father will expose me and will know what my life is made of. In my head, as I drive, I hear his beleaguered, monotone, 'Didn't I send you money last month to fix that awful-looking bang on the hood, hmm? Suppose you spent it on something more important? This car looks like it belongs to a tramp.' Jesse's voice breaks through this in-brain chatter:

'Mom' (uttered with the anguish of someone enduring a particularly strenuous bathroom experience), 'don't get all nervous tonight. Every time we visit Grandpa it's the same thing. You start acting like a child, like you're afraid to speak or let him know things.'

'Yeah,' chimes Daniel, 'and I don't want tuna fish again. I eat cheeseburgers. If he's really a millionaire, let him buy us food we'll eat.'

'It's not the money. It's the kosher thing. Respect, that's all.' Suddenly I realise how very much like him I sound. We drive on in silence, and in the ten minutes it takes to reach the Sea View, half of me goes missing. I'm getting into mode, a neutralising of self so thorough that the very man who made me won't even begin to recognise what he's fashioned. That telling admonition hangs between us as we clamber through the gates. Before I've even dislodged the key from its socket, the valet is hovering by the window. I want to tell him I'll park it myself to avoid the charges, but that doesn't fit with the image I've concocted. In my fictional life, I can afford to valet park, so I take the chance that my father will shove a few bills in my direction at dinner, under the table, of course, away from his wife's surveillance. Car dispensed with, we trot through the varnished wood-and-glass doors, the marbled floors, past the ornate, gilded mirrors that catch me off guard in their glare (God almighty, I think, he'll never stop talking about the extra thirty pounds, and my hair, I forgot to give him advance warning about the cut), past the concierge who appears to have fallen asleep under his cap and is emitting sounds that indicate immediate need for a respirator, towards the reception desk. In the kind of jittery body language that's become my trademark, I signal for the boys to take a seat on the row of variously uncomfortable high-backed chairs that adorn the middle of the lobby. I venture off towards Mary, the self-same receptionist I've approached upon arrival for the past eighteen years.

'Can I help you?' she inquires without a hint of recognition, in the kind of imperious County Kerry accent I used to abhor back when I lived in Ireland.

'I'm here for Mr Woolfson, the same Mr Woolfson I've been visiting for the past twenty years.'

'Oh, that Mr Woolfson,' she ventures finally, 'from Dublin, is it?' at which point she picks up the phone and dials his room. After the prescribed twenty-six rings, someone answers and informs her, whereupon she informs me, that they will be down shortly.

The boys, slouched on brocade, look as if they're about to be subjected to a colonic irrigation, so I amble off to the shop where I'm greeted by the same rack of dusty magazines and fossilised perfumes that have been there on the past ten visits, and the cashier cum society dame who's been boasting the same towering champagne frosted hair-do for just as long. But she manages a smile, and God knows in such austere and superficial surroundings, that touches me. Finding nothing published post-1994, I return to the lobby. I catch a glimpse of my father and Adele peering through the elevator doors. Just as I'm about to wave, the doors close.

'That was Grandpa,' the boys announce. 'Why didn't he get out?'

I'm suddenly overwhelmed by a barrage of surreal memories: my father driving through Miami streets in a rental car, trying to get from one lane to another, without bothering to indicate, probably because he couldn't find the mechanism, the near crash that ensued, Adele's panic and his calm retort, 'They drive very poorly here in America'; or the time he promised to attend Jesse's baseball game and I found him stuck on a corner a block away (in a different rental car), with the wipers zigzagging frenetically across the windows, the horn blaring, the lights pulsating, everything moving but the car itself. When he finally noticed me, he looked up and said, 'I should have taken the Lincoln.' By the time I pointed out that the car was still in park, the game was all but over.

I watch the elevator lights go from the second to the third, the fourth, the seventh to the tenth floor and back down again. When they finally exit in the lobby, they're as exhausted as if they'd just flown in from Africa on a one-engine plane. Immediately he comments on my haircut (makes you look twenty years younger) and, for openers at least, tenders no mention of the thirty pounds that hang loosely from my hips. He says the boys look well, and why wouldn't he, they're groomed to the nines. His wife smiles evenly in our direction – a good sign.

He wants to go to some Jewish chicken palace that he's tracked down through the concierge. She wants 'anything' kosher, the boys want hamburgers, and I want somewhere nice and quiet that serves excellent wine. I really need a drink. We hail a taxi, and head for Forty-first Street, home of all things Jewish. By the time we arrive, we're hyperventilating from the squash. Avi's chicken palace looks about as appetising as Denny's at dawn. We hover in the doorway. My father glances around, smiles that rueful grin of his and suggests that I embark on a reconnaissance mission of the nearby eateries. Eventually, we settle on a posh Italian establishment two doors down.

The meal progresses in typical fashion with the waiter spilling a few precious drops of Merlot on my father's polyester garment within the first five minutes, Adele rubbing frantically to erase the damn spot, followed by the proverbial interrogation of the chef regarding the absence of meat stock from the dishes, the typical humming and hawing over the orders and the inevitable *faux pas* that ensue when your life is a covert operation. Jesse and Daniel have never quite captured the need for stealth. Why can't Grandpa know that we're broke despite all the money he sends, that we never go to synagogue and don't intend to, that you have sex with a woman, that you loved that woman, that she is gone, and now you are sad? They have no context in which to place the lies and half-truths that serve as the narrative of our lives for my father, or the tacit agreement that he and I have forged over the years: I pretend to be more like the daughter he wants; he continues to send me money. I rationalise this pact with the knowledge that he cannot face his eldest daughter and her two black sons on Irish turf. I've heard enough of his Israel speeches to understand my options. I have stayed away and learned to excel at pretence. I have become adept at something else too: I know how to steel myself against the arc of memory.

I sit across from Adele who is still smiling, albeit with some strain. I see her thin, painted lips move. She is talking about her grandson, the one they visit each weekend in Leeds, the one whose nappies my father changes, the one who slips into his bed on Saturday mornings, the only one in a long line of toddlers who can actually claim the attentions of a grandfather. The Messiah, we, my brothers, sister and I have titled him, for the remaining grandchildren, though bound by blood, receive precious little of his time, far less of his love. This child is special to him, very special because he belongs to her, or at least to her daughter. I see the warmth in her face as she describes his antics, a typical grandmother's love. And the pride in my father's eyes.

Messiah dispensed with, she moves on to her next love, Gribbets the cat (named, quite cleverly I think, after a machine my father's company uses to dissect foam), how he miaows and pesters when they return after a night out until they give him the choice piece of salmon they've salvaged, how he's treated like royalty in the prestigious cat hotel he frequents when they travel (which is often), how he hides in my father's study, and chases his own tail. There's kindness to her voice when she speaks of this cat. She passes his photo across the table. He humanises her; I recognise that. Yet, floating along the edges of the moment, there is something else. The stranglehold of our mutual history. The past I can't let go.

Snap, snap, Jesse's fingers spark against my face. 'Earth to Mom, dinner's over, come back.' And this from the young man who has studiously perfected the art of the blank stare, who can sit for hours at a stretch without the merest twitch of a facial muscle. I see that my father is negotiating with the waiter about an item on the bill. A soup that wasn't ordered, or rather that was ordered and returned because it turned out to have chicken stock. In response to the waiter's heavy South American accent, my father has opted for the Lubavitch/Eurotrash twang he seems to produce any time he engages in conversation, even, momentarily, with a foreigner. As kids we used to laugh at this, how quickly his intonation switched, how incomprehensible he became given the slightest opportunity. Tonight, though, it is more endearing than funny. I listen to him grapple for words in the language he has spoken all his life and want to hug him.

'How much should I leave for the tip?' he asks then. Always a sore point, and often during our outings, I end up adding to whatever paltry pittance he's deposited on the table, no matter how broke I am at the time.

'Ten per cent?' he continues.

'Good God, *no*,' I exclaim in horror, 'at least fifteen.'

'Easy enough for you to say,' he snaps back. 'When you're earning and taking me out for dinner, you can leave twenty per cent.' I don't feel like hugging him any more. I feel like running from those watered-down eyes.

Then it starts.

'You have got to change, Shivaun,' he says, 'or you'll never amount to anything. I won't always be around to pick up the pieces, you know. You won't have me for ever.'

I look down and see that I am holding Gribbets's picture in my hand. I have been staring at it, probably for a full three minutes. Adele is looking on eagerly, waiting for my response.

'He sure is a character that cat of yours,' I say finally, though I'm thinking that the creature probably eats better than I do, certainly sleeps better in his posh little hotel. Jealous of a damn feline. I must be going insane.

'Yes, that's what you'd call him. A character,' she says and laughs.

Meanwhile the waiter has recovered from the Merlot spill and is standing to my side, proffering an eloquent speech about the desserts for the evening. He's holding some creamy concoction that bears a striking resemblance to a penis. My father opts for a cappuccino, and I can't say I blame him. The boys, of course, order the most expensive items on the menu. They've produced all of three sentences apiece throughout the meal, each in response to a question from my father. School, baseball, synagogue! Yes, double yes, NO!

'Are you still working in that Center, with the children?' my father inquires, to break a brief silence.

'The gang kids,' I say, 'no, I told you I'm teaching English at the university now.'

'Oh yes, I remember. Teaching foreign students, is it?'

'No, Daddy, teaching literature, composition, creative writing, teaching.'

'Really, and how much does that pay? Hope it's better than that other place. What was it you did there again?'

I can't believe what I'm hearing. Just nine months ago, in a different Italian restaurant, on a different night, I'd proudly produced my portfolio of newspaper clippings, photographs and awards: Center changes lives, Gang kids turn around. Woolfson says . . . Woolfson confirms . . . Woolfson states . . . Picture upon picture.

'I still think,' he says, 'with all the money I've put into your education, bright as you are, you should be earning a decent wage. You could work in a bank, in a corporation, anywhere you want.'

The cavernous pit in my stomach that always surfaces in his company opens. On this particular night, the fissure inside of me is unusually large. As I sit beside him in this elegant restaurant, I want very much for him to know that I found love, that it has gone, and because of that, I need him. I want him to know about Cece (the girl he'd proclaimed was so nice when he met her at Jesse's bar mitzvah), to know that she brought me chicken soup in bed when I was sick, that she called when she said she would, that she bent on her knees to scrub my wasted kitchen floor until it shone, that she made love to me like she meant it. And promised to stay for ever. I want him to turn his face towards mine and to listen. Really listen. What I desire from him now is that same careful tenderness he displayed when I was a kid, sick with fever, when he'd appear, out of the shadows by my bed, feel my brow, hand me my medicines, and sit by me until I slept. I want my father back. Not the business associate he's turned into, whose sole interest in me seems to be how much I am costing. But instead he talks about his hip operation, and how painful it was, and the trip he's just taken to Israel, via Budapest, and the lovely Jewish people he met there. Because he finances my world, he is able to ignore it with tremendous ease. It is not the world he wants for me. What I find when his wine-soaked eyes meet mine is disappointment. Nothing else.

FORTY-TWO

We're back in the Sea View lobby.

The boys are on the hard chairs. Adele has gone up to change. My father orders a stiff whiskey from the bar and guardedly hands me a wad of notes. I stuff them inside my bra (a residual from the M days) without counting them.

'Is that how you handle money?' he asks. 'No wonder you never have any. You'll lose that.'

'I won't. It's very safe.'

Silence.

There's not much to talk about when money is out of the way.

'With your luck,' he says then, 'somebody will rob you on the way to the parking lot. That's the kind of thing you attract. You buy cars that don't work, get jobs that don't pay, houses that fall apart. I just don't understand how you could have turned out like this. All the opportunities you've had. All I've done for you, and still . . .'

'Stop,' I say quietly, 'please stop. I'm doing better now, since I got the degree. Much better.'

'Ah, degree, *schemee*, where did it really get you? You still can't work in this country. I tell you Israel is where you need to be. You don't need papers, don't need permits. You're a Jew, the boys are

Jews, that's all that matters there. But of course, why listen to me? What do I know? You and all your high-flying plans. Not once have you said, OK Daddy I'll do it your way, just once, and see. Not once. Never.'

The boys have roused. They glare at me. Speak, they are saying, speak up for yourself. Be an adult, for God's sake.

I am silent.

'What time should I get you in the morning,' I ask finally, 'for the lawyer?'

'Oh yes, the lawyer, suppose he'll want another $10,000 out of me. Are they getting anywhere at all? Have they said you'll be able to get work papers? Americans, they charge you every time they blow their nose. Maybe it's all for naught.'

'What time then?' I ask again.

'Nine o'clock,' he says, rising from his chair.

The visit is over.

We drive back across the Causeway in silence. I feel inside my bra, pull the wad out at the traffic lights and count three one-hundred-dollar bills. Less than last time, better than nothing. I'll be able to keep the electric on, pay half the phone bill and buy some groceries. All of a sudden I feel dizzy. The wine is slowing me down. The lights change. I stall. I can't seem to push forward. A police car pulls up alongside me. He stares straight at me. I don't have insurance. Haven't paid my tickets, have no resident alien card. Fuck. 'Don't show your fear,' I say to myself. 'Hold it in. Keep moving, and he'll mind his own business.' I glide away from the traffic lights, slowly, like I haven't been behind the wheel of a car in twenty years. I'll be arrested for drunk driving, thrown in the back of that police car, my wrists bound in steel. I can't go back there.

'What the hell is wrong with you, Mom?' Jesse asks suddenly. 'Why are you driving all over the road?'

'The police,' I say, 'right there behind us. Jesus, don't look around. It'll draw attention.'

'Mom, the way you're driving is what's going to draw attention. Why would they stop you? What have you done? Forgot to pay the tickets again?'

'Shit man, Mom's off to jail,' Daniel says, 'like the last time. They stopped her for that illegal turn and I sat down real low in the car. It was late at night. The guy took pity on us, let her go, because of me. Don't think it'll work this time, Mom.'

I rifle through my bag, pull out my bottle of blood pressure pills and pop one in my mouth. I remember being stopped, not having any, feeling like I was going to die, right there, on the side of the road, with Daniel hunched up in the front seat.

'Chill, Mom,' Jesse says then. 'We're driving home from a night out. We are going over this Causeway, down our street, and into our house.'

The police car passes and speeds out of sight.

I'm tired of feeling that everything can be taken from me in an instant. The terror has embedded itself so deeply in me, it feels like part of my body. Those dreaded sounds and images – sirens blasting, doors clanging, cold stares, hardcore walks and furious talk – have infiltrated my brain and corrupted it. I can't think straight. My arms tingle. I start to sweat. Every moment of the last twenty years weighs down on me. I don't know where I am, where I'm headed or how to get there. I've read about symptoms like mine. They belong to men and women who've seen horrific things, who've lived unspeakable lives and witnessed death too close. They pull at their own hair, make marks on their skin and fidget. They talk to themselves in a shuddering vocabulary that lives under their breath. They are the ones who cannot stay still, who crave answers and who continue to question even when they have them.

'Stop off at Rafik's for some drinks, two for me, two for Bro,' Jesse says then. The clarity in his voice jerks me back. I look around and see beautiful eyes and expansive smiles breaking across finely sculpted features. They were afraid. Now they are calm.

'OK, I say, and Reese's Pieces, two each, right?' This is our life together: soda and chocolate treats.

Next morning I'm up early. I wait for my father in the lobby. He finally emerges sporting an Adele-inspired ensemble: slacks, Hushpuppies, shiny polyester shirt and a wool cardigan, emblazoned with boldly coloured rectangles. He's losing more than his memory, I think. But he's smiling. On the drive through the city he tells me about the previous evening. He'd had a meeting planned with a business associate he'd never met, only knew that the guy would be wearing a brown jacket. So he spots a likely contender in the lobby, goes up to the man, introduces himself, has a ten-minute conversa-tion about business, before realising that he has the wrong guy. That's my father, I think, as I listen. That's the man I love, with the dry wit, the offbeat way of looking at the world.

I haven't lost him yet.

We sputter down Brickell Avenue (I'm hoping he won't comment on the strange noises from the engine) with its lavish condos, banks and corporate offices.

'This is where I used to send you the money, to the Allied Irish Bank, right?' he asks.

'Yes,' I tell him, amazed that he remembers, 'but it's gone now, moved out of Miami. The Steinberg Torchell offices are up there on the left, the tallest ones on the block.'

'Impressive,' he says. 'No wonder the fees are so high.'

I don't want to get into it with him, not right now anyway, but I think he's wasting his money. Steinberg might harbour the most expensive legal eagles in Miami but they don't do immigration, at least not the kind that I need. But the recommendation came from his Lubavitch connection and he refuses, as usual, to listen to anything I have to say. And, after all, it is his money.

They lead us through a marbled entrance, up into a glass elevator that looks out over Miami Bay. Stunning. Then into a hushed corridor, where elegantly attired men and women glide noiselessly through the hallway. Even the phones barely make a whimper. Finally, we're taken to the twenty-fifth floor, the penthouse restaurant where we're met by Henry Ryan, middle-aged, ruddy face and heaving chest, and Lawrence Cohen, younger, Jewish and sharp. We spend the next fifty minutes talking about golf, fiddling with the salmon on our plates, sipping chilled wine, totally ignoring a lunch that will surface a month later on the bill at a cost of $1,000. By the time it gets round to the coffee, we approach the matter at hand.

'Your daughter has a very difficult case here,' says heaving chest, sounding as if every breath is his last.

'I'm aware of that,' my father responds, 'that's why we've hired you. Now do you think you can help?'

'What we need from her,' interjects Cohen, 'is a kind of narrative breakdown of the events surrounding her arrest and after. I'm off to Nevada next week, very important case. Have her write it all out. I'll take it on the plane with me, as leisure reading, you know. Should be more entertaining that those awful airline mags they offer.'

Suddenly I feel transparent, like they're looking right through me on to the broad view of Miami Bay. I stare off into the distance, following the detached trail of their eyes, and imagine that I can see that awful building, with its three-inch windows, cement exterior and iron gates. The place where I almost lost my mind.

'Shivaun,' my father is saying, as his hand scratches across a cheque on the table, the latest instalment, 'you'll provide them with the information they need, right! Now if you say you're going to do it, you have to keep your word. Lawrence here will be waiting for the document. They can't possibly help you if you don't help yourself.'

'Yes, yes,' I say, drawing my eyes back in from the Bay. 'I'll write it all out. It's right here in my head.'

I deposit him an hour later on the steps outside his hotel. We hug briefly, but fiercely, and I know if I look into his eyes I will find tears. Driving away I spot his stooped frame, moving slowly through the lobby, towards the reception desk where he will press poor Mary from Kerry, or wherever it is that she's from, for his faxes, his phone calls, his urgent messages. I know too that he'll make his way gingerly up to his room where he'll pour himself a double whiskey before settling into an afternoon of work that doesn't need to be done: long, handwritten faxes dispatched to his staff in Ireland who will spend hours deciphering his illegible scrawl. But the writing of them, the act of hand on paper, will take his thoughts away from the morning's meeting and the daughter who just didn't turn out right.

FORTY-THREE

The house looms ahead.

The irony of that is not lost on me: finally finding the home you want and, at once, losing the person with whom you wish to share it. I open the front door and see her bulging cardboard boxes, strewn heavily across the floor of the back room, the enclave she claimed we'd fill with wide armchairs and classy magazines, so we could sit together, look out at the garden and read on Sunday mornings.

All the mornings have rolled together since she left.

I lie against the boxes, breathe in the smell of her, the lingering presence that's clamped itself over my home like a dead-weight. I can't shift it. So I do what I always do: go back in time, replay the story.

Maybe it was the night she finally met my writing students that did it. I'd been putting it off for months. But the last class, after their reading, we ended up at Periccone on Brickell. The students, by turns, complimented my teaching and each time they did, Cece placed her hand on my head and patted me lovingly. It felt like an enormous weight. She was nervous, I could tell, desperate to make a decent impression. The noise in the room was deafening, but above it all, I could hear her constant and increasingly heightened prattle. I sat there, gripping my utensils, suddenly disabled. Everything in the room liquefied, everything, that is, but the sound of her voice. I glared over at her then.

'Stop,' I wanted to shout at her, 'please, please be quiet.' And if, in that moment, I had been able to frame my truth in words, I would have said, if not aloud, at least to myself, 'because I don't want them to think you are crazy.' If, in that moment, I could have accessed the self-awareness that so often surfaces in retrospect, I would have understood that my terror belonged to a small, frightened child, the little girl whose mother had been taken away, strapped to a machine and shocked into submission, to the child still in love with the mother who talked too loud, laughed too hard and danced way too suggestively. All I knew then was that I had to interrupt Cece. So I did, with some offhand comment that steered the focus away from her and on to someone else. On the drive home, she asked,

'Why do you always have to shut me up? Why are you so ashamed of me?' I looked at her then, at her little-girl self, the one who had been sent away, belted into place and fed pills that blanched her brain. That was the price she paid for seeing; that was what they had done to her, the mother and the man who almost broke her. I wanted to take her in my arms and make her better because I have been trained to make everything all right for people who are not all right. But I also wanted to break her. Because I was fed up with how she saw me: a woman who let the world happen to her. Because at night when she called me baby or angel, when those words floated through the darkness towards me, I felt safe and warm. Yet, in an instant, I became her demon, and she'd spit other words at me, vile, obscene words about the men I'd loved and the things I'd done. And for the moment, I was all the things she said I was: trust-fund baby at forty, still running for cover when the rent was due, a battered princess who'd suck her daddy's dick for a dime. I often wanted to ask her if she could see what her rage did to me, how I disappeared in it. Most of all, I wanted to tell her that I needed her love, her compassion, not her hatred or her fear. I wanted her to know that I was no longer all that I used to be, but that I was still, and would always be, some of what I was.

And that's the truth of it. I know this as I sit clutching on to a bit of cardboard, running my fingers through her belongings. The fact is, in her presence, I become again the small child who sat at a window on a cold Dublin night and watched as her mother's back receded into the darkness, until it was engulfed by shadows and disappeared. I can't have my mother back, but I want Cece to look at me again with love, to touch me again with desire.

I'm not sure I'll make it without her.

FORTY-FOUR

I call her.

Yes, she'll see me. Maybe a movie.

We get to the new complex on Lincoln, and in the strange five-year-old voice Cece's taken to using, she tells me she wants nice treats, sodas, and popcorn, yogurt-covered pretzels and ice-cream. She devours them all, quickly, like a child. On the way home, she feels sick, but she wants pizza from Steve's anyway so I buy her that too. Outside Deb's house, I hold her close, feel the motion of her breath against me. I see myself touching her naked body. I can imagine my fingers running over her skin, along the scars, all the places her pain has been etched in blood, but she disengages from me quickly and lets herself out of the car. I follow her up to Deb's living room. She sits opposite me, a lifeless look on her face.

'Won't you even consider getting back together?' I inquire, desperate.

'It's very interesting,' she answers, 'this sudden claim of love. Next time you're with someone, you'll treat them right from the start. Next time you'll love them and cherish them. Next time,' her voice spirals 'you won't take them for granted. I'm going to be loved, and it's not going to be by you. Don't you understand, Shiv?'

She's shouting now.

'I don't want you anymore. I've outgrown this relationship. I'm not coming back. Do you get that?'

Deb appears suddenly in the corner of the room. Go, leave her, Shiv, her face says, walk away, save yourself. I pick myself up and trudge away.

Hours later, I sit in my bedroom alone; slowly a recollection forms, of the night my mother appeared on our doorstep, a few years after she'd left. She was in her bedclothes, half naked, holding on to the silver candelabra and the ancient vacuum cleaner.

'Your mother's run away,' my father said when I went downstairs to see what was going on, 'we're putting her up in the Orwell Lodge tonight, until I can secure a place for her at Grangegorman.'

I didn't want her to ever go back there.

The next morning Moira and I took my mother shopping. She wanted a dress and a miniskirt, a pair of jeans and a halter top. We waited in the car while she made her purchases.

'What's wrong with Mummy?' I asked Moira.

'Well, it's complicated, love. The doctors call it a diminished responsibility, like when someone can't live up to their duties.'

'And they think hooking her up to some machine and pumping her with electricity is going to help her face her responsibilities.'

'Not so much that, more like shift her out of the rut she's in?'

'Why did she get so angry when we were little?' I ask then.

'Ah love, it's not badness that's in your mammy, it's like a collapse. She was too young to be minding a child like Roberta. Then when she died, and her own mammy left her a week later, well I don't think she ever recovered is all. And your father's family isn't the easiest to get along with.'

'I know that. They never understood her. Always said she was too high and mighty for her own good.'

'Well, they should see her now.'

She floats towards us in a tight skirt and luminous lime-green top. She's waving to the shop clerk through the windows. Her smile is radiant. Her eyes are glittering. She tumbles into the car, light and laughter. 'Now then, girls, where are we off to?'

We dropped her at the Orwell Lodge, where we saw her into a cosy room on the fifth floor. All night, I worried about her.

'She'll be lonely,' I told my father, 'maybe we should just bring her here.'

'Shivaun, I know what I'm doing. We can't get too involved. Tomorrow I'll take her to the doctor's and she'll get the help she needs.'

Finally, I went to bed, but I was still wide awake when the phone rang hours later. My mother had taken it upon herself to run naked through the hallways of the Orwell Lodge. I watched my father put on his heavy winter coat and walk out to the car. A while later, he shepherded my mother into the house and told me to prepare the guest room. I tucked her into bed like a little girl, pulled the covers tight up around her neck, sat beside her and held her hand until she started to fall asleep. Then I left. Outside the door, my father told me to go back in and take out the razor he'd spotted on the nightstand, and 'any other dangerous-looking objects', he added.

I remember how responsible I felt. I think of Cece as a teenager, strapped to a bed in a mental ward, loaded up on Thorazine, and as an adult on those awful nights just before she left when she ate, vomited and ate again, then lay beside me shaking, calling out for her mother. I think too of the day I noticed criss-crossed lines carved into her ankles in blood. I recognise now how reluctant I have been to explore what my misgivings surrounding Cece are made of. I suddenly remember a poem I wrote to my mother as a teenager that I never got around to showing her. Frantic to find it, I rummage through old boxes. At the bottom of a crate, I come across a crumpled sheet of paper, covered in blue scratches. I can barely decipher the words, but these lines hit me: '*And I will spend my life falling in love with you. I will look to find you in every woman I meet.*'

From my mother I learned to laugh until our sides ached. I learned about love and loss, grief and madness, about stepping out and fitting in, about friendship and acceptance, about generosity and betrayal. She defied tradition when she and Teresa sat at our kitchen table and joked like old friends as they mindlessly folded sheets. She frequently raided my father's wardrobe to unload the contents on to unsuspecting vagrants. Our home often resembled a Salvation Army hostel cum animal shelter, and at any given time Tree Tops housed a horse, three cats, a few dogs and a bird (usually with a broken wing). There was the old candlestick merchant she kept in business, the tinkers whose horses she fed, the burned child in the hospital upon whom she lavished an assortment of gifts. My mother was a dichotomy: kindness and insight contrasted with an irrepressible desire to break into pieces. A child always on the verge of psychosis. I often stopped by the window of the outhouse in the garden to watch her paint, and I'd marvel at the sight of her splashing vibrant colours across the canvas. But I also watched her facial muscles tense as she whipped me with long slender fingers that left their mark. I was always amazed at her capacity to cause hurt.

I understand, as I acknowledge this, that I found in Cece that same unhinged quality, the erratic, impulsive trait that takes me home to such ancient places and that triggers in me such fear. And I know too where I hid in the face of her loving: behind lifeless looks and harsh responses so that my small, sad heart could stay open, even though loving her walked me by the hand back into the minefield of my youth, the minefield that exploded daily all around me in my mother's fists and my father's violent words.

As I sit with the crumpled, yellow paper in my hands, I stare into a dead space as if to locate the parts of me that slipped from my grip somewhere on the way to this moment. I face the year ahead and see that I will not survive it, not in Miami. Not alone. It occurs to me then that I must leave this country. I have lived for the past decade awaiting this moment, anticipating the instant when I would be set free, and it has arrived now not as a joyous occasion but as an edict simply to move on. And for a second I feel like a captive, trapped in the forest, frightened to return to civilisation. I think of the friendships I have formed here; of Deb with her cackling laugh, with whom I have spent every holiday for the past fifteen years, whose home is like my home; of Margaret, the first person I met in Miami, who used to walk Jesse back and forth in his stroller, when Julio was missing and I was losing my mind and who, today, stops in after work for a cuppa or a bottle of wine; of Janice, who reminded me of my mother the day I met her, with her cigarettes, morning coffee, airs and graces, dark glasses and voluptuous manner; of Josie with her soothing cello sounds; and of Cece, whose absence I cannot yet comprehend. These people have loved me. They nursed me when I was sick, lent me money when I was broke (which was often), laughed with me, cried with me, lived with me. I do not know yet how to walk away, but I know that I can no longer stay.

FORTY-FIVE

—◆—

The phone rings.

My father.

'Well, have you thought about your situation?' he demands, in a voice that's unusually austere.

'What situation?' I ask.

'Your work situation, getting a proper home, a proper life. I can't support you for ever.'

'I thought we went through all that today.'

'We did, but without results. I need answers, Shivaun, a plan of action. You're not a child any more. You're a middle-aged woman.'

I feel like a child.

'I can't really think straight right now,' I say. 'I don't expect you to understand this, but I've just come out of a three-year relation-ship and I'm really upset.'

'Who was he? I never knew about any three-year relationship you were in.'

'That's because I never told you. Anyway, it wasn't a he.'

Long silence.

'Oh, I see. For a woman who's supposed to be so smart, some-times you act very stupidly. Is that the kind of thing you want? Is that the way you want to bring up your children?'

'It just happened.'

'Just happened, Shivaun. That's not a life for you. I should have known something was going on. It's that big girl, isn't it? The one we met at the bar mitzvah. No wonder she was always answering the phone. And here I am killing myself, paying your bloody rent, so you can live like that. I won't stand for it, you hear me. Forget buying a house in Miami. I'm pulling you out of there.'

He's screaming.

I can imagine his hand waving up and down by his side on the other end of the phone, just like when I was a teenager off out with Pat. Back then he always told me I was raising his blood pressure and threatened to have a heart attack, and sometimes I thought he would. Today, though, I sense he doesn't have the energy for the histrionics.

The phone goes dead in my hand.

Through the night I dream; I see myself suspended in midair, with my feet dangling. I push downward, frantic to connect with solid ground. But I'm stuck, padlocked to nothingness. Suddenly a wind comes, a gentle gust that lifts me up and carries me away. Even in my dream I recognise it as a form of deliverance. In it I experience a soaring redemption, as if, in that instant, the last strings that are tied to the balloon that represents my life, holding me in place, are cut. Not cruelly, but calmly. Irrevocably.

FORTY-SIX

◆

'What do you guys think about moving?'

It's a simple question, one I've asked a hundred times before.

They're sitting on the edge of my bed in their soiled baseball gear.

'Here she goes again,' says Daniel. 'Where to this time, Mom? New York, Atlanta, San Francisco? You decide to move every three months and we never go anywhere.'

'London,' I say.

'England. Hell no,' interjects Daniel. 'That's where it rains non-stop, the food is lousy, and everyone has bad teeth.'

'Why London?' Jesse asks seriously.

'Well, it's better than Dublin if you're mixed, and maybe it wouldn't be such a good idea to be so close to my dad after being away so long. But I've got to get out of Miami.'

It starts just like that, the plan. Followed by a series of discussions with my sister in London who pledges to help set me up in the city that has been her home for the twelve years since she left Dublin.

'You could make it here, Shiv,' she says. 'It won't be easy, but I'll be there to see you through.'

A house is found, on the edge of north London, near hers. Tickets are purchased. A date is set.

I tell Cece. For a minute her eyes get all soft. In them, I catch the tiniest trail of her love for me. I watch closely.

If she asks me to stay, I will.

She doesn't.

At night, alone, I struggle with the decision. Here I go yanking my sons head first out of their lives. I look at those lives: Jesse fighting tooth and nail to make it on to some shitty community college team where the coach keeps him perched precariously on what he euphemistically refers to as the 'bubble', some haphazard, fledgeling spot he's reserved for players yet to prove themselves. But no matter how well Jesse plays, how many home runs he hits, he can't get off that damn bubble. It's down to percentages, the coach explains, something to do with bringing in a new pitcher, losing a catcher, recruiting an outfielder. Maybe then, there'll be a place for him on the team. Meanwhile, Jesse's looking tired and old, running into walls with his studies, tearing up his lists of goals and close to tears most of the time.

And he's had enough of it, enough of being yelled at on the playing field, jerked from games moments before the scouts arrive to see him, enough of waiting by the phone for the major leagues to call. Enough.

'I don't want to do this any more, Mom,' he says one evening, 'but I'm afraid to quit, afraid there'll be nothing else for me in life. Afraid I'll turn into a loser, working at McDonalds on minimum wage when I'm forty.'

'If you've had enough, then walk away,' I say. 'London or no London, you can't go on like this, never knowing from one minute to the next if you're on or off. Living off someone else's whims. Walk away.'

He does.

★

Daniel follows suit. Hands in his uniform and boots one dark evening after practice.

'I'm not a quitter,' he tells me, 'I just decided I couldn't take that shit any more. Raking the field for hours, being screamed at like I was an idiot. It's not for me.'

That night I am proud of the young men I've raised who know enough to know that you never have to pay for your life with your life. Know more than I ever did.

With baseball no longer in the equation, we sit and talk calmly. Jesse's excited about the prospect of change, as long as he can get into college. Wants to study creative writing. As it happens, he's damn good. Daniel's concerns are more practical. Who will give him the kind of fade haircut he's used to, where will he purchase his Fubu, Mecca and Boss clothes, where will he buy his CDs, DMX, Dr. Dre? What kind of gyms do they have? I tackle these issues one by one, and when I convince him that he will no longer have to study chemistry or even maths, but can concentrate instead on graphic design, photography and the subjects he likes, he consents. Reluctantly.

They spend a lot more time with their father in the months before we leave. Travelling across the Causeway in my car to sit with him, his wife and small daughter, Jennifer, in their cramped apartment on the beach. So much wasted time, they say. And so little time left. After one of these visits, they arrive home and Daniel retreats immediately to his room. When I enter hours later, I find him stretched on his bed, crying.

'I've said my goodbyes now,' he tells me. 'I'm ready.'

FORTY-SEVEN

⏤▲⏤

Two weeks to go.

I'm sitting in the pale blue writing room.

Surrounded by boxes. Mine this time. Sealed according to the shipper's instructions. Boxes filled with books, because after all these years here, that's all I want to take with me. Everything else has been sold: the TVs, VCRs, dining tables, lamps, kitchenware, desks. I need none of it. Twelve boxes I have. Twenty-one years of living packed into twelve cardboard crates.

I try, as I sit, to fathom what America has meant to me, what it has taken and what it has bestowed. I feel as if I have lost half my life here, but I know too that it is here that I became a mother and carved out a life. But living here has come at such exorbitant cost, for I have been taunted day after day by a pressing need to create and to instigate. I am good, I have discovered, at making things happen. I have embodied the Nike slogan. I have embraced the patriarchal mindset that suggests you are only as valuable as what you produce. And I have produced. The black portfolio I carry in my briefcase says so – exhibits, courses, centres, events, writings, newspaper clippings, artworks – they are all a testament to the bulk of my output. But they don't take into account the seepage factor that takes hold in this city, for no matter how bulky that portfolio became, my momentum trickled away as steadfastly as sand eroding. Miami is built on land reclaimed from swamp and sea. And those of us who live here have to fight hard against the wearing away of spirit, determined to make something stick, to plant something firm, forgetting all too often that you cannot build on that which is eaten away day in, day out, by nature.

There are other factors: for two decades I have battled what I've come to view as a primarily American outlook, the type of positive thinking which calls upon individuals to bypass and neutralise their personal truths in favour of a more optimistic collective reality. 'Don't worry, be happy' is the message. But there is no obvious benefit to me in pretending that I feel fine when in actuality I don't. On the contrary, there is something comforting to me in saying I feel like shit when I do, in admitting that I'm scared, depressed, sad, that I am affected, deeply so, by the world around me. I don't know how to subscribe to the kind of perpetual self-improvement philosophies that I have encountered so frequently here. They frighten me, and I have often wondered how I am ever to align my consciousness, which feeds on darkness and shadows and gravitates towards the uglier, less seemly aspects of life, with the upbeat attitudes of those around me. And because the stance that comes most naturally to me is grounded in a need to experience both the beauty and horror of life, I am drawn towards the edges.

I would rather travel out of my way to some back-lot liquor store graced by winos and hookers in tattered clothes to purchase cigarettes and beer than set foot in a Walgreens, or an Eckerds. I purposely take detours through Overtown, Miami's first black neighbourhood, where I'm comforted rather than intimidated by the sight of men and women sitting on crates outside run-down churches, shouting and jostling over five-dollar bills. The sounds of human endeavour so readily apparent there reach me and bring me to life. But something happens to your life, to what you believe in and who you are, when it is inherently contradicted by the people and situations that frame you. Over the years, I've witnessed what I can only interpret as a collective dread that springs into being in this country around issues that cannot be explained away, instantly demystified with one-word answers: good, bad, black, white, Madonna, whore, winner, loser. I have discovered that what masquerades as acceptance is instead a kind of shaky stranglehold which would have the inhabitants of this nation think as one. Difference here is no more tolerated than in those countries which people die trying to escape from so that they can come and live in the free world. Yet, in this land of free speech, where so many words, vacant, empty words are spoken, not enough is said.

Not nearly enough.

And it has been with Cece that my conflict with America, or what I perceive as the American way, has found its most charged playing field. We are fundamentally different, Cece and I. She wants to be happy above all else; I don't understand happiness as a goal, or a way of life. She is afraid of reliving her past. I am terrified that I will forget mine. She wants a life filled with light and beauty and is horrified by that which is ugly; I seek to unearth, at once, the magnificence and the dreadfulness of existence. The world to me is so much more than hope and love, so much larger than inspiration and affirmation. It is dirty and vile, crammed with hatred and fear. I know this, know it intimately in fact, because I survived what I view now as an unspeakable childhood, and its remnants live on in me and call upon me to name its horrors. And because my life has been so tainted, I need to acknowledge and to accept the baseness in others. The world is not all good. I am not all good, and in denying the sheer unadulterated humanity of it all, I disown a chunk of personal history that I cannot afford to lose.

I have lived an unfathomable life, from the nights back in Dublin when my mother beat me, then lied in my father's face, then forced me to tell lies on her behalf; to nights later on in my adolescence, when my father himself sided with his new wife against his own children, and dispatched me from his house; to times here in Miami when I was lied to and betrayed by Julio, beaten by M, rammed from behind by Jose and belittled by Cece herself. Bottomless and unsound as that life has been, it is all that I know, the total record of me to this moment. And perhaps this is what America has taught me: with all of its crashes and collapses, my life, as it stands, is deserving of celebration.

Celebration. Sounds like something off a fucking Marianne Williamson tape. At least that's what the cynic in me says. But I'm beyond being disparaging at this point. Because I want my life to mean something. To amount to something. To be worth it.

'Shivaun, Shiv . . . aaaun', a voice travels up the stairway. I recognise it immediately as Margaret's. I hear her puttering about in the kitchen and imagine her shaking her head as she shuffles through my cabinets in search of a pair of unchipped wineglasses. I know we'll spend the afternoon, as we often do lately, seated in my bare living room, getting drunk, moving closer because we know our time is short. Celebrating, as it were, our lives.

FORTY-EIGHT

I've taken to walking everywhere.

Because I can no longer cope with the eternal road-works that stall traffic on virtually every Miami street. I enjoy the daily outings to the corner with its panhandlers and hookers. I smile at them, and they smile back. Sometimes I give them money. More often I don't. There is a playground at the end of my street, filled with poor, black children in frayed clothes. There are dogs in every garden that bark and yelp as I pass, a bar on the corner and an AA meeting hall next door.

I'm clearing the way for departure.

I don't know what lies ahead. I don't know that it even matters. What's important is that I'm getting out. But I struggle with the transition. Every night I get drunk. Every morning I wake up with a heaving chest and the taste of cigarette butts in my mouth. I am obsessed with the notion that I will die here in Miami, just cease to be in the early hours. And the choice that surfaces in me each day is beyond physical landscapes, beyond the intricacies of language and culture. It is, in essence, about living and dying. Why do I focus so stubbornly on death? What is its erotic lure? I can imagine only that in it I will rest. Finally rest. In the back of my mind lies immense guilt about the way I have lived here and the things I have done. Part of me believes that I won't make it out of this country alive. But another part, the intuitive part that has fought so hard to stay afloat, powers me forward with a trembling certainty.

FORTY-NINE

⁓

The house is packed.

We fly to London in the morning. Sue, my rocker friend, backed by Kentucky the bassplayer, and a gal thrashing away on a drum set, are storming through a blistering rendition of 'Mustang Sally.' Margaret's in the kitchen, depositing the tank of beer she lugged in through the front door. Deb's over in the corner describing some new essential oils and aromatherapy products to an enchanted crew. Janice is sitting to the side, dark shades on even though it's close to midnight. Patri and Chelala are engaged in a heated discussion about communism or lesbianism or some other ism, or maybe the zoning laws for dogs on Miami Beach (they have two) where they've just purchased a condo. Cielito's swaying to the music, a beer bottle in each hand. Cece's floating about, by turns ecstatic, then gloomy like she's just lost her mother. Jesse's swirling those Latin hips of his, bending his ample butt into Cathy, the Dominican bombshell who worked with me at the Centre for years. Daniel and his friends have had too many Coronas and are beginning to turn green.

The noise in the room is near riotous. But it's a happy noise. I watch my friends with a keen eye, knowing this may be the last night I ever spend with them. I see that Deb has moved on to an astrology reading. Sue has stopped playing and Chelala has taken over, singing one of those haunting Cuban ballads that make my heart ache. Cielito's moving in on Daniel's friend's mother. Jesse and Cathy have slipped outside. Suddenly, everything goes still. Liquid in its clarity. I stand in the open doorway, hovering between the new and the old, the life I'm about to leave and the uncertainty that rests on the other side of it. Faintly, I hear chatter from the front lawn. A car pulls up next door. I walk down the stone pathway towards the street. The scent of jasmine clings to the air. It was one of the first things I noticed about this house, how fresh and clean it smelled. And when I arrived six months ago, that gave me hope. Tonight, it fills me with sadness.

My eyes travel along the sidewalk, strewn with boxes, a few lamps, a broken table, a torn blanket, all the things we couldn't get rid of in the yard sale. An old Haitian lady walks past, the weight of the day slowing her down. She stops a moment, picks up a lamp and looks up at me. 'Take it,' I say, 'take whatever you want.' She fills her basket and lumbers forward. The night is silent and sparkling clear. I gaze upward towards the sky: blue, black and heavy with stars. 'I will miss you, Miami sky,' I say quietly. I stand for a long time, inhaling the night air, pulling deep into my lungs floating memories to carry with me. I turn finally to face the house. Through the sheer drapes, I see heads bobbing, bodies moving. I see faces filled with laughter. And other faces, like Cece's, that turn to despair when no one is looking. And I see love. I see the very thing that's capable of drowning loss, of setting a life right, the thing that gives rise to its own celebration.

I have never been here before.